LET JUSTICE ROLL

Religious Forces in the Modern Political World

General Editor Allen D. Hertzke, The Carl Albert Center,
University of Oklahoma at Norman

Religious Forces in the Modern Political World features books on religious forces in politics, both in the United States and abroad. The authors examine the complex interplay between religious faith and politics in the modern world, emphasizing its impact on contemporary political developments. This new series spans a diverse range of methodological interpretations, philosophical approaches, and substantive concerns. Titles include:

LET JUSTICE ROLL

Prophetic Challenges in Religion, Politics, and Society

Edited by Neal Riemer

Rowman & Littlefield Publishers, Inc.

ROWMAN & LITTLEFIELD PUBLISHERS, INC.

Published in the United States of America
by Rowman & Littlefield Publishers, Inc.
4720 Boston Way, Lanham, Maryland 20706

3 Henrietta Street
London WC2E 8LU, England

British Cataloging in Publication Information Available

Library of Congress Cataloging-in-Publication Data

Let justice roll : prophetic challenges in religion, politics, and society / edited by Neal Riemer.
p.   cm. — (Religious forces in the modern political world)
Includes bibliographical references and index.
1. Religion and politics.   I. Riemer, Neal, 1922– .
II. Series.
BL65.P7L43   1996   291.1'77—dc20   95–47042   CIP

ISBN 0–8476–8192–0 (cloth : alk. paper)
ISBN 0–8476–8193–9 (pbk. : alk. paper)

Printed in the United States of America

♾ ™ The paper used in this publication meets the minimum requirements of American National Standard for Information Sciences---Permanence of Paper for Printed Library Materials, ANSI Z39.48-1984.

Contents

Acknowledgments

Several chapters in this volume (those by Paul D. Hanson, Michael Walzer, Rosemary Radford Ruether, Cornel West, and J. Mitchell Morse) are based on papers originally given at a Drew University Graduate School Colloquium on "The Prophetic Mode and Challenge in Religion, Politics, and Society," 18–19 April 1985, and which subsequently appeared in *The Drew Gateway* edition of Winter 1984/Spring 1985 under my guest editorship. Our thanks go to Drew University's Theological School for permission to draw upon these papers and also my introductory chapter for this volume.

I also want to pay a special tribute to the prophet Amos for giving us the title of this volume.

Finally, I want to acknowledge the many keen conversations with my wife, Ruby, that have deepened my understanding of the prophetic voice.

Preface

Why is a fresh exploration of the prophetic mode and challenge in the domains of religion, politics, and society in order? This question takes on heightened interest in light of the changing world of politics shaping up after the end of the Cold War, and of the soul-searching that inevitably accompanies the advent of a new millennium—here the millennial year 2001. There are several related answers.

First, we can always profit from an up-to-date, critical exploration of the concept of the prophetic, especially one in which political scientists, as well as students of religion and society, take seriously the contribution that the prophetic mode and challenge can make to our political and social lives. In this volume, then, we will take a fresh look at the prophetic mode and challenge: its biblical and historical roots; its historical and contemporary expression; its central values, characteristics, and manifestations; its strengths and weaknesses. We will pay special attention to the relationship between the prophetic paradigm and politics and will ask especially about the relevance of the prophetic mode and challenge in the modern world.

Second, exploring the prophetic mode and challenge in religion, politics, and society helps us to bring to bear on our contemporary and future problems the insights and understanding—ethical, empirical, and prudential—of the prophetic mode. Philosophy, science, social science, and literature can, of course, contribute to our approach to these problems. Yet we cut ourselves off from a vital and illuminating religious contribution when we ignore the prophetic mode.

Third, we must appreciate that as the prophetic mode and challenge may nourish the secular world, so too philosophy, science, social science, and literature may have contributions to make to our fuller understanding of the prophetic mode and challenge. We may, in other words, not only find problems and weaknesses in politics and society that the prophetic mode may help us address; we may also find problems and weaknesses in the prophetic that philosophy, science, social science, and literature may help us to overcome. Particularly disturbing is the age-old, and ever present, problem of distinguishing between true and false prophets, between bona fide and bogus prophets, between those—religious or secular—who are genuinely in the prophetic tradition and those who are not. Here, then, we seek to investigate the creative interaction between the religious and the secular to the mutual benefit of both domains.

Without attempting to preempt the rich definitions and exegesis of the prophetic that will follow in this volume, let me, in the interest of initial clarification, indicate very briefly what the prophetic (as it will generally be understood in this volume) is and is not.

When we speak of the prophetic we are *not* primarily talking about predicting or forecasting the future, although those in the prophetic tradition (religious or secular) may—indeed, must—communicate to society the ethical, empirical, and prudential implications of current behavior or trends. According to the biblical tradition, the prophet is a person who speaks God's word and passes judgment on those who respect or violate God's word. The characteristics of the prophetic, as it becomes a part of our secular as well as our religious understanding, are (1) a passionate commitment to such values as love, justice, freedom, peace, well-being, and moral excellence for all; (2) a dedicated commitment to criticism of existing societies in light of their fulfillment or nonfulfillment of those prophetic values; (3) a strong commitment to action, both covenantal and constitutional, to fulfill those values, to honor the commandments, and to narrow the gap between prophetic values and existential reality; and (4) a thoroughgoing commitment to continuous prophetic scrutiny and futuristic projection in order to anticipate problems and ensure our long-range societal health. These characteristics will be emphasized and illuminated in the articles in this volume. Readers are encouraged to probe the meaning, and to analyze the relevance, of these characteristics in the domains of religion, politics, and society.

We shall seek, then, to explore in the essays that follow the origins, development, historical uses, present understanding, and future tasks of the prophetic mode and challenge. We shall speak to, and invite our readers to reflect upon, a number of crucial questions:

(1) Does the Bible provide us with the classic paradigm of the prophetic mode and challenge? (And what are the several interpretations of that paradigm?)

(2) What can we say about the religious evolution of the prophetic mode and challenge? (And what factors account for the expression or repression of the prophetic?)

(3) How does the prophetic mode and challenge manifest itself in politics and society—and in political philosophy, history, and literature? (And what is the nature of the interaction between the religiously prophetic and secular interpretations of the prophetic?)

(4) Can we identify a secular prophetic mode and challenge? (And can a secular prophetic mode and challenge be long sustained in a world that rejects

belief in God, revelation, covenant, and commandment?)

(5) Can a higher law, based only on human reason, science, the ethics of the Enlightenment, and the practice of constitutional democracy, suffice to keep the prophetic consciousness alive? (And what kind of consensus can we get on such a higher law?)

(6) What is the relevance of the prophetic mode and challenge to global and domestic peace, liberation theology, the feminist movement, the battle against racism, the fight against poverty, and, lest we forget, the struggle against other forms of oppression and degradation in contemporary society? And what is the relevance of the prophetic mode and challenge to future generations? (Can a prophetic politics provide us with a model that may wisely and effectively guide us in dealing with these issues?)

(7) Is it important for us to distinguish between true and false prophets, between the genuinely prophetic and the falsely utopian? (And how do we do so?)

(8) Is it really possible to achieve an integration of prophetic ethics, social-scientific understanding, and democratic and constitutional statecraft to enhance the strengths, and remedy the weaknesses, of each? And to avert the dangers of false prophets and cheap prophecy? To avoid the sterilizing ethical neutrality and empirical shortsightedness of much modern social science? To overcome the complacency and timidity of so much contemporary politics? (Can such an integration lead to the articulation of a prophetic social science that will guide us as we enter the twenty-first century?)

Readers are invited to join the contributors to this volume in exploring these important questions. Our hope is that the essays that follow will stimulate a creative, ongoing dialogue on the meaning and relevance of the prophetic mode and challenge in our contemporary world.

1

The Origin and Nature of Prophetic Political Engagement in Ancient Israel

Paul D. Hanson

The Bible and Politics

Neal Riemer, in *The Future of the Democratic Revolution: Toward a More Prophetic Politics,* sees in the prophetic mode a reliable basis for exposing the weaknesses of Machiavellian, utopian, and liberal democratic politics, and a promising means for moving "to a higher level of politics that can more effectively ensure vital civilized life, healthy growth and creative [human] fulfillment."[1] And he describes very clearly the contribution of biblical tradition to this mode of political reflection and action. Michael Walzer, in chapter 2 of this book, portrays the paradigmatic task of prophets within a society as that of judging "the people's relations with one another (and with 'their' God)" and "the internal character of their society"—in other words, the task of social criticism.

I am greatly encouraged by the efforts of these two political philosophers to recover the prophetic dimension of Hebrew Scripture. For too long now we have been satisfied with a very unprophetic, popular interpretation of the Bible that has comforted the comfortable and left the oppressed to their oppressors. Many people in our religious communities have private interests in protecting that particular elitist reading of the Bible. The Bible, however, is a document that stands solidly on the side of evenhanded justice and equality. But it does not adopt a utopian mode for advancing universal justice. Rather, it is characterized by an unflinching realism that commends itself for reflection to people seeking to make lasting contributions to social reform. Given the sterility of the popular domesticated reading of Scripture and the particular role that reading has played in reinforcing inadequate and often recklessly dangerous social and political positions, it is heartening to see philosophers and thinkers of the stature of Walzer and Riemer dedicating themselves to a new look.

As a student of the Bible and a concerned citizen, I am intrigued by the possibility of reviving the prophetic mode as a credible and perhaps even critically important perspective within today's political arena. We must proceed in the exploration of this possibility, to be sure, with full awareness that our presuppositions, our institutional and societal structures, and the realities of the world around us differ considerably from those of the ancient world within which Israelite prophecy once flourished. We know all too well with what enthusiasm and frequent harm the Bible is being translated into programs for political action throughout our world today. Leaders who exercise caution in drawing quantum physics or economic theory into their arguments often reach into the world of the Bible in perfect confidence that its meaning is simple and transparent. What are we to say to those cynics who will now ask, and with justification, How is your application of biblical prophecy any more legitimate than that of Ralph Reed, Jerry Falwell, or Hal Lindsay?

I operate with the hermeneutical assumption that application of any ancient source to a modern setting is legitimate only if based, first, on a critically informed understanding of the ancient documents in question and the phenomena described therein, and second, on a careful consideration of possible intrinsic connections between the ancient phenomena and their modern counterparts. In the case of the prophetic mode, applicability depends on the commensurability of essential ingredients within the two loci, the ancient and the modern.

Prophecy in Ancient Israel

It is my desire first to describe the essential characteristics of prophecy in ancient Israel and to sketch the stages through which prophecy passed in its roughly five-hundred-year history. For illustration I shall cite specific texts. With this characterization in hand I shall return to the question of the applicability of the biblical model of prophetic critique to our own world, although I will keep that section brief, since other chapters will focus specifically on the prophetic in the contemporary world.

We begin with the phenomenological observation that prophecy can be divided in the ancient Near East in general into two types, as Robert Wilson has shown in his book *Prophecy and Society in Ancient Israel*.[2] One type of prophecy he calls central prophecy; it is supportive of the interests of institutions and authorities of a given society. The other type, which he calls peripheral prophecy, stands outside the mainstream and exercises criticism over against it. The ancient Near Eastern texts that we possess, especially those from Mesopotamia, are generous in supplying examples of central prophets. Every king had his troop of prophets to support his decisions in battle or in domestic disputes, and as the story, in 1 Kings 22, of Ahab consulting his four hundred prophets illustrates, Israel's kings were no exception.

But what the court prophets proclaimed is of little interest to us. And in this we are already anticipated by the students of the tradition of antiquity. Biblical tradition preserved not the words of the political supporters of the powers that were, but the words of the reformers, the harsh critics of kings and nobles and priests, those less interested in supporting official policy than in exposing it to a very distinct and unflinching critique from an independent perspective. The term peripheral, however, is unfortunate, I think, and should be replaced, for it is open to the interpretation and misunderstanding that the majority of Israel's recorded prophets acted from a position outside of an effective sphere of power. No one in Israel looked upon the prophets as peripheral or powerless, not even their most cultivated despisers. When Elijah confronted Ahab as the latter entered the vineyard he had recently confiscated, the king responded to the prophet with the question "Have you found me, O my enemy?" and with those words exposed his dread before this "troubler of Israel."[3] The prophets were not peripheral. They were located centrally within a very distinct sphere of power, and their impact on their society can be understood only if that sphere is understood, for it assured them not only a hearing before kings and nobles, not only a circle of dedicated disciples, not only a fifth column in times of duress, but also the potential of a popular following capable of sweeping societal change. The prophets were thus spokespersons of a recognizable order. They were neither utopian dreamers nor self-indulgent individualists. They were spokespersons, empowered citizens, representing a distinct order of reality. This needs further clarification.

Too often in scholarship, and certainly in popular understanding of prophecy, attention is focused on the psychology of the prophets, with the result that ecstatic experiences and esoteric actions have been described in terms of highly individualistic propensities. The prophets are characterized as extraordinarily sensitive persons open to dimensions of reality of which normal people are scarcely aware. I do not want to discount the insights given to us in a classic psychological study such as that of Johannes Lindblom.[4] Nevertheless, we must recognize another dimension, and I think a far more important one, to ancient prophecy in Israel. The prophets—at least those whose words are preserved in the Bible—spoke out of a distinct tradition, drew upon a carefully developed worldview, and defended a social system characterized by well-defined values and warrants. This can be seen in the high degree of consistency that characterizes their description of the moral and covenantal mandate placed before Israel by its God. Not uncommonly, one can recognize a reference in the prophets to the Decalogue, as in Hos. 4:1–3, or to the Book of the Covenant, as in Amos 2:6–8. This indicates the degree of specificity with which these prophets drew upon a received tradition.

Especially if the prophetic mode is to be considered seriously as viable within the modern realm of politics, it is important to recognize the ancient prophet's location within a clearly defined tradition and to understand the importance of that connection for the prophet's effectiveness as an agent of social reform. It is a widely held view in our society that prophets are, and always have been, solitary individualists acting out of a private and inscrutable impulse. What, then, is the significance of the fact that Israelite prophets addressed reality from the perspective of a distinct and definable tradition?

First of all, it meant that the prophet assessed the world from a unified view of reality, a view that had undergone years and years of testing by previous generations. And because that worldview was distinct from the prevailing one—remember that the prophets lived during the period of the monarchy—it supplied an independent vantage point from which existing social and political realities could be scrutinized and judged. The simple fact that the prophetic tradition was different from the prevailing one, however, is in itself of limited significance. The value of the perspective and standards of judgment the prophetic worldview provided depended rather on the essential nature of the difference between itself and that which it sought to evaluate and change. Before we can proceed further, therefore, it is necessary that we describe the relationship between prophecy, on the one hand, and its host system, the monarchy, on the other.

In considering that relationship, bring to mind any one of Israel's major prophets, for example, Elijah, Amos, Isaiah, or Jeremiah. In each case we find an individual, though holding no official office in the government, exercising a great deal of influence in the land, especially through pronouncements highly critical of the reigning king and other persons of wealth and power. It is patently clear that these prophets do not view their world from the same perspective as those in power, and thus frequent clashes over values and priorities are inevitable. Whereas kings generally think in terms of securing the land against foreign invaders by military alliances and increased chariotry, and often justify the forfeiture of their subjects' rights on the basis of the ostensibly loftier concerns of the crown, the prophets persistently begin with the intrinsic value of the individual regardless of social status.

What is the deeper significance of this disparity? Using contemporary terms we can recognize on one level a clash between offices, and if one sees a sort of check-and-balance system in ancient Israel, we can say that each of these—the king as well as the prophet—was exercising the prerogatives of his office. But on a deeper level, a genuine clash between ideologies can be detected. The order of reality embraced by the prophets is different from that held by most of Israel's kings. We need to examine these divergent orders of reality, defining them and seeking to identify their sources.

The Ideology of Kingship

Fortunately, we know a great deal about kingship and its ideology in the ancient Near Eastern world of which Israel was a part. No Israelite king was slavishly dependent on foreign models. Nevertheless, there are substantive lines of continuity, for example, between the ideology of the Davidides in Jerusalem and some of Babylon's kings. The source of our knowledge of ancient royal ideology is the extensive mythological and historical literature unearthed by archaeologists in the last century and a half, together with information provided by the Bible.[5]

According to the ideology of kingship, the governance of this world was intimately tied to the governance of the entire cosmos. The link between the two was as intimate as the relationship between the king and his god. Therefore we can understand kingship only if we first understand the divine realm from which it derived its authority.

Foremost among the tasks of the gods was the maintenance of the harmony of the cosmos. This was a most difficult task, for a host of divine beings preferred chaos. One of the most significant of all myth types is therefore the conflict myth, seen for example in a Babylonian version in the *Enūma eliš*.[6] The myth describes a deadly threat to the pantheon posed by Tiamat, or Monster Sea, and her creatures. Marduk is commissioned by the pantheon, meeting in divine assembly, to defeat Tiamat and reestablish order. It was the ensuing conflict that established the universe. Marduk cut Tiamat in half, fixing the upper half of her carcass as the sky, the bottom half as the firmament of the earth. The sky in turn he supported with mountain peaks. Beyond the sphere of order thus established, there churned the murky waters of primordial chaos. Portals in the two half shells controlled the influx of the appropriate amount of rain and subterranean water to fructify the earth. To regulate days and nights, months and years, Marduk set the heavenly bodies in their courses. In acknowledgment of his accomplishments, the gods appointed Marduk to be king over them.

Earthly kingship was thought to derive from this heavenly kingship. The king's realm was a mirror image, greatly reduced to be sure, of the divine realm. Each earthly king had a patron deity, for the gods had divided the nations among themselves. Even as one can find the cosmology sketched above reflected in Gen. 1, so too one can recognize a reflex of myth in the division of the nations among the gods in Deut. 32:8–9. To each god a nation is assigned, with Israel falling to Yahweh. The fortunes of his god in the divine assembly determined the fortunes of a given king. As the authority of the successful king of heaven depended upon his establishing and maintaining cosmic order, so too the authority of an earthly king depended on his establishing and maintaining mundane order. In this, two endeavors were paramount: (1) securing the land from enemy attack through military strength and skill, and (2) maintaining harmony within the kingdom through economic stability and enforcement of the laws of the land. The royal court functioned in intimate connection with the temple and priests, inasmuch as support of the military and the distribution of food supplies were both regulated by the sacrificial system of the temple cult. A sacral rationale was given to this whole system through the claim that the disruption of the flow of offerings into the temple would deprive the cosmic rulers of vital needs, with the woeful result that they would be distracted from their lofty responsibilities of maintaining cosmic order, thereby leading everything, including human habitation, to collapse into chaos. The social and political implications of the mythopoeic ideology were clear: Subjects, from priests to slaves, were to be faithful above all in fulfilling their assigned duties in the cosmos by being obedient. They were to support and defend monarchy and temple in all things, for upon the strength of these institutions depended the viability of the entire universe.

Israelite Prophecy and Its Ideology

In describing Israelite prophecy and its ideology, ancient Near Eastern texts outside the Bible are less helpful. In spite of numerous efforts to connect the prophetic movement with phenomena in Mesopotamia and Egypt, the only light that has been shed is on central or cult prophecy. The office of critical prophecy seems to be unique to Israel, a fact intimately related to its roots in the traditions of the tribal Yahwism of the premonarchical period.

This refers us back, therefore, to the question of the nature of the tradition from which prophecy drew its unified view of reality and hence its critical perspective. Though it is true that in a historical sense prophecy originated with the monarchy, on a deeper, more critical level, its origin must be located in the founding experiences of the Hebrew people, what we can call metonomically "the Exodus." This tradition furnished a critical perspective from which monarchy could be evaluated, inasmuch as it was born of a set of circumstances vastly different from those described in the etiological myths of kingship. Whereas kingship was described in terms of a primordial drama within which the gods established one (quasi-deified) human as privileged head of the society, the early Yahwistic tradition recalled a historical drama in which Yahweh, in defiance of earthly potentates, embraced the cause of the most lowly of the earth and of them made a nation chosen to be a blessing for, and a teacher of, all people.

Now, if prophecy originated historically, not during the period of the Exodus but in the early years of the monarchy, why did it base itself on the earlier Exodus tradition? The answer to this question brings us back to the contrast between the ideology of kingship and the ideology of prophecy. In the introduction of kingship, the prophets recognized facets of a sociopolitical order resembling that which had earlier secured the bondage of their ancestors in Egypt. We can conceptualize this contrast by picturing Egyptian society as a pyramid. Basically, the system from which the Hebrews had been liberated and which their descendants saw reimplanting itself in Israel was a social pyramid with the deity at the top, followed by the divine king, and then in a progressive descent moving through the social classes to the slaves at the bottom. Metaphysically, this was imagined as an emanation of divinity, from its purest embodiment in the Horus-king down to its weakest concentration in the rocks and clay of the ground. Everything to some degree embodied divinity, but in a harshly stratified sense. The pyramid, then, symbolized the past history of the Israelites, the period of their being held in bondage by a strictly stratified social system.

The prophetic appeal to the early Exodus tradition was an urgent appeal back to the model that, according to Yahwistic belief, had supplanted the model of the stratified Egyptian pyramid. That alternative model arose when the Hebrews, as members of the slave class located at the oppressive base of the pyramid, encountered a God who, rather than holding them in their allotted position as a requisite for social and cosmic stability, actually defied the divine and royal powers of Egypt and delivered them from their bondage. The prophets, in harking back to Exodus tradition, were thus appealing to the essential nature of early Yahwistic community and a unique quality of life that was being endangered by the reintroduction of the socioeconomic order of monarchy, an order appealing to mythic warrants, predicated on an ideology of special privilege, and dedicated to the preservation of the "law of the king" against all change and challenge (cf. 1 Sam. 8:9–18).

Let us pause for a moment here to delineate this Exodus tradition from which the prophets drew their critique and their reforming vision. Consider its essential characteristics. First of all, it confessed that the ultimate Reality that unifies all reality was Yahweh, a unique deity known as champion of the weak, the lowly, and the oppressed of the earth. This Reality in turn relativized all other powers, thus establishing equality among human beings. Of course this ideal remained largely inchoate in the early period. There were still slaves in early Israel, and the vision of egalitarian community remained thwarted. Nevertheless, the monotheistic thrust in that early confession that the God who gave birth to Israel was one God, a God who showed special concern for the weak and the oppressed, was in essence powerfully egalitarian. This principle was acknowledged by the faithful within Israel through worship.

Second, the fitting social response to this gracious deliverance by God was defined as the communal embodiment in family relations, social structures, and economic institutions of the qualities manifested in Yahweh's delivering act. Chief among the qualities that the community sought to embody were righteousness and compassion. Righteousness was understood to be a just moral standard applying impartially to all people, rich and poor, strong and weak, resident and alien. Compassion was defined as the outreach of this people, privileged by God's deliverance, towards those excluded by the very definition of belonging provided by its just standard of righteousness, whether that exclusion was caused by sickness, indebtedness, or accident of birth.

We find then a triadic concept of community predicated on the sole worship of Yahweh and embodying the qualities of righteousness and compassion. This triad in turn became that which defined and safeguarded the community's habitation, what we might call the orbit of *shalom*. Within the biblical context we can understand shalom to be the God-given blessing that nurtured the wholeness of all members of the society and fostered harmony among them. It gave rise to institutions as concrete as the *nahala*, or family inheritance, which was the plot of land given to each family as a basis for its economic viability, as well as to notions like the jubilee, the year occurring every half-century when all debts were to be forgiven, all forfeited property restored, all broken relationships healed.[7]

This concept of community, with its triad safeguarding shalom, was not regarded as a trifling matter. It was seen as the sine qua non not only for the viability of this one community, but for the family of the nations (as already suggested by the Abrahamic Blessing in Gen. 12), and even for the entire universe (cf. Hos. 4:1–3 and Isa. 24). There thus developed out of the humble beginnings of the escape of a band of slaves from Egypt a remarkably encompassing vision of the redeemed community as a nucleus essential for the health of the entire cosmos.

Originating in a revolutionary historical experience, this concept of community fostered in Israel a dynamic ontology of renewal. The God who broke the bonds of the first Hebrew slaves would continue to break bonds wherever they were found until all humans were free. On the basis of this ontology sociopolitical structures emerged within the triad of shalom that, if we for a moment use modern terminology, can be seen to resemble features of modern democracies. First, I believe one can recognize a rudimentary form of constitution, formulating the cardinal principles of the community and tracing their origin to Yahweh's deliverance of a slave people from Egypt (Exod. 20:2–7). This relation between principles and their origin in antecedent divine activity (Exod. 20:2) suggests that the values of this society were understood to be traceable to events of its past (i.e., its epic). Obedience was thus something other than mindless adherence to impersonal authority. Obedience was grateful response on the part of those living within the freedom and well-being that flows from grace within a covenant relationship.

We can perhaps go on to suggest that the principles of the constitution were translated very concretely into something resembling a Document of Human Rights, found in Exod. 20:22–23:19, the so-called Book of the Covenant. The Book of the Covenant is a hodgepodge of different laws and even types of laws, but all of them unite around the theme of safeguarding the dignity of the human within the society.

Finally, the constitution and the document of human rights were undergirded by an epic, commonly referred to by biblical scholars as a historical credo. This was the narrative core around which the first five books of the Bible grew. Originally in poetic form, it was likely recited by the early tribes of Yahweh at cult centers like Gilgal, Shechem, and Shiloh. In the ancient Hebrew community the epic was not just some sort of narrative embellishment added to the hard legal and institutional apparatus of the society. Rather, it gave expression to the soul of the community. It described that community's essential nature and offered the possibility of constant renewal of that nature through memory, through recitation, through re-creation of an open, dynamic, and radically egalitarian/inclusive ontology. The early Yahwistic community ideal simply cannot be understood apart from this epic. It explains why early Yahwistic tradition was important for the prophets not merely because it offered a contrast to kingship, and not merely because it was old. No, that early tradition explained the meaning of this people's existence by referring back to its birth in a miraculous passage from bondage to freedom, a miracle that established Israel's life upon pure, undeserved divine grace.

In the Book of the Covenant, we see this vital function of the epic, this function of calling Israel back through memory to its essential nature and motivational center. Remember that we are dealing here with a document written before kings had arisen in Israel, and preserved in a form unaltered by the later kings. Consider first Exod. 23:9: "You shall not oppress a stranger. You know the heart of a stranger, for you were strangers in the land of Egypt." That is a marvelously radical pronouncement within a world economy predicated on the exploitation of captured slaves, captured often as they went wandering through your land. Protection of the sojourner? Why? Because of a memory: "You were a sojourner." Or consider Exod. 22:21–24: "You shall not afflict any widow or orphan. If you do afflict them, and they cry out to me, I will surely hear their cry; and my wrath will burn, and I will kill you with the sword, and your wives shall become widows and your children fatherless." Perhaps the formulation here is a bit strong for our modern taste, but we must not let that obscure the message. The God Yahweh, in a manner perfectly consistent with the earlier act of deliverance, would punish those liberated slaves who forgot their past by enslaving others. Finally, consider Exod. 22:25–27: "If you lend money to any of my people with you who is poor, you shall not be to him as a creditor, and you shall not exact interest from him. If ever you take your neighbor's garment in pledge, you shall restore it to him before the sun goes down, for that is his only covering, it is his mantle for his body; in what else shall he sleep? And if he cries to me, I will hear, for I am compassionate." The order of the universe boils down to a mantle—that is, to the concrete and the particular—because that is, after all, the level upon which the vital center of the universe is maintained.

These examples illustrate how the triadic notion of community presupposed by the prophets is intimately tied to the central theme of the early epic, the theme of deliverance. They show how intimately related within the Yahwistic notion of community were the two sides of the wholehearted response to the gracious God: on the one side, worship acknowledging the Sovereignty of the One true God; on the other, obedience to the Torah. The full life is thus epitomized in joyful worship and loving obedience. Together they secure the foundations of a genuinely humane community.

Having located the source of the ideology of the prophets in early Yahwism, we are in a better position to explain their attitude toward kingship. Important in this context is Samuel's speech in 1 Sam. 8. It is predicated, as Kyle McCarter has demonstrated, on an early prophetic tradition.[8] In it Samuel warns the people concerning their request for a king: This king will take your sons and make them charioteers, your daughters and make them bakers and perfumers, a tenth of your land and the best of your fields, and then—and here is the bottom line—you shall become slaves. The basic problem that the prophets had with kingship was that it threatened to undo the intricate order of shalom to which God had given birth in the Exodus. And it raised that threat by placing a penultimate authority in the place where only the ultimate authority, Yahweh, could rightfully stand. In other words, in relation to the triad of worship, righteousness, and compassion, the king began to encroach upon *Yahweh*'s position at the top of the triad by defining righteousness on the basis of the *king*'s rule of the land, and by limiting the showing of compassion to those enjoying a privileged status within the nation-state. Therefore we find the warnings in 1 Sam. 8 ending with the blunt assertion "and you shall become slaves." In other words, you will reverse your whole epic and end up where you came from. Kingship threatened to return Israel to point zero, with the added bitter irony that the king under whom they would suffer would no longer be a foreigner, but one of their own blood. But the people ignored Samuel's warning, and replied: "No, but we will have a king over us, that we also may be like all the nations, and that our king may govern over us and go out before us and fight our battles" (1 Sam. 8:19).

Israel found herself on the horns of a dilemma. Historically, the introduction of kingship was inevitable. If Israel had not adopted the centralized structures of kingship, she would have been defeated by the Philistines. Yet those same monarchical structures that promised political salvation threatened the very soul of this nation. To this very ambiguous situation, prophecy gave reply in 1 Sam. 12. This chapter is an important one to consider, given a common tendency among students of the Bible to adopt a simplistically negative attitude towards kingship. The prophet Hosea offers a similar corrective, for in Hos. 1:4–5 we encounter a prophet who has determined that prophetically inspired reforming zeal has been carried to excess, threatening the order, imperfect though it was, that kings maintained in the land. We must be prepared to recognize the carefully nuanced position of Israel's prophets toward their kings, and in this connection 1 Sam. 12 is helpful. Here Samuel grants that kingship was introduced because of the sinfulness of the people, and that it posed a serious threat. But he proved himself unwilling to concede the future to self-aggrandizing kings either by escaping into a utopian vision or by thrusting himself into a suicidal form of resistance. No, Samuel proceeded to challenge the people to reclaim the new system, fallen though it was, for their cherished Yahwistic ideals born of the Exodus: "Fear Yahweh. Serve Yahweh faithfully, with all your heart; for consider what great things Yahweh has done. But if you still do wickedly, you shall be swept away, both you and your king." This is a clear formulation of prophetic realism. It acknowledges that structures of society, forms of government, and economic institutions are flawed, even evil. But this is precisely the nature of the context within which the people of vision are called to be faithful. In this context the prophet is the one dedicated to keeping alive the vision of the godly, moral life amidst the ambiguities of a sinful—that is, human—political and social order. "Moreover, as for me," adds Samuel, "far be it from me that I should sin against Yahweh by ceasing to pray for you; and I will instruct you in the good and the right way."

These words of Samuel refute those who assert that biblical prophecy, by offering simple answers to unambiguous situations, has little to contribute to the complex problems of a pluralistic and largely secular world. 1 Sam. 12 moves prophecy into honest confrontation with the kind of social and religious ambiguity that marks our world. The prophets were not dealing with simple sociopolitical problems!

What was "the good and the right way" to which Yahwistic prophecy was dedicated? It was rooted in the notion of the covenant community born of the Exodus from Egypt. It amplified the vision of a former slave people called from nothing by Yahweh's saving grace to be a community of peace dedicated to God and extending to all people (regardless of race or class) the compassion and righteousness first received from God.

Kings and Prophets Contrasted

Against this background we can now venture to contrast the ideologies of kingship and prophecy, in order to grasp better how prophecy functioned in ancient Israel. Kings in that ancient world were primarily dedicated to establishing and maintaining order, security, and prosperity. Their methods included military force, foreign alliances, taxation, control of power through dynastic succession, and manipulation of religious institutions to bring them into conformity with their imperial objectives. That is what one expects of kings. To defend their privileged status they appealed to the myth of primordial conflict. The reality they projected was thus one precariously balanced on the abyss of chaos and requiring superhuman leaders to maintain order. What was required of the average citizen in turn was absolute, unquestioning obedience. The royal model was what later thinkers would designate a Machiavellian political mode. The chief beneficiaries of this system were the royal court, the military generals, the temple priests, and the mercantile class. Those most often victimized by the system were found among the small landowners, women, the working poor, and nonresident aliens. Within the earlier tribal confederacy the freedom and rights of such persons had been protected by the laws of the Book of the Covenant (Exod. 21–23). Under the monarchy, owing to the insatiable appetite of kings and land barons for new acquisitions, these vulnerable classes were commonly forced into indebtedness and slavery. Yet those officiating over the system would have contended that these were the inevitable costs of social stability and economic prosperity.

Prophets, on the other hand, were dedicated to the rights of individuals, especially of those exploited by the imperial system of might and order, a system that rationalized poverty, exploitation of labor, high taxation, and indebtedness as aspects of political order and national security. The prophets remained less convinced than their political leaders by the royal notion of order and prosperity based on the myth of conflict. For them the world was ultimately ordered not because of the superior power of a king, but because Yahweh reigned, thereby securing humans from the threat of chaos. The cosmos was not threatened in the first instance by cosmic forces, but by acts of human disobedience and cruelty. Yahweh could be trusted to maintain order in the universe even as humans were commanded by God to respect the moral ordering of life within their human habitation through acts of justice and mercy. Within the relationship thus established, harmony could arise that would embrace the entire world.

With this understanding of reality, the prophets were actually able to accept kingship, but in a qualified sense that set them apart from the central prophets in Israel and other nations. Kingship represented not an unchangeable, inevitable, or eternal order, but a human institution. They were able to give an account of its origins in historical decisions and mistakes. It was thus an institution, like all human contrivances, that was capable of good and ill, requiring constant surveillance, conscientious critique, and caring guidance. Under no circumstances could it be exempted from criticism by an appeal to divine decree or metaphysical uniqueness. Whether it contributed good or evil depended strictly on the principles by which it was guided, which led the prophets outside of the structure of kingship itself for that guidance. As for the person of the king, the prophets refused to concede that he was closer than any other mortal to the deity. Like every other citizen, the king was to respond to the true king Yahweh by a life of obedience to the Torah, and like every Israelite he stood under God's judgment.

The Characteristics of the Prophetic Mode in the Bible

Against this historical background, we can begin to define the salient characteristics of the prophetic mode.

First, we can recognize a visionary modality. The prophets' messages and their activities were predicated on a vision of a harmonious sociopolitical order that ultimately was derived from a gracious God. This vision was born historically of a liberation experience and thus was radically egalitarian in thrust and dedicated to a deep sense of justice. This is the transcendent side of prophecy.

Second, there is a pragmatic or practical or realistic dimension. The prophets' lives were dedicated to translating that vision into the concrete realities of their society. This worldly side of prophecy is an important corrective to those who would use biblical prophecy to justify renunciation of involvement in social and political institutions in favor of a world-disdaining spirituality. It took radical dedication to hear God, in the heavenly council, saying, "Go and say to my people," and to obey that command, given the sacrifice and struggle obedience was sure to entail.

Third, we recognize a revisionist dimension or facet. Dedication to translating the vision into everyday realities disallowed the prophets from formulating a final version of the vision and the sociopolitical program it implied. For example, we can discern a development within prophecy from the limited vision of a legendary figure like Elisha, who, irritated by some youngsters calling him baldhead, cursed them and delivered them to be torn by bears, to Amos and Second Isaiah, proponents of a broadly embracing vision of justice and world peace. Such a revisionist tendency can be seen as the inevitable effect of constant application of the vision to the changing conditions of this world. The need to reformulate the vision pressed itself upon those who took this world seriously. This tendency can be seen also in connection with the concept of the messiah, the anointed one, as it developed beyond the courts of an oriental despot to the domain of the Creator and Redeemer of the entire creation.

This revisionist impulse was closely related to the prophetic view of God's arena of action. A historicist perspective is at the root of this revisionist tendency. Since the setting of God's activity was history, historical events had to be taken seriously, had to be factored into the formulation of the vision; hence the need for revision. For example, what could royal Jerusalem tradition, a tradition celebrating a Davidic messiah, do with Cyrus, a foreign conqueror who seemed to be accomplishing God's purposes? It named Cyrus the new messiah, a rather shocking revision of an earlier nationalistic concept of divine rule. Appreciation of the revisionist impulse should not make us overlook the precariousness of such an open-ended, dynamic ontology of events. Even the prophets of Israel made some memorable mistakes. Perhaps we should not be so quick to condemn a prophet like Hananiah, deemed a false prophet by Jeremiah for prophesying the imminent breaking of the yoke of the king of Babylon (Jer. 28). Though history vindicates Jeremiah, Hananiah's message of restoration would also have its time, as indicated by the salvatory themes of Second Isaiah. Prophetic engagement with the real issues of politics and society is a precarious business. I am reminded of something I learned from Professor Klaus Scholder in Tuebingen, Germany, about Dietrich Bonhoeffer. Right after Hitler's invasion of France, the Confessing Church met in conference in Berlin to decide what response should be made. Bonhoeffer is reported in the minutes of this meeting to have suggested that the Confessing Church was obliged to look more closely at Hitler in light of such a resounding victory. Such are the ambiguities of history, here confusing even a modern saint, if but for a moment.

Therefore, a word of caution is called for. We have tended to describe prophecy as a unified phenomenon. And such oversimplification is often necessary for heuristic reasons. But in one sense prophecy could not be a unified phenomenon precisely because its ontology was historically grounded. Its dynamic, historical orientation forced it to be particular, to take sides, to make pronouncements within concrete and often ambiguous situations, resulting in broad diversity both synchronically and diachronically. The prophetic mode is no haven for those seeking spiritual repose. The mode offering eternal repose is myth, and it continues to attract many people as it did in antiquity. It is not surprising, for example, to see fundamentalism forsaking the historical particularity in the ontological open-endedness of prophetism with its honest confrontation with ambiguity and opting for the timeless myth of an infallible doctrine that yields clear answers to all social, political, and religious problems.

The inevitable result of this dynamic ontology, courageously applied to changing conditions by the prophets, was diversity. Contrast Amos and Isaiah, who reflect two very different theologoumena. Amos condemns kings and royal structures while Isaiah upholds a Davidic-Zion theology. Or contrast Isa. 56–66 with Haggai and Zachariah. Picture Haggai trying to reconstitute the nation by motivating the people to build the temple so that Yahweh would again bless Israel. In effect, he was reviving the old orthodoxy: Renew the economic structures of the land by building the temple and restoring the sacrifices, which after all were the means of gathering the basic commodities for redistribution by the king. To this, "Third Isaiah" had the audacity to reply: "Heaven is my throne and the earth my footstool; what is this house [i.e., temple] which you would build for me?" (Isa. 66:1). Here we see prophets daring to disagree with one another as they struggle to apply their vision of God's order of justice and mercy to the realities of their world.

A diachronic move through prophecy also reveals a great deal of diversity, from prophets against kings in the early stage, to prophets against the nation when we come to Amos and Isaiah, to prophets for the nation in Second Isaiah, to prophets for an open society in Ruth and Jonah, to prophets envisioning cosmic collapse and a new creation in apocalypticism.

From Theocracy to Prophetic Engagement with an Alien Order

In basing their relationship to the dominant regime of their time on a tradition from an earlier era, the prophets were not blindly replicating a pattern of the past. The concept of community that they embraced, the concept predicated on the triad of worship, righteousness, and compassion, arose within a world in which the religious community and the nation were one entity. That was the world of tribal theocracy. The law of the land, of the judicial court, and of the marketplace was the law of God. Community and society, gemeinschaft and gesellschaft, were coextensive.

The prophets sought to preserve the concept of community predicated on worship, righteousness, and compassion within a world ordered on the basis of other concepts, especially the ideology of kingship appealing to mythic warrants for the special status of the monarch over against subjects. As spokespersons for a perspective that respected the dignity and equality of every human without distinction, they inevitably came into conflict with the authorities of the state. The community of compassion and justice became a remnant within a larger society that in large part derived its identity from other values. The circles of the prophets, as citizens of a nation that by virtue of its secular values could never be their essential home, thus foreshadow the communities of resistance and protest that exist within our secular world. Like the prophets, those who today view reality through the prophetic mode find that their call to citizenship implies not ultimate, but penultimate, allegiance. They give their best to their nations not by unquestioning acceptance of authority, but by vigilant critique based on a vision of impartial justice and universal peace that transcends every human institution and national regime. It is this "dual citizenship" of the prophet that creates the commensurability between biblical prophecy and prophetic activity today that is essential for the viability of the prophetic mode in contemporary political process.

Examples of Prophets Engaged in Politics

Let us consider a few illustrations of how specific prophets applied their vision and translated their concept of community into the social, economic, and political realities of their time.

The Israelite army is in the battlefield. King David remains at home in the safety and comfort of his fortified city. His eyes fall upon Bathsheba, wife of Uriah, one of his foot soldiers. He takes her to himself and must get rid of Uriah as a consequence of the resulting pregnancy. After the death of Uriah, the prophet Nathan comes to David. He tells the story of a rich man who, though possessing large flocks, took the sole possession of a poor man, his little beloved ewe lamb, and roasted it for a houseguest. David is indignant: "As Yahweh lives, the man who has done this deserves to die!" To this Nathan replies, "You are that man" (2 Sam. 12:5–6). We witness here a clash between the monarchical notion of special privilege, supposedly a necessary part of a strong kingdom, and the strict sense of egalitarian justice defended by prophecy.

Rehoboam is about to succeed his father, Solomon. The elders come to him representing the *eda* (the congregation of the earlier tribal confederacy). They plead with him to lessen the forced service and heavy taxation Solomon had placed upon them, promising to serve him faithfully if he did. The reply which the crown prince gives them is heartless: "My father made your yoke heavy, but I will add to your yoke; my father chastised you with whips, but I will chastise you with scorpions" (1 Kings 12:14). Then a prophet comes along and tears away from Solomon's son ten of the tribes, anointing a rival king to assume rule over these ten tribes instead. Here we witness the opposition between the ideology of might preserving order and the communal concept of evenhanded righteousness.

In 1 Kings 21 a vintner named Naboth is visited by King Ahab, who seeks to force him into selling his family *nahala* (inheritance), a vineyard, because it is needed for palace expansion. Naboth pleads that he cannot, for according to early Yahwistic custom his land had been placed in the sacred trust of his family by Yahweh forever. Yahweh owned the land. Each family had a nahala, and was not permitted to sell it; it was held in sacred trust. Ahab, coached by his Canaanite wife, Jezebel, hires false witnesses to testify against the stubborn subject. Naboth is killed. Ahab takes possession of the vineyard. The prophet Elijah appears and brings a stinging word of judgment from Yahweh against the king. Here too we find a biting attack against special privilege and prerogative from the perspective of an egalitarian sense of justice.

In Amos we see the conflict between the prophet and the priestly defender of the crown, Amaziah. The prophet has dared to speak out against the king, for which he is severely attacked by Amaziah, who seeks to silence him. "Never again prophesy at Bethel," he is warned, "for it is the king's sanctuary, and it is a temple of the kingdom" (Amos 7:13). Here is a classic conflict between those who would identify religion with patriotism and those who insist on a religious commitment that acknowledges as ultimate no loyalty save loyalty to God.

In Hos. 4:1–3, we find a prophet giving expression to the Yahwistic triad of shalom and identifying the confessing community as a nucleus essential for the viability of the whole. First Hosea, in brief words, characterizes the keystone of community as acknowledgment and worship of Yahweh alone (4:1). Then he refers to representative commandments from the Decalogue (4:2). Finally, he describes the nucleus community within its natural habitation, ordered by God, but now threatened by human disobedience (4:3):

Hear the word of the Lord, O people of Israel.
　for the Lord has a controversy
　with the inhabitants of the land.
There is no faithfulness or kindness,
　and no knowledge of God in the land;
there is swearing, lying, killing, stealing, and committing adultery;
　they break all bounds and murder follows murder.
Therefore the land mourns,
　and all who dwell in it languish,
and also the beasts of the field,
　and the birds of the air;
　and even the fish of the sea are taken away. (Hos. 4:1–3)

To this indictment one might add Isa. 24, which extends the vision of judgment to embrace the entire cosmos. For what reason? Not because of some whimsical act of the deity, but because "the land lies polluted under its inhabitants; for they have transgressed the laws, violated the statutes, broken the everlasting covenant" (Isa. 24:5). We see in microcosm both the notion of society that the prophets draw from early Yahwistic tradition and their vision of the consequences of human repudiation of God's gracious sovereignty.

After the catastrophe in fact occurred, we find a new stage of prophecy, represented by Second Isaiah: "Comfort, comfort my people" (Isa. 40:1). Here the heavenly heralds are sent out to tell the nation that her warfare is ended, that a harsh stage of Yahweh's dealing with the people is over. Beyond tragedy, grace again prevails. But the people are restored not only for their own blessing, but in order that God's Torah and God's salvation might reach all peoples (cf. Isa. 42:1–17 and 49:1–6).

The Applicability of the Prophetic Mode

Our examples of the political engagement of prophets of course could be expanded, but they suffice as background for further reflection. Perhaps we can promote such reflection with several suggestions regarding the applicability of the prophetic mode that arise from our survey of biblical prophecy.

As suggested at the outset, the question of applicability is tied to the question of whether intrinsic connections exist between the history of ancient Israel and our own nation's history, for only upon the basis of such connections can we argue for the continued validity of the model of prophetic critique and reformation. I believe that such connections can be demonstrated.

Robert Bellah in *The Broken Covenant* has suggested that we as a country have strayed from our mandate, our Constitution.[9] In effect, we have broken our covenant as a people, violated our constitutional foundation. Neal Riemer has argued that we need to look back to the creative breakthrough of James Madison and his associates if we are to rediscover the model of transformation through ongoing revolution.[10] A connection immediately suggests itself. Above we drew attention to early Israel's "constitution," the Sinai covenant with its Decalogue. It would be interesting to compare this covenant document to our founding document, the U.S. Constitution. We can go on to draw connections between the Book of the Covenant, with its protections of human rights, and the Bill of Rights, for both elaborate on the cardinal principles of the founding documents. More than this, Israel's historical credo bears similarities in function to our own national epic (incomplete as it is). Both relate stories of the passage from bondage to freedom under God's providence and thereby strengthen the resolve of the nation's citizens to live as a free people, not only in the sense of withstanding the efforts of others to enslave them, but also in the sense of withstanding the temptation to enslave others.

Moreover, the epic, when functioning properly, provides a creative dynamic for the renewal of the revolution. The revolution in Israel was not completed in its foundational stages. Here one must be on guard against the kind of romanticizing of Israel's early history that flaws Norman Gottwald's *The Tribes of Yahweh*.[11] The revolution was not completed by early Israel. One can detect in the Book of Judges the confusion of that early period, marked by rampant idolatry and violence. The patriarchal bias of the Yahwistic cult illustrates another aspect of the persisting captivity of God's covenant people. The history of Yahwistic slave laws offers a third example of the unfinished revolution. Though the Book of the Covenant gives noticeable examples of social breakthrough, its provision for the release of slaves is limited to males. But the revolution against slave structures continued, as evidenced by the reformulation of the law of release in Deuteronomy to cover male and female slaves, and the total prohibition against the enslavement of Hebrews in the Book of Leviticus. The Yahwistic social revolution, supported by the dynamic and open-ended Yahwistic ontology, was ongoing.

Is it possible to regard as an extension of that revolution and its underlying ontology our struggle today over human rights and international justice? To be sure, when one considers how many years intervened between the Exodus and the Emancipation Proclamation, one is not permitted to indulge in facile optimism. We face the distinct danger that our legal system will fall under the power of those holding to an ideology of privilege and that our foreign policy will be transformed into an ideal of reenslavement of major parts of the world. There is also the attendant danger that by romanticizing the past, we will freeze our epic into a static myth. We have already seen that this is an inappropriate use of a national epic, which should never become a primordial myth. Rather, the epic must remain an open invitation to a people to keep moving forward on the basis of the vision arising from its story and with a clear awareness of its imperfections and the unfinished nature of its task. We need only consider the history of Native Americans to be shocked out of a facile reading of our history. Our epic, like Israel's, functions properly only if it reminds us of our revolutionary beginnings and remains a source for the renewal of our own critical ontology in the face of ever present reactionary forces.

We therefore venture to suggest that this function of the epic in renewing our sense of a dynamic ontology provides a meaningful connection between ancient Israel and our country and is thus an important aspect of the prophetic mode. If this is so, it is important to note that one of the vital applications of our epic and the ontology it implies is found in prophetic critique and renewal.

It is therefore not a casual option, but an urgent mandate, that we redirect our attention to the prophets lest the ideal of a free democracy be lost. And like the prophets, we will do well to consider the story of the Exodus a paradigm that sheds light on our own history as a free people struggling to preserve its precious freedom against disturbing odds.

In considering such proposals, however, it is important to emphasize that the traditions of the Bible do not imply any special status for the United States among the family of nations. A similar comparison could be made with the epic and founding documents of any nation. We are dealing with analogies that can be useful in clarifying the continued validity of the prophetic mode in the political process, and not with arguments for the superior status or destiny of any modern nation.[12]

Prophets are necessary today, as they were in ancient Israel, to keep us in touch with our foundational stage of life. For in remembering our epic and the values, morals, and sociopolitical ideals drawn from it, we clarify the vision that enables us to be agents of reconciliation and healing in our society and world. In forgetting, we abet social decline and moral decay, for more than a cognitive exercise is involved in remembering and forgetting. History is not just a tale to be retold, but the source of our being, the fashioner of our character, and the determiner of our destiny. For this reason it is a matter of great urgency that we relearn the significance of words such as these: "You shall not oppress a stranger. You know the heart of a stranger, for you were strangers in the land of Egypt" (Exod. 23:9).

Notes

1. Neal Riemer, *The Future of the Democratic Revolution: Toward a More Prophetic Politics* (New York: Praeger, 1984), 253.

2. Robert R. Wilson, *Prophecy and Society in Ancient Israel* (Philadelphia: Fortress Press, 1980).

3. 1 Kings 21:20 (Revised Standard Version). All biblical citations are from the RSV.

4. Johannes Lindblom, *Prophecy in Ancient Israel* (Oxford: Basil Blackwell, 1962).

5. This material is most conveniently collected in James B. Pritchard, ed., *Eastern Texts Relating to the Old Testament* (Princeton, N.J.: Princeton University Press, 1969).

6. Ibid., 60–72.

7. For a full treatment of the origin and development of his triadic notion of community in Israel, see Paul D. Hanson, *The People Called: The Growth of Community in the Bible* (New York: Harper & Row, 1986).

8. Peter Kyle McCarter Jr., *1 Samuel,* vol. 8 of the Anchor Bible (Garden City, N.J.: Doubleday, 1980), 18–23.

9. Robert N. Bellah, *The Broken Covenant: American Civil Religion in Time of Trial* (New York: Seabury Press, 1975).

10. Riemer, *Future of the Democratic Revolution,* 149–55.

11. Norman K. Gottwald, *The Tribes of Yahweh* (Maryknoll, N.Y.: Orbis Books, 1979).

12. Cf. Paul D. Hanson, "The Role of Scripture in Times of Crisis," *Word and World* 1 (1981): 116–27.

2

Prophecy and Social Criticism

Michael Walzer

My aim in this essay is to understand the practice of prophecy in ancient Israel. I don't mean the prophet himself; I am not interested in the psychology of inspiration or of ecstasy. Nor do I mean the prophetic texts; these are painfully obscure at many points, and I don't possess the historical or philological knowledge necessary to decipher them (or even to offer speculative readings of disputed passages). I want to understand prophecy as a social practice: not the men or the texts, but the message—and also the reception of the message. Of course, there were prophets before the ones we know, seers and soothsayers, oracles, diviners, and clairvoyants; and there is nothing very puzzling about their messages or about their audiences. Foretellings of doom and glory will always find listeners, especially when the doom is for enemies, the glory for ourselves. The people say, says Isaiah, "Speak unto us smooth things,"[1] and that's what the professional prophets of courts and temples commonly do.[2] It's only when these foretellings are set within a moral frame, when they are an occasion for indignation, when prophecy is also criticism, provocation, a verbal assault on the institutions and activities of everyday life, that it becomes interesting. Then it's a puzzle why people listen—and not only listen but copy down, preserve, and repeat the prophetic message. It's not a smooth message; it can't be happily heard or readily followed; the people, most of them, don't do what the prophet urges them to do. But they choose to remember his urging. Why?

It is here, writes Max Weber, "that the demagogue appears for the first time in the records of history."[3] But that's not quite right (as Weber himself suggests later on in his *Ancient Judaism*), for though the prophets spoke to the people and, arguably, on their behalf, they do not seem to have sought a popular following, nor ever to have aspired to political power. Weber is closer to the truth when he argues that the prophecies, written down and circulated in the cities of Israel and Judah, represent the earliest known example of the political pamphlet.[4] But the suggestion is too narrow. Prophetic religion embraced not only politics but every aspect of social life. The prophets were social critics, the first social critics in the West, and we can learn from reading them and from reading about them something of the conditions that make criticism possible and of the place and standing of the critic in the society he criticizes.

Prophecy and Covenant

The first thing to notice is that the prophetic message depends upon previous messages. It isn't something radically new. We can detect a certain theological revisionism in some of the later prophets, but none of them presents an entirely original doctrine. For the most part, they disclaim originality—and not only in the obvious sense that they attribute their message to God. It is more important that they continually refer themselves to the epic history and the moral teaching of the Torah: "He hath showed thee, O man, what is good. . . ." (Mic. 6:8). The past tense is significant. The prophets assume the previous messages, the divine "showings," the immediacy of history and law in the minds of their listeners. They have no esoteric teaching, not even for their closest disciples. They speak to a large audience and, for all their anger, they seem to take that audience for granted; they assume, writes Lindblom, "that their words could be immediately understood and accepted."[5]

This assumption has its correlate in the social structure of ancient Israel: a loose, localized, and conflict-ridden set of arrangements that stood at some distance from the unified hierarchies of Egypt to the west and Assyria to the east. In Israel religion was not the exclusive possession of royal bureaucrats. Prophecy in the form we know it would not have been possible except for the relative weakness of priesthood and bureaucracy in the everyday life of the country. The necessary background conditions are indicated in the prophetic texts: justice is done (or not done) in the "gates" of the city, and religion is discussed in the streets.[6] The Bible clearly suggests the existence among the Israelites of a strong lay and popular religiosity. This had two aspects, individual piety and a more or less common moral theology; taken together, the two made for a culture of prayer and argument that was independent of the more formal religious culture of pilgrimage and sacrifice. Sustained, no doubt, as Weber says, by "circles of urban intellectuals," this informal religiosity also reached beyond such circles.[7] Had it not done so, the prophet would never have found his audience.

Or prophecy would have taken a wholly different form. I will try to illustrate one alternative possibility out of the Book of Jonah, a tale about a prophet sent by God to the city of Nineveh, where the appeal to Israel's history and law would obviously make no sense. But first I need to say something more about the conditions under which the appeal does make sense—most crucially, about the strength and legitimacy of lay religion. In part, this is a matter of popular practices, like the practice of spontaneous prayer that Moshe Greenberg has recently revealed to us.[8] But there is also what we might call an idea, or even a doctrine, of lay religiosity. The doctrine is entirely appropriate to a covenantal creed, and it is more clearly set forth in Deuteronomy, the crucial exposition of Israel's covenant theology. The precise relation of Deuteronomy to the prophetic movement is a subject of ongoing scholarly debate. Did the prophets influence the Deuteronomic writers, or the writers the prophets? It seems likely that influence worked in both directions and in ways that we shall never wholly understand. In any case, a large number of passages in the prophetic books echo (or anticipate?) the Deuteronomic text as we now have it, and the covenantal tradition that Deuteronomy elaborates is surely older than Amos, the first of the literary prophets.[9] So I shall take the book to suggest the doctrinal background of prophecy: a normative account of the informal and unpriestly culture of prayer and argument.

I want to look briefly at two passages, the first from the end of the book, the second from the beginning. Whether either of these was part of the manuscript "discovered" in the temple in Jerusalem in the year 621 B.C., I can't say; nor can anyone else. But they share the spirit of the original as a covenantal document.

> For this commandment which I command thee this day, it is not hidden from thee [Hebrew: *felah*, alternatively translated, it is not too hard for thee]; neither is it far off.
> It is not in heaven, that thou shouldest say, Who shall go up for us to heaven, and bring it unto us, that we may hear it, and do it?
> Neither is it beyond the sea, that thou shouldest say, Who shall go over the sea for us, and bring it unto us, that we may hear it, and do it?
> But the word is very nigh unto thee, in thy mouth, and in thy heart, that thou mayest do it. (Deut. 30:11–14, Authorized [King James] Version)

Moses, indeed, climbed the mountain, but no one need do that again. There is no longer any special role for mediators between the people and God. The law is not in heaven; it is a social possession. The prophet need only show the people their own hearts. If his is a "voice in the wilderness" (Isa. 40:3), it is not because he has embarked on a lonely or heroic quest for God's commandments. The image recalls the history of the people themselves, their own wilderness time, when God's voice was the voice in the wilderness, and reminds them that they already know the commandments. And though they may need to be reminded, the knowledge is readily renewed—for the Torah is not an esoteric teaching. It isn't hidden, obscure, difficult (the Hebrew word has all these meanings, as well as "marvelous" and "set aside," as a sacred text might be set aside for a body of specially trained priests). The teaching is available, common, popular, so much so that everyone is commanded to speak about it: "And these words which I command thee this day shall be in thine heart: And thou shalt teach them diligently unto thy children, and shalt talk of them when thou sittest in thine house, and when thou walkest by the way, and when thou liest down and when thou risest up" (Deut. 6:6–7).

Prophecy is a special kind of talking, not so much an educated as an inspired and poetic version of what must have been at least sometimes, among some significant part of the prophet's audience, ordinary discourse. It is not only ritual repetition of key texts, but heartfelt prayer, storytelling, doctrinal interpretation. The Bible provides evidence for all of this, and prophecy is continuous with it, dependent upon it. Though there is conflict between the prophets and the established priesthood, prophecy does not in any sense constitute an underground or, as we shall see, a sectarian movement. In the dispute between Amos and the priest Amaziah, it is the prophet who appeals to religious tradition, the priest only to reason of state (Amos 7:10–17). Prophecy aims to arouse remembrance, recognition, indignation, repentance. In Hebrew, the last of these words derives from a root meaning to turn, to turn back, to return, and so it implies that repentance is parasitic upon a previously accepted and commonly understood morality. The same implication is apparent in prophecy itself. The prophet foretells doom, but it isn't only fear of coming disasters but also knowledge of the law, a sense of their own history, a feeling for the religious tradition, that motivates his listeners. Prophetic admonition, writes Moshe Greenberg,

> presupposes common ground on which prophet and audience stand, not only regarding historical traditions but religious demands as well. The prophets seem to appeal to their audience's better nature, confronting them with demands of God that they know (or knew) but wish to ignore or forget. . . . There is more than a little optimism underlying the generations-long succession of reforming prophets; it reflects the prophets' confidence that, in the final analysis, they had advocates in the hearts of their audiences.[10]

Two Prophets: Jonah and Amos

Contrast this view, now, with the example provided by the Book of Jonah. This is a late (postexilic) tale commonly taken to argue for the universalism of divine law and divine concern—though universalism is, as we will see, an ancient argument. Perhaps Jonah is an ancient tale, retold sometime after the return from Babylonia as an attack upon the parochialism of the Judean restoration. The immediate issue of the story is the reversibility of divine decree, an issue raised at least implicitly in the earliest prophets.[11] That God himself is capable of "repentance" is suggested by Amos (7:3), and there is a striking example even earlier, in the Exodus story. But I want to stress another feature of the Book of Jonah and contrast the content of Jonah's message with that of the prophets in Israel. The contrast would be sharper if the Jonah of the tale could be identified with the prophet Jonah son of Amitai mentioned in 2 Kings 14:25, a contemporary of Amos, but it does not depend upon the identification. For my immediate purposes the provenance of the tale and its author's intentions matter less than the tale itself. I shall take the "plot" literally and pass over its possible ironies. When he prophesies doom in Nineveh, Jonah is necessarily a different sort of prophet than Amos in Beth-El or Micah in Jerusalem, for doom is the entire content of his prophecy. He can't refer to a religious tradition or a moral law embodied in covenantal form. Whatever the religion of the inhabitants of Nineveh, Jonah appears to know nothing about it and to take no interest in it. His prophecy is a single sentence: "Yet forty days and Nineveh shall be overthrown" (Jon. 3:4).

Now, "overthrown" is the verb used in Genesis to describe the fate of Sodom and Gomorrah, and it serves to assimilate Nineveh to these two cities. All three are charged with a general wickedness and "violence" (another repeated word). In the case of Sodom this is at least minimally specified: its immediate form is the sexual mistreatment of guests and strangers. But we actually know very little of the internal life of Sodom or of the moral history or commitments of its citizens. And we know even less of Nineveh. Jonah tells us nothing at all: This is prophecy without poetry, without resonance, allusion, or specification. Jonah comes and goes, an alien voice, a mere messenger, unconnected to the people of the city. Even the regard for the people that God teaches him at the end is only a rather abstract "pity" for the "six score thousand persons that cannot discern between their right hand and their left hand" (Jon. 4:11).

This last phrase probably refers to the children of Nineveh; the adults, it appears, have some discernment, for they repent of their "violence." Though Jonah does not say anything about it, there is some moral knowledge to which they can return, some basic understanding that God and his prophet alike presuppose. Of course, Nineveh has its own moral and religious history, its own creed, its own code, its own shrines and priests, its own gods. But it is not Jonah's purpose to remind the people of what is their own; only a local prophet could do that. What Jonah achieves is simply this: The people recognize and turn away "from the violence that is in their hands" (Jon. 3:8). What is this "violence" whose recognition does not depend upon a particular moral or religious history?

The first two chapters of the Book of Amos provide an answer to this question. Here the prophet "judges" a group of nations with which Israel has recently been at war, and he provides a brief, though sometimes obscure, account of their crimes. Damascus "threshed Gilead with sledges of iron," a reference, apparently, to extreme cruelty in warfare; Gaza "carried away captive a whole captivity"; Tyre violated a treaty; Edom pursued "his brother with the sword, and did cast off all pity"; Ammon "ripped up the women with child of Gilead"; Moab burned the bones of the king of Edom, denying him honorable burial. All these are crimes of "violence," and in all of them the victims are enemies and strangers, not fellow citizens. These are the only crimes for which the "nations" (in contrast to Israel and Judah) are punished. The prophet judges Israel's neighbors only for what Weber calls "violations of a form of international religious law . . . presupposed as valid among the Palestine peoples."[12] Of the everyday morality of these peoples, their domestic practices and institutions, Amos, like Jonah in Nineveh, has nothing to say.

Amos's judgment of the nations suggests not a late but an early and minimal universalism. The existence of some kind of "international" law, fixing the treatment of enemies and strangers, is already apparent in the story of Sodom and Gomorrah, to which Amos refers casually (4:11) as if his audience knows it well. The author of the Book of Jonah, centuries later, adds nothing to the argument. God will punish "violence" wherever it occurs. But alongside this universalism there is a more particularist message, delivered only (at least by Israelite prophets) to the children of Israel: "You only have I known of all the families of the earth; Therefore I will visit upon you all your iniquities" (Amos 3:2).

All your iniquities, domestic as well as international: the elaboration of this phrase constitutes the particular morality, the substantive argument of the prophets.

The Prophets' Concern for the People of Israel

The concern of the prophets is for *this* people, their own people, the "family" that came up out of Egypt (Amos 2:10). (I will ignore for my present purposes the political division between the rival kingdoms of Israel and Judah; the two share a history and a law, and prophets like Amos go back and forth between them.) Jonah has no personal interest in Nineveh and no knowledge, as I have already argued, of its moral history. Hence Martin Buber is wrong to call the Jonah story a "paradigm of the prophetic nature and task."[13] The paradigmatic task of the prophets is to judge the people's relations with one another (and with "their" God), to judge the internal character of their society—exactly what Jonah does not do. Prophetic teaching, writes Lindblom more accurately, "is characterized by the principle of solidarity. Behind the demand for charity and justice . . . lies the idea of the *people,* the people as an organic whole, united by election and covenant," singled out, we might say, by a peculiar history.[14] Committed to this solidarity, the prophets avoid sectarianism just as they avoid any larger universalism. They attempt no further singling out; they make no effort to gather around themselves a band of "brethren." When they address their audience, they always use inclusive proper names—Israel, Joseph, Jacob. Their focus is always on the fate of the covenanted community as a whole.

For the same reason, the message of the prophets is resolutely this-worldly. Theirs is a social and workaday ethic. Two points are crucial here, both of which I take from Weber, whose comparative perspective is especially illuminating.[15] First, there is no prophetic utopia, no account (in the style of Plato, say) of the "best" political or religious regime, a regime free from history, located anywhere or nowhere. The prophets don't have philosophical imaginations. They are rooted, for all their anger, in their own societies. The house of Israel is *here,* and it needs only to be ordered in accordance with its own laws. Second, the prophets take no interest in individual salvation or in the perfection of their own souls. They are not religious adepts or mystics; they never advocate asceticism or world-rejection. Wrongdoing and rightdoing alike are social experiences, and the prophet and his listeners are involved in these experiences in accordance with the principle of solidarity, whether or not any given right or wrong act is their own. Utopian speculation and world-rejection are two forms of escape from particularism. The two always take culturally specific forms, of course, but they are in principle available without regard to cultural identity: Anyone can leave the world behind, anyone can come to "nowhere." The prophetic argument, by contrast, is that *this* people must live in *this* way.

The prophets invoke a particular religious tradition and a particular moral law, both of which they assume their audience knows. The references are constant, and while some of them are mysterious to us, they were presumably not mysterious to the men and women who gathered at Beth-El or Jerusalem to listen. We need footnotes, but prophecy is not, like some modern poetry, meant to be read with footnotes. Consider, for example, these lines from Amos, which follow close upon the famous passage about selling the righteous for silver and the needy for a pair of shoes: "And they lay themselves down beside every altar upon clothes taken in pledge" (Amos 2:8).

The reference here is to the law of Exod. 22:26–27 (part of the Book of the

Covenant): "If thou at all take thy neighbor's raiment to pledge, thou shalt deliver it unto him by the time the sun goeth down: For that is his covering only, it is his raiment for his skin: wherein shall he sleep?" The prophet's complaint makes no sense without the law. Whether the law was already written down (as seems likely in this case) or known only through an oral tradition, the point is that it was known—and, judging from the form of the reference, commonly known. It is also worth saying that neither the law nor the morality behind the law is universally known. We have different ideas about the pledge (the pawn), and it is not obvious that our ideas are unjust.

But the prophets don't only recall and repeat the tradition, they also interpret and revise it. Even here, they don't act alone; prophecy has a prehistory in the tradition itself. The new emphasis upon the social code of Exodus, a code that has its origin in the experience of bondage and is designed to guard against a repetition of that experience, is rooted in discussions and arguments that must have gone on, that are easy to imagine, in the cities of Israel and Judah. Amos can hardly have been the first person to realize that the law of the pledge, say, was being violated. He speaks against a background of urban growth and class differentiation that gave that law, and all the Exodus laws, a new relevance.[16] Similarly, the prophetic deemphasis of ritual sacrifice is rooted in popular piety, in the rejection or avoidance of priestly mediation, in a spontaneous acting out, through individual prayer, of the ancient dream that all Israel would be a "kingdom of priests and a holy nation."[17] Still, it is the prophets who most clearly draw the connection between piety and conduct and who most explicitly use the Exodus laws as a weapon of social criticism.

As before, I shall follow here the argument of Amos, in whose work both the new emphasis and the new deemphasis are dramatically displayed. We must assume the social changes that precede and motivate Amos's prophecy: the introduction of greater and greater inequalities into what had been, and still was ideally, an association of freemen. No doubt, inequality of some sort was already ancient, else there would have been no ancient social code aimed at limiting and ameliorating its effects. But by the eighth century B.C., the years of monarchic rule had produced in and around the court and in the growing cities a new upper class feeding on a new lower class. Archaeological finds confirm the development: "the simple, uniform houses of the earlier centuries had been replaced by luxurious dwellings of the rich on the one hand, by hovels on the other."[18] Amos is, above all, a critic of this new upper class, whose members are increasingly capable of, and committed to, what we now call a high standard of living, with winter houses and summer houses (3:15), couches of ivory (6:4), sumptuous feasts, and costly perfumes: "That drink wine in bowls/ And anoint themselves with the chief ointments" (Amos 6:6).

The prophet's caustic description of all this is often characterized as a kind of rural puritanism, the dislike of a countryman for city fanciness.[19] Perhaps there is something to this view, though I have already suggested that prophecy draws upon urban practices and arguments. In any case, Amos's main charge, his critical message, is not that the rich live well, but that they live well at the expense of the poor. They have forgotten not only the laws of the covenant, but the bond itself, the principle of solidarity: "They are not grieved for the hurt of Joseph" (6:6). More than this: they are themselves responsible for the hurt of Joseph; they are guilty of the Egyptian crime of oppression.

Amos's word for "oppress" is *'asok;* he uses the Exodus word *lahatz* only once (6:14), when he is describing what will happen to Israel at the hands of an (unnamed) foreign power. The shift in terminology suggests nicely how Amos (or unknown speakers or writers before him) responds, within the tradition, to a new social experience. *Lahatz* means to press down, to squeeze, to crush, to constrain, to coerce. The range of meanings evoked by *'asok* is quite different: to maltreat, to exploit, to wrong, to injure, to extort, to defraud. *Lahatz* has political, *'asok* economic, connotations. Of course, Egyptian oppression was also economic in character, and in eighth-century Israel and Judah the oppression of the poor was upheld by the monarchic regimes. Amos condemns both the "great houses" and the "palaces." But the primary experience was of tyranny in the first case, extortion and exploitation in the second. The new bondage had its origin in commerce—usury, indebtedness, default, and confiscation; its setting was more significantly the market than the state. Amos addresses himself specifically to avaricious merchants:

Hear this, O ye that would swallow the needy,
And destroy the poor of the land,
Saying, When will the new moon be gone, that we may sell grain?
And the Sabbath, that we may set forth corn?
Making the ephah small, and the shekel great,
And falsifying the balances of deceit;
That we may buy the poor for silver,
And the needy for a pair of shoes,
And sell the refuse of the corn. (Amos 8:4–6)

The address, indeed, is doubly specific: it is to avaricious *Israelite* merchants, who can hardly wait for the end of Israel's holy days, when business dealings are forbidden, so that they can return to the business of extortion and fraud. Amos suggests a hard question: What kind of religion is it that provides only temporary and intermittent restraints on avarice and oppression? What is the quality of worship if it does not direct the heart toward goodness? As the prophet describes them, the oppressors of the poor and needy are scrupulously "orthodox." They observe the festival of the new moon, they keep the sabbath, they attend the religious assemblies, offer the required sacrifices, join in the hymns that accompany the priestly rites. But all this is mere hypocrisy if it doesn't translate into everyday conduct in accordance with the covenantal code. Ritual observance alone is not what God requires of Israel. Pointing toward the real requirement, Amos evokes the memory of the Exodus: "Did ye bring unto Me sacrifices and offerings in the wilderness forty years, O house of Israel?" (5:25). In the Exodus story as we have it, they did; perhaps Amos has access to an alternative tradition.[20] But the practice of sacrifice is not, in any case, what was to be learned from the experience of liberation. Indeed, if oppression continues, nothing has been learned, however many animals are sacrificed.

This is the standard form of social criticism, and though later critics rarely achieve the angry poetry of the prophets, we can recognize in their work the same intellectual structure: the identification of ritual pronouncements and "respectable" behavior as hypocritical, the search for core values (to which hypocrisy is always a clue), the demand for an everyday life in accordance with these values. The critic begins with revulsion and ends with affirmation:

I hate, I despise your feasts,
And I will take no delight in your solemn assemblies.
Yea, though ye offer me burnt-offerings and your meal-offerings,
I will not accept them. . . .
Take thou away from me the noise of thy songs;
And let me not hear the melody of thy psalteries.
But let justice well up as waters,
And righteousness as a mighty stream. (Amos 5:21–24)

The only purpose of the ceremonies is to remind the people of their moral commitments: God's law and the wilderness covenant. If that purpose is not served, then the ceremonies are of no use. Less than no use: for they generate among rich and avaricious Israelites a false sense of security—as if they were safe from divine wrath. The prophecies of doom, which make up so much of Amos's message, are designed to dispel that sense, to shatter the confidence of the conventionally pious: "Woe to them that are at ease in Zion" (6:1). Neither "woe" nor "hate" constitutes the substance of Amos's argument, however; the substance is "justice" and "righteousness."

But how does the prophet know that justice and righteousness are the core values of the Israelite tradition? Why not sacrifice, song, and solemnity? Why not ritual decorum and deference to God's priests? Presumably if Amaziah had offered a positive defense of his own activities at Beth-El, he would have given us a different picture of Israelite values. How then would the argument between Amaziah and Amos move toward closure? Both priest and prophet could cite texts—there is never a lack of texts—and both would find supporters in the crowd that gathered at the shrine. I suppose that disagreements of this sort don't move toward closure. Nor would they even if God himself were to intervene, for all he can provide is another text, subject to interpretation exactly like the earlier ones. Still, we can recognize good and bad arguments, strong and weak interpretations along the way. In this case, it is significant that Amaziah makes no positive claims at all. His silence is a kind of admission that Amos has reached to the realities of Israelite religion—also, perhaps, that he has found, as Greenberg says, advocates in the hearts of the people. That doesn't end the disagreement, and not only because the prophet is apparently forced to leave Beth-El while Amaziah continues his priestly routines. The claim that God is better served by scrupulous worship than by just dealings with one's fellows, even if it is only made implicitly, has an enduring appeal: worship is easier than justice. Still, Amos has won the only kind of victory that is available: He has evoked the core values of his audience in a powerful and plausible way. He suggests an identification of the poor in Israel with the Israelite slaves in Egypt and so makes justice the primary religious demand. Why else did God deliver the people, this people, from the house of bondage?

Prophecy as Social Criticism

Amos's prophecy is social criticism because it challenges the leaders, the conventions, the ritual practices of a particular society and because it does so in the name of a particular social code. I have already distinguished this sort of prophecy from the sort represented by Jonah in Nineveh. Jonah is a mere messenger who makes no appeal to a social code (though he may appeal, without saying so, to a kind of international law). A second distinction is also useful, not between prophet and messenger, but between prophet and missionary. The missionary carries his social code with him wherever he goes, and when he challenges the practices of the society he enters (but doesn't join), he does so in terms that are likely to be, at least at first, incomprehensible to the members. They will understand only insofar as they are converted. The work of the missionary is often a critical activity; it may begin a long process of social change, as elements of his code are naturalized into the local religious or moral culture, connected to certain ideas within the established tradition, juxtaposed to others. But the missionary is not properly called a social critic. Later on, social critics may use the tools the missionary has supplied (though not only those) and judge their fellows in ways not possible before he came. But they won't be

trying to convert their fellows to a new way of life, only offering a new interpretation of an old way.

The social critic properly understood is himself a member. It is not only that
he criticizes his fellows, but that he suggests reforms that they can undertake
while still remaining *fellow* members of the same society. Amos, of course,
can be read differently. The prophecies of doom are so powerful and unrelenting that, on some interpretations, they overwhelm any possible argument for
repentance and reform. Then the pleas for justice and the promises of divine
comfort at the end seem unconvincing—as if they come (as many commenta-
tors believe, at least of the promises) from another hand.[21] The animating pas-
sion of the book as a whole, however, is surely a deep concern for "the hurt of
Joseph," a powerful sense of solidarity, a commitment to the covenant that
makes Israel . . . Israel. It isn't only his anger but also his concern and commitment that make Amos a critic. He aims at an internal reformation that will
bring the new oppression of Israel, or of poor and needy Israelites, to an end.
That is the social meaning he has in mind when he repeats (or anticipates) the
Deuteronomic injunction, "Seek good, and not evil, that ye may live" (Amos
5:15; cf. Deut. 30:15–20).

Amos also prophesies, as we have seen, against nations other than Israel.
Here he is a critic from the outside, like Jonah, and he limits himself to external behavior, violations of some sort of international law. I don't mean to suggest, however, that the provisions of Israel's covenant have no general validity.
No doubt, one could abstract universal rules from them—above all, one universal rule: *don't oppress the poor* (for oppression is, as Weber writes, "the
pre-eminent vice" in the eyes of the Israelite prophets).[22] And then one could
judge and condemn the oppression of Syrians, or Philistines, or Moabites by
their avaricious fellows in the same way that the prophets judge and condemn
the oppression of Israelites. But not, in fact, in the same way; not with the
same words, images, references; not with regard to the same practices and religious principles. For the power of a prophet like Amos derives from his ability
to say what oppression means, how it is experienced, in *this* time and place,
and to explain how it is connected with other features of a shared social life.
Amos has an argument to make about oppression and religious observance,
and it is one of his chief arguments: that it is entirely possible to trample upon
the poor and to observe the sabbath. And from this he concludes that the laws
against oppression take precedence over the sabbath laws. The hierarchy is
specific; it invites the prophet's listeners to remember that the original point of
the sabbath was "that thy manservant and thy maid servant may rest as well as
thou" (Deut. 5:14). Prophecy would have little life, and little effect, if it could
not evoke memories of this sort. We might think of it then as an academic exercise. In a strange country, Amos would resemble Samson in Gaza. Not eyeless,

but tongueless: he might indeed see the oppression, but he would not be able to give it a name or speak about it to the hearts of the people.

Of course, other nations can read and admire the Israelite prophets, translate the prophecies into their own language (footnoting the references), and find analogies in their own society for the practices the prophets condemn. Just how wide the actual range of reading and admiration is, I am not sure. It obviously doesn't coincide with the possible range, and it may well be limited to those nations whose history is in some significant sense continuous with the history of Israel. In principle, though, it could extend further than that. What would it mean if it did? It's unlikely, I think, that what distant readers would learn from the prophets would be a set of abstract rules—or, again, a single rule: *don't oppress the poor.* If they knew what oppression was (if they could translate the Hebrew word *'asok*), they would already know that much. The rule, though it might have different references and applications, would be familiar. More likely, distant readers would be moved to imitate the practice of prophecy or, perhaps, to listen in a new way to their own prophets. Whether prophecy, in one form or another, was already established among them or successfully reproduced, it is the practice, not the message, that would be repeated. Readers might learn to be social critics; the criticism, however, would be their own. Indeed, the message would have to be different if the practice was to be the same, else it would lack the local vividness and historical reference that prophecy (and social criticism) requires.

The case is different with regard to Amos's prophecies against the nations. Here it is precisely the message that gets repeated: don't violate treaties, don't kill innocent women and children, don't transport whole nations into involuntary exile. Confirmed from many sides, these rules are incorporated into a law of nations that isn't all that much more extensive than the "international" law of Amos's time. But their prophetic utterance is quickly forgotten. For the utterance is not specific to the rules; vividness and reference are alike unnecessary. Is there some philosophical distinction between the two sorts of rules, against violence and against oppression? The two have the same linguistic form. But they are not the same. The rules against violence arise from the experience of international relations, the rules against oppression from the experience of internal relations. The first regulate our contacts with strangers; the second regulate our common life. The first are stereotyped in form and application; they are set against a background of standard expectations, based on a narrow range of shared experience. The second are complex in form and various in application; they are set against a background of multiple and sometimes conflicting expectations, rooted in a long and dense history. The first tend toward universality, the second toward particularity.

It is a mistake, then, to praise the prophets for their universalist message.

For what is most admirable about them is their particularist quarrel, which is also God's quarrel, with the children of Israel. Here they invested their anger and their poetic genius. The line that Amos atttributes to God, "You only have I known of all the families of the earth," could have come also from his own heart. He knows one nation, one history, and it's that knowledge that makes his criticism so rich, so concrete, so detailed. We can, again, abstract the rules and apply them to other nations, but that's not the "use" that Amos invites. What he invites is not application but reiteration. Each nation can have its own prophecy, just as it has its own history, its own deliverance, its own quarrel with God.

> Have not I brought up Israel out of the land of Egypt,
> And the Philistines from Caphtor,
> And Aram from Kir? (Amos 9:7)

Notes

1. Isa. 30:10 (Masoretic Text). Unless otherwise noted, all biblical citations are from *The Holy Scriptures (Masoretic Text)*, updated ed. (Philadelphia: The Jewish Publication Society of America, 1955).

2. See the opening chapters of Johannes Lindblom, *Prophecy in Ancient Israel* (Oxford: Basil Blackwell, 1962) and Joseph Blenkinsopp, *A History of Prophecy in Israel* (London: SPCK, 1984).

3. Max Weber, *Ancient Judaism,* trans. H. H. Gerth and Don Martindale (Glencoe, Ill.: Free Press, 1952), 268–69.

4. Ibid., 272.

5. Lindblom, *Prophecy,* 313.

6. On the importance of "the court in the gates," see James Luther May, *Amos: A Commentary* (Philadelphia: Westminster Press, 1969), 11, 93.

7. Weber, *Ancient Judaism,* 279.

8. Moshe Greenberg, *Biblical Prose Prayer as a Window to the Popular Religion of Ancient Israel* (Berkeley and Los Angeles: University of California Press, 1983).

9. See Anthony Phillips, "Prophecy and Law," in *Israel's Prophetic Tradition,* ed. Richard Coggins, Anthony Phillips, and Michael Knibb (Cambridge: Cambridge University Press, 1982), 218.

10. Greenberg, *Biblical Prose Prayer,* 56.

11. Yehezkel Kaufmann, *The Religion of Israel,* trans. Moshe Greenberg (Chicago: University of Chicago Press, 1960), 282–84, argues that the Book of Jonah as we have it dates from the eighth century B.C., but few scholars agree with him.

12. Weber, *Ancient Judaism,* 302.

13. Martin Buber, *The Prophetic Faith* (New York: Harper & Brothers, 1960), 104.

14. Lindblom, *Prophecy,* 344.

15. Weber, *Ancient Judaism,* 275, 285, 313–14.

16. See Martin Smith, *Palestinian Parties and Politics That Shaped the Old Testament* (New York: Columbia University Press, 1971), 138 ff.

17. Greenberg, *Biblical Prose Prayer*, 52.

18. Smith, *Palestinian Parties*, 139.

19. For example, Blenkinsopp, *History of Prophecy,* 95, and Henry McKeating, *The Cambridge Bible Commentary: Amos, Hosea, Micah* (Cambridge: Cambridge University Press, 1971), 5.

20. McKeating, *Amos, Hosea, Micah,* 47.

21. May, *Amos*, 164–65, but see McKeating, *Amos, Hosea, Micah,* 69–70.

22. Weber, *Ancient Judaism,* 281.

3

Politics and the Prophetic Tradition in Christianity

Glenn Tinder

"Why does man feel so sad in the 20th century?" Walker Percy asks, and it is an arresting question for an age in which attaining happiness has become something like a point of honor.[1] A likely answer is that, preoccupied with avoiding sadness in the immediate moment, we have become incapable of hope. We do not look ahead with expectancy. Because of the historical disasters and disappointments of our century, and of a commercialized culture, the spiritual content of which is summed up whenever a restaurant meal is served with the injunction "Enjoy!" we have lost the inclination and ability to live consciously into the future. But to find authentic life in the present moment is impossible. We are temporal creatures and are bound to feel sad if we cannot live with hope.

This, at any rate, is the answer suggested by the prophetic tradition. To speak summarily, this is a tradition, present in Judaism, Christianity, and elsewhere, which calls for historical expectancy. Hope—hope that is not merely personal but also social and political—is indispensable to an integrated life; where it is lacking, sadness is inevitable. To articulate this answer to Walker Percy's question is my purpose in this essay. I shall do this in terms of one particular version of the prophetic tradition, that of Christianity. My concern will not be to show that there is such a tradition in Christianity. It is well known that there is; that can be established merely by mentioning such names as Paul, Augustine, and Reinhold Niebuhr. My concern will be rather to show as clearly as possible the nature of the prophetic tradition in the Christian vision. Prophetic elements that are not merely compatible with Christianity, but integral to it, have often been neglected, even by great Christian writers. The result is not only to distort Christianity but to impoverish the prophetic outlook. By casting Christianity in its true prophetic form, I hope to convey something of the spiritual richness that can be embodied in prophetic hope.

I must note, however, that this concern arises from an interest not only in

Christianity and the prophetic vision but also in the possibilities of our over-coming the sadness inherent in the hedonistic preoccupations our society so assiduously cultivates. The twentieth century will be very much on my mind. I believe that the prophetic tradition has an important bearing on our situation today. I believe, too, that this tradition is available in some measure to every-one and is not restricted to Christians. I shall try to show why this is so.

Christian Prophetic Hope

There is something strange about arguing that Christianity is a prophetic reli-gion, for Jesus, in Christian eyes, was not one of the prophets. Rather, he was the fulfillment of prophetic expectations; through his life, the reign of God, anticipated by the prophets, began to be realized. In Christian faith, Jesus was in some sense the end of history and the end of historical expectancy. How, then, can Christianity be a prophetic faith?

The answer, of course, is implicit in the word "began": with Jesus the reign of God *began* to be realized. Jesus can be identified in a way that distinguishes him from the prophets, yet does not dim the prophetic purport of his teaching and life, by saying that he was the "chief cornerstone" of God's kingdom—a phrase from the Old Testament but explicitly recognized in relation to his own mission by Jesus himself.[2] With Jesus the forming of the kingdom of God began, but the completion still lies ahead. Jesus recast the historical expec-tancy expressed by the prophets but did not end or in any way weaken it. To be more specific, Jesus recast the prophetic tradition by becoming himself the object of prophetic expectancy. Thus Karl Barth can write that "the real New Testament says clearly that He who came is also He that comes." And he adds that the New Testament in this respect "takes its place naturally alongside the Old Testament. It is only the sharpened and clarified message of the expecta-tion in which Israel was already living."[3]

At this point one might ask what makes hope prophetic. Why speak of *prophetic* hope and not merely of hope? It cannot be simply in order to distin-guish from other kinds of hope the hope expressed by those we call prophets, for then the question is not answered but only rephrased: Why do we call them prophets? We can begin to see the distinctive character of prophetic hope by noting the assurance with which it is held; it is hope that cannot fail and thus can be sustained even when it has no apparent empirical grounds. It can live as "hope against hope." Such assurance points in turn toward a source of hope that transcends human calculations and human powers. Prophetic hope arises from transcendence, or God. This being so, yet another characteristic of prophetic hope is brought into view: it pertains to nations and peoples, not just to one hopeful person. Grounded in transcendence, it is historical, rather than merely personal. In sum, prophetic hope is in spirit indefeasible, in origin transcendental, and in scope all-encompassing.

Where exactly the line between prophetic hope and ordinary hope should be drawn in particular instances is no doubt disputable. It is surely not disputable, however, given the preceding definitions, that prophetic hope was called forth by the life and teaching of Jesus. Although not a prophet in the usual sense, Jesus was a prophetic figure. Preaching the imminent coming of the kingdom of God, and in his life—his unqualified love, his healing, his feeding of the multitudes—seeming to be the vivid presence of the kingdom of God, he created intense expectancy. Simultaneously prophet and messiah, he gave prophetic hope unprecedented dramatic force. Granted, as the centuries unfolded and God's kingdom did not visibly break into history, prophetic expectancy declined. Christianity came often to be identified with established institutions, and Christian leaders lost the inclination to view the existing order with the principled mistrust inherent in Jesus' original proclamation. Yet prophetic expectancy has flared up again and again among Christians, and it has become clear in our own time that the disappearance of such expectancy creates a breach between Christian faith and the faith of Jesus.[4]

Jesus did not merely claim that the kingdom of God was coming *sometime,* however, but that it was *near at hand,* and it may seem that this poses a serious problem. Has not Jesus' claim been long since disproved? The impression that it has, I suggest, comes from taking literally a proclamation that in truth was meant metaphorically. Nicolas Berdyaev somewhere says that "time is always on the verge of eternity," and perhaps that statement expresses as clearly as plain terms can the meaning of Jesus' metaphor. Time leads into eternity and is, so to speak, under the immediate command of eternity. Jesus dramatized the subordination of time to eternity with the use of a temporal metaphor—the kingdom of God is at hand. But to translate the temporal metaphor into a literal forecast, into expectations of an event to occur in a certain number of years, is to conceptualize the relations of time and eternity within a temporal framework—clearly an invalid procedure.

The metaphorical character of Jesus' proclamation does not deprive it of practical import, however. First of all, there is its personal import. Jesus meant for those who heard him to be continually attuned to eternity. Perhaps this does not sound practical at all, but it may be understood to mean living in continual readiness for experiences of insight and mutuality that, to the eyes of faith, are foreshadowings of the kingdom of God. Our sadness in the twentieth century often arises not from global conditions but from the emptiness and dreariness of personal life. The personal conditions may be caused by the global conditions. Nevertheless, to have faith that the kingdom of God is at hand is to transcend, through hope, the void in one's immediate experience. Prophetic hope should have roots in the most subtle and intimate intuitions of personal life. And, indeed, unless it does, it must be regarded as a mere hypothesis, without compelling claims on the allegiance of individual human beings. The expectancy for which Jesus called becomes real when it is lived in every moment of solitude and in every face-to-face encounter.

Faith in the imminence of the kingdom of God also has a universal dimension, however, and this dimension too has practical significance. Jesus anticipated an event impending over not only moments and hours but also centuries and millennia, an event not only urgently personal but also comprehensively human. He announced a new humanity. He himself, as the Christ, became the authoritative sign of this humanity. Christianity is distorted when it becomes a religion of purely personal salvation. After all, Jesus proclaimed a *kingdom*. One is saved as a participant in a new creation; and since the new creation is accomplished in some measure in time and on earth, one is saved as a participant in history. One must live as a responsible member of the human race, a race to be defined in terms not of biology but of a common drama—of sin and redemption, of death and life.

This imperative leads inevitably into politics. This is so in spite of the fact that there was little if any political content in Jesus' teaching. Perhaps any political commitment by Jesus would have entailed historical relativization of a kind incongruous with representation of the *eschaton*. In Christian faith, Jesus was the Son of God. The rest of us are merely human, however, and it is incumbent on us in our mere humanity to accept our historical immanence and to enter responsibly into a state of historical relativity. We must allow ourselves to be recast as potential embodiments of the new humanity. That responsibility cannot be separated from politics, for politics is the activity in which human beings relate themselves to one another on a global scale. In short, politics is required by love. Translating love into political principles and programs is a task infested with complexities and uncertainties. It is unavoidable, however, for it is inherent in the work of envisioning human beings in the light of Christ.[5]

Once the political dimension of faith in the imminence of the kingdom of God is seen, the Christian prophetic attitude comes clearly into view. All human beings, in all places and all societies, are envisioned in the context of a human renewal that is not merely an ultimate possibility but is assured and is now occurring. In this context, every established society comes under moral and historical judgment—moral judgment that exposes its imperfections, and historical judgment that reveals its impermanence. The prophetic figure of Christ becomes the center of a politics of hope.

We must note one distinctive characteristic, aside from being centered on a particular historical figure, that attaches to the Christian version of prophetic hope.[6] This is eschatology, or the idea that history leads to an end beyond history. There are no good grounds for regarding this characteristic as a source of political weakness. The old objection that by offering "pie in the sky," Christian eschatology encourages acquiescence in earthly injustice is—if we are talking of doctrinal implications and not merely of erring human inclinations—without substance. There is nothing in the impending entry of eternity into time that can justify dereliction from the commands of love. Far weightier is a consideration on the other side. Human imagination runs far beyond historical possibilities; images of heavenly paradise cannot be altogether expunged from even the most caustically skeptical mind. In this sense, hope is *essentially* eschatological. If hope is confined to history, then, in spite of every human effort to dramatize the glories of historical progress, history will be seen as ultimately meaningless. Hence, eschatological hope gives rise to a sense of political responsibility that is more assured, stubborn, and resourceful, and less vulnerable to historical disappointment, than does hope that is merely historical.

Christian Prophetic Virtues

Faith, love, and hope constitute, as everyone knows, a classical delineation of Christian virtues. They were given this status by Paul and have always figured largely in theological discussions of Christian life and conduct. All three virtues are prophetic. All three place human beings within history, orient them toward the future, and impose responsibilities that are in part political.

Faith

Even Christians have often failed to take fully into account that the God they worship is not enthroned in the heavens, superior to the tragedies of human history. He is a crucified God. To say that is not to state a general principle but rather to express the Christian belief that, in the person of his Son, God was executed on a particular day by particular human beings who were agents of the Roman imperial government and of a particular Roman emperor. Such a belief is absurd to secular intelligence. The point here, however, is that it envisions God as involved in the fullest possible measure in human history. It is worth noting, too, that so thoroughly historical a vision of God was not a Christian aberration. It arose naturally from Jewish attitudes and faith. The first act attributed to God in the Old Testament is the creation of day and night, following one another in succession, thus constituting time and the basis for history. And the pages following Gen. 1 do not present abstract concepts of God, but rather recount particular historical deeds—deeds of God and of a particular people chosen by God as his medium of revelation and atonement.

If God entered into history, then for human beings to seek God by withdrawing from history would be not merely anomalous or unnecessary, but sinfully perverse; it would be to seek God where, on biblical testimony, God is not to be found. If God lived and died in history, then surely those who would enter the company of God must also live and die in history. This is no less true for Christians, I suggest, than for Jews. It may seem otherwise because of the otherworldliness suggested by the eschatological dimension of Christianity. But for Christians as for Jews, God approaches human beings in their full, concrete—that is, historical—lives; they must respond to God where God approaches them. And this task is inescapably political. Responding to the God who in Jesus proclaimed the imminence of his kingdom cannot mean anything other than trying to make that kingdom as real as historical circumstances permit. Societies must be judged and reshaped.

Sharpening our consciousness of the prophetic character of Christian faith has perhaps been the major theoretical contribution of liberation theology. The Crucifixion and Resurrection have been interpreted according to standards suggested by the story of the Exodus of the ancient Hebrew tribes from Egypt—as divine acts of human liberation, calling for human responses. In my opinion, Pope John Paul II's concern about the overall soundness of liberation theology has good grounds.[7] But at least on one point, liberation theology is nearer to true Christianity than the views of many Christians who mean to adhere unwaveringly to orthodox doctrine, and that is in its vision of the general nature of reality. The Christian universe must be understood comprehensively as a story, not merely a structure. The structured universe is the setting for a drama of sin and redemption. Moreover, the drama comprises all of life and not merely a detachable sacred component; secular history as well as sacred history has meaning. This, too, liberation theology has insisted upon, and the point is irresistible. The God of Christian faith is not a specialist, dealing with one segment of life. His claim is on all of life, the secular as well as the sacred, the political along with the ecclesiastical. This is implicit in the First Commandment: "You shall have no other gods before me" (Exod. 20:3). Every realm of existence is under one God.

Love

In Paul's analysis, love is unlike faith; it does not "pass away" (1 Cor. 13:8–13).[8] This might lead one to suppose that love reflects an eternal moment and is unattended by the "not yet" that obviously accompanies faith. But simply to note the character of *agape,* the love Paul was concerned with, indicates that such an inference would be invalid. It is the essence of agape that it is not determined by the immediate empirical actuality of the one who is loved. It envisions a human being in accordance with the destiny revealed and ordained in Christ; it looks ahead. This is presumably why Paul says of love that it "bears all things, believes all things, hopes all things, endures all things" (1 Cor. 13:7). In a word, love is prophetic.

It is prophetic, moreover, not only in its expectancy but also in its range—a range one might term "political." Although love is indissolubly concrete—characterizing a relationship with one particular person—it is marked by universality. It is a perception in one person, the "neighbor," of the new humanity ordained for all. This is to say that love, for Christians, is the perception in another human being of the kingdom of God. If that is true, it has political implications. Obligations that pertain here and now to one other person pertain also, however differentiated by circumstances and instrumentalities, to the entire human race.

These, at any rate, are implications of the Christian concept of love. These implications point toward prophetic politics. Love, like faith, roots one in a concrete, perhaps quite uncomfortable, set of circumstances; it does this by binding one to particular human beings, human beings who are themselves rooted in concrete situations. But these circumstances are also historical, since the particular human beings who are loved are loved for a humanity that is not exclusively their own but belongs, through Christ, to the entire human race, even though it is distinctively embodied in each particular person. Moreover, there is loyalty to the new humanity only where there are efforts to make it real within the present time. Hence, it is not a personal task alone but also political.

Hope

We have been speaking of hope all along, for, as is now apparent, hope is not a distinct and separate virtue standing on a common footing with faith and love. It enters into the essence of faith and love. Thus, to experience and meet the claims of faith and love, but to do so without hope, would be an impossibility rather than a partial fulfillment of Christian morality.

The concept of hope thus makes fully explicit the prophetic character of Christian life and Christian virtue. Seen from a Christian perspective, the life we carry on in history, within the forms given it by social and political institutions, is emphatically unacceptable. This is due primarily to sin. Our actions are always more or less misguided and our motives more or less reprehensible. The evil in human beings is not overcome by society, although society is needed for creating order; this is evident in the extreme selfishness of groups, classes, and nations. Order is created primarily, as the framers of the American Constitution well knew, not by eradicating evil but by dividing it, so that evil is checked by evil. The cross is a powerful symbol of our life in the world; the human need for redemption is proved by the murder of the redeemer. Hope is the virtue that enables us to take cognizance of such conditions without cynicism and to suffer from them without resentment or despair.

Hope spontaneously fuses our sense of actualities and of possibilities. If we always could simply abandon threatening and onerous situations, hope would have no occasion. Hope is realistic; it opens our eyes to the palpable conditions of our lives. It does this, however, by freeing us from fear. It enables us to understand that oppressive conditions are impermanent and that they bear possibilities of life and happiness that are not visible to the finite and iniquitous creatures who inhabit them.

In a nation where private life is as heavily emphasized as it is in America, we tend to read such comments in personal terms. They are political, too, however. My own suffering and happiness is never an isolated fact; it is related to conditions that are fully explicable only as global conditions. Hence, I apprehend my own personal situation only if I apprehend it as a universal situation. In like fashion, the hope I have for myself and my friends is spiritually valid only so far as it is a hope for all human beings. It is not permitted, so to speak, to hope selfishly and exclusively. Hence, when I ask what action the hope I have requires, I must think not only of myself but of nations and peoples. Plainly, the idea of hope encapsulates the prophetic and political consciousness implicit in all of Christian life.

The Nature of the Christian Prophetic Attitude

We are now in a position to take note of how fundamentally the prophetic outlook differs from all of the major present-day ideologies. Doing this will enable us at once to see more fully the nature of the Christian prophetic attitude and to begin taking cognizance of its political implications.

It is immediately manifest that the prophetic outlook is quite different from classical conservatism such as that voiced by Edmund Burke. It is not enough, however, simply to say that the prophetic outlook is much more critical of established institutions. The reason for this must be brought to light. Christianity tends to subvert all human hierarchies. It does this through the principle of agape, which implies that every human being, regardless of wealth, power, or social rank, must be accorded unqualified respect. This is because every human being, without regard to temporal and institutional distinctions, has been honored by God through Christ. To love one another as Christ commanded is to honor one another in the manner of God. Established rank is irrelevant. This is perhaps the most explosive notion that has ever entered the human mind, for no social order can emerge wholly vindicated from the critical examination it demands. The worst societies are entirely condemned, and even the best are placed in question. Conservatism of the sort that reveres old and established institutions, mainly because they are old and established, becomes impossible.

It may be objected that Christianity in fact has not been socially explosive. Slavery and serfdom, social inequality and political absolutism, and other drastic violations of the principle of personal dignity have been allowed by Christians to stand unshaken for centuries. The factual accuracy of the objection cannot be denied, and it points to a great Christian failure. But I suggest that the reason for the failure lies not primarily in any hypocrisy or spiritual weakness on the part of Christians, but in the fact that it took a long time for the prophetic outlook to be fully developed and understood. Not until the time of Augustine, in the fifth century, was the bare notion of meaningful history clearly formulated. And not until the time of Hegel, one might say, was there a serious effort to see historical meaning not only in sacred history but in secular history as well. And not until that time could the concept of prophetic politics be fully understood. The result was that the Christian evaluation of the individual person was left, as it were, suspended in the heavens, detached from history. Only recently have humans come—albeit with tragic diversions, such as Marxism—to apprehend their affairs as having a momentum and direction determined by a Logos that bestows on every human being an unearthly glory. That this has released the critical and destructive power inherent in the idea of the infinite value of every individual is apparent all about us—in the uprising of American blacks, of women, and of nonindustrial peoples. The principle of personal dignity has been brought down to earth with revolutionary (and often far from beneficent) results.

It must be recognized that there is a fashionable Christian Left to which revolutionary talk comes all too easily. Conservatism embodies insights that prophetic expectancy cannot safely ignore: that stability, even the stability provided by an imperfect order, is a prime necessity of human life; that human beings are persistently fallible and selfish, hence not to be trusted as social engineers; and that even with the wisest and most fortunate leadership, no earthly kingdom can ever be transformed into the kingdom of God. In its Christian form, the prophetic outlook assumes that even though history unfolds meaningfully, it ends inconclusively if not tragically. The doctrine of original sin, along with biblical visions of catastrophic end times, renders such a view unavoidable.

Nonetheless, in Christianity stability is a practical, not sacred, value. Given the Christian view that human beings are persistently and ingeniously selfish, we must bear in mind not only the dangers of revolution, but also the near-certainty that long-standing traditions and customs will embody—perhaps along with some of the accumulated wisdom affirmed by conservatives—unjust privileges and advantages for dominant groups. And we must recognize that established elites and authorities, typically much respected by conservatives, are apt to display the pride and selfishness reflective of original sin even more flagrantly than the general run of the human race. Thus Luke asserts that the revelation of God in Christ has "put down the mighty from their thrones, and exalted those of low degree" (Luke 1:52), and Paul, writing to the Christians in Corinth, notes that "not many of you were wise according to worldly standards, not many were powerful, not many were of noble birth" (1 Cor. 1:26). Small comfort for conservatives! A social elite, unlike an individual human being, must always be viewed with skepticism rather than unreserved respect, and a social order is never sacred.

It is surprising that Christianity has so often played a conservative role in history. This is no doubt partly because the Christian doctrine of sin has made Christians fearful of revolutionaries and reformers. But they should have been fearful of conservatives and of established authorities as well. That they were not, at least not sufficiently so, is probably to be explained by the fact that the Christian clergy have normally themselves been among those established authorities.

It must be admitted too that eschatology—"pie in the sky"—may often have worked to give Christianity a conservative cast. As we have already seen, there is no inner logic connecting eschatology and conservatism. On the contrary, fidelity to the eschaton entails a critical and reformist attitude toward the established order. That is only one edge of the sword, however. The other edge is that faith in the coming of a transcendental kingdom may provide established powers and privileged groups with a plausible (although not logically compelling) excuse for neglecting evils in existing kingdoms. That Christianity has used the latter edge of the sword more often than the former is probably owing to the fact that Christianity has in most societies, since the time of Constantine, been formally or informally an established religion.

One may reasonably feel, accordingly, that Christianity has been considerably damaged by its "success"; its prophetic essence has been diluted. If Christianity now is "failing," if "God is dead" and we are entering an age of unbelief, this need not be viewed by Christians as an unalleviated disaster. No doubt there are dangers of the kind Dostoyevsky discerned; already countless multitudes all over the world have tacitly or openly embraced the nihilistic principle that "all is permitted." Nonetheless, if Christians were again to become a small and scorned minority, there might be benefits; for one, there might be a recovery of the prophetic spirit.

Doesn't all of this imply, however, that while the Christian version of the prophetic outlook must be sharply distinguished from conservatism, it conforms with the general pattern of radicalism? To call Christianity radical would not, in my view, be entirely erroneous. It would nevertheless be misleading. This can quickly be made clear if we take Marx as representative of secular radicalism and compare his doctrine with Christianity.

As often noted, there are striking resemblances between the Marxist and Christian visions: Both anticipate the rise of a new humanity from wretchedness and suffering; both see the new humanity emerging among the poor and despised and against the resistance of the wealthy and powerful; both rely on a mysterious destiny that is thought to be at work in human affairs; and both have a dialectical conception of this destiny, with unity arising from conflict and life from death. These resemblances have made possible not only Marxist-Christian "dialogue" but even a Marxist form of Christianity, liberation theology. As soon as such resemblances are defined, however, the gulf between Marxism and Christianity comes plainly into view. The gulf is between the historical and the eschatological. The proletariat is a triumphant worldly power, whereas Jesus ends his public, visible life on the cross (the Resurrection was not a publicly visible event, as the New Testament makes clear). Communism is realized within, the kingdom of God beyond, history.

The distance between Marxism and Christianity may be measured by comparing their attitudes toward human sin. For Marx, such qualities as selfishness and cruelty would be largely overcome by historical developments; for Christians, such qualities underlie and shape historical developments, and thus survive and contaminate every historical achievement. Plainly stated, for Marx there is no sin; for Christianity, sin is the primary determinant of the human state.

One word may be used to summarize the attitude toward historical realities and events that arises from the doctrine of original sin and distinguishes Christians from secular radicals; the word is "skepticism." This may strike readers as odd, for Christians are supposedly "true believers," while skeptics are usually atheists or agnostics. But Christians attentive to the political meaning of their faith are not true believers when it comes to historical powers and agencies. They regard them with abiding mistrust. On the other hand, the history of left-wing attitudes—toward the Communist Party, the Soviet Union, China, Cuba, Vietnam, and most recently, Nicaragua—shows that radicals are far from consistently skeptical in regard to historical powers and agencies. Often *they* are true believers.

The consistent historical skepticism of Christians obviously makes for a very different kind of political responsibility than that typically evinced by als. Christian skepticism does not stifle the disposition to criticize established order—at least there is no good reason why it should, for that disposition is grounded in faith and love and is nothing other than the prophetic spirit. Admittedly, Christians have to struggle more continuously than do secular radicals with the question of what sorts of changes are worthy of being tried, given the conditions created by human sin; and they are never, as secular radicals are almost continuously, buoyed up by the confidence that in one nation or another the major problems of collective life are being definitively solved. But there are advantages on the Christian side.

For one thing, Christian politics is not vulnerable to the shattering disappointments that have been recurrently experienced by the secular Left during the twentieth century. It looks on all human efforts with a guarded attitude. Further, Christian politics is sustained by a hope that is arguably commensurate with human nature in a way that radical hope is not. Even though Marxism has inspired heroic action, the hope it offers is, in Christian eyes, fatally limited; it is confined to the world and history. Dostoyevsky voiced typical Christian suspicions of secular hope in a swift characterization of human nature. "Shower all earthly blessings upon him," Dostoyevsky wrote of man, "drown him in happiness, head over ears, so that only bubbles should be visible on the surface, as on the surface of water; bestow such economic prosperity upon him as would leave him with nothing else to do but sleep, eat cakes, and only worry about keeping world history going—and even then he will . . . out of sheer ingratitude, out of sheer desire to injure you personally, play a dirty trick on you."[9] The idea that there is no full and lasting earthly satisfaction is not without implications for historical action. If pie in the sky is the only kind of pie that can finally meet the desires that arise from man's infinite imagination, then Christianity may be better able to sustain realistic and enduring political effort than is secular radicalism.

If, however, prophetic Christianity is neither conservative nor, in the usual meaning of the word, radical, the question arises whether it is not simply liberal. In a sense it is. If liberalism means adopting a critical attitude toward every existing and possible social order and accordingly placing a premium on liberty, as offering room both for a life not dictated by law and custom and for reformist activities, then prophetic Christianity is liberal. But liberalism is traditionally not so spare a creed as that; it seeks "the good society."[10] This aim, embracing the eventual solution of all major social problems and the achievement of an ideal order, reflects two qualities in traditional liberalism that separate it decisively from prophetic Christianity: worldliness and confidence in human goodness. Liberal hopes are ordinarily framed with little or no regard to transcendence. They are consequently confined to history and presuppose human reasonableness.

In these ways liberalism is like secular radicalism; this is obvious. Less obvious is that it is also, in these ways, like conservatism. Conservatism, too, affirms the possibility of a good society, although such a society must be reached by slow, historical development rather than by deliberate social engineering. And although conservatism reflects a keener consciousness of the evil in human beings than do liberalism and radicalism, it presupposes the possibility of evading the influence of this evil through political caution, respect for tradition, and deference toward traditional authorities. It goes without saying that there are many variations among individual writers, conservative, radical, and liberal alike, and that not all fit neatly into one or another ideological category. Nonetheless, modern politics has been shaped far more than earlier politics by ideology, and the major marks of ideology are anticipation of a good society in this world and confidence in human goodness. These marks are evident in the main political outlooks dominant since the French Revolution.

The uniqueness of prophetic Christianity becomes apparent. Only limited confidence is placed in human beings, regardless of the conditions under which they act; every historical prospect is therefore regarded with critical reserve. Yet these attitudes do not create a disposition to settle for any workable order whatever. This, of course, is because Christian faith is in the coming of the kingdom of God and thus calls for social criticism and reformist action. I do not maintain that Christian prophetic attitudes can be represented in a clear and coherent political ethic or political program. According to Christian doctrine, human life is lived on the boundary line between history and eternity. Hence it is subject to competing demands—those of power and agape, of the feasible and the paradisiacal, of worldly prudence and transcendental boldness. Those who try to practice a prophetic Christian politics must probably be confused and uncertain more of the time than are people following one of the ideologies. But this does not demonstrate that their principles are defective. Many of the worst things done in our century have been done by people who were not nearly so confused and uncertain as they ought to have been.

Still, if prophetic politics is not carried on in accordance with a clear idea of the nature of a good earthly society, isn't it necessarily bereft of all standards of action and isn't it condemned to political futility? These questions bring us to a position from which we can see fully the political purport of prophetic Christianity and understand why it has particular relevance to our times.

The Prophetic Stance

Prophetic Christianity does not tell us what kind of society and polity are best, but rather how we should stand in history and in the political universe. True, it

prescribes broad standards, such as liberty and equality. But these mean different things in different circumstances and are never fully realized (for example,
the idea of a society offering limitless liberty and complete equality is self-
contradictory, since society as such entails limits on liberty and inequalities of
power and status). Political philosophers typically translate their principles
into a definitive ideal; Plato and Aristotle, Rousseau and Hegel, all are examples. This cannot be done on the basis of prophetic Christianity. To speak of
eschatological hope is to speak of expectations that in their very nature defy
historical fulfillment. For prophetic hope, there is no ideal earthly society.
There is, however, an ideal stance; there is a way of standing in relation to historical affairs that is in all circumstances valid. I shall call this the "prophetic
stance."

This stance might be summarily described as one of simultaneous detachment and availability: detachment expressing the awareness that no historical
agencies or programs warrant unreserved commitment, and no historical
achievements unqualified approbation; availability reflecting attentiveness to
all that is being said and done in history, and readiness to act when opportunities are offered. In theological terms the prophetic stance is waiting for God in
history—watching for signs of God's will and being prepared to act on them. It
means avoiding the idolatry of established institutions implicit in conservatism
and avoiding also the presumption and pride typically present in resolute radicalism. But the prophetic stance is not only a relationship with the past and
future. It is also a way of living in the present time. It means occupying atten-
tively and responsibly a concrete situation, a set of limits and possibilities
defining the immediate moment. It means bearing the burden of the here and
now, cognizant of a past that cannot be uncreated or legitimately forgotten, and
alert to intimations of a future—a future both universally human and intimately personal—that gives us both hope and guidance.

Such a stance spells solitude in the sense that no historical relationships or
groups can be exempted from, or entirely vindicated by, the critical examination prophetic responsibility requires. The very idea of prophetic hope implies
standing apart, that is, transcending through expectancy every immediate association. But the solitude of prophetic hope is, so to speak, communal. It involves the deep human connectedness implicit in paying attention to the voices
and the needs of other people. (Simone Weil called attentiveness the "rarest
and purest form of generosity.")

An ideal stance may seem a poor substitute for an ideal society. But I suggest that it is far more useful. Ideal societies can bring inspiration and guidance, but they inevitably bring disappointment as well, and sometimes they
inspire atrocious political behavior. What we need more than political ideals
and programs is an understanding of how to relate ourselves to the ideals and

programs we encounter in the political world and how to relate ourselves to the realities those ideals and programs supposedly illuminate, but always in some measure obscure. We need an understanding, for example, of what to do when political plans that had seemed resplendent have come to fruition in banality and boredom, or perhaps in totalitarianism and violence.

This is a pressing need for individuals, since each one of us is swept along by a largely incomprehensible and highly dangerous stream of events. Is it legitimate in chaotic times to ignore politics and cultivate the pleasures of private life? Must I make political choices, at least to the extent of voting, even when I am confused or uninformed? Should I sometimes support programs that are humanitarian even if they are unrealistic? Can I fulfill my political responsibilities merely by reading newspapers and voting? Today we can hardly even try to carry on moral lives unless we can answer such questions, and they are questions that all ask, in one way or another, How should I stand?

Societies as well as individuals have an urgent interest in this question. Fascism is a stark example of what can happen to societies in which most individuals feel entirely lost. Where people are too confused and desperate to think soberly about political issues or to take political responsibility, dictatorship is inevitable and totalitarianism possible. Incapable of citizenship, people entrust themselves wholly, sometimes hysterically, to a leader, a party, a movement.

It is above all the idea of the prophetic stance that led me to say at the outset that prophetic Christianity has particular relevance to our times. Most times, of course, are in some way troubled, but surely our times are worse than many. Someone has said that this is the worst century so far, and it is a plausible assertion. The monstrous outcome, in the Soviet Union and elsewhere, of the Communist movement; the Nazi death camps; the turmoil and bitterness prevailing almost everywhere in the nonindustrial world—such realities as these make ours an unusually trying era. And the shadows are deepened by less frightful, but still disquieting, phenomena such as the uninspiring results of socialism and reformist liberalism and the vacuous popular culture of the liberal democratic nations. The question of whether and how to assume political responsibility is in substance the question of how to live as one human being among numberless multitudes of human beings—a great many of them confused, despairing, and violent.

My major claim for the prophetic tradition in Christianity is that it indicates how this can be done. It helps us see how one can be human in inhuman times. I do not mean, of course, that the bare idea of prophetic hope can miraculously make us capable of standing in our authentic humanity amid the confusing historical currents of our age. A mere idea does not have that kind of power. The idea must be infused with life—in Christian terms, with grace; only thus can it undergird the personal and political bearing by which we are rightly related to our human companions in history. But the idea of the prophetic stance does provide a general description of that bearing.

What good does that do, however, for people who are not Christians? A Christian might respond that the prophetic stance is a ready possibility for religious Jews, and perhaps for Muslims, since they adhere to parts of the same religious tradition as do Christians. But what about people who adhere to an Eastern faith, or to no organized faith at all? What about agnostics and atheists? Obviously, there are many such people today, and we therefore face a critical question. It is, in sum, whether the concept of the prophetic stance has universal validity.

It may seem that a Christian cannot possibly grant such validity, for that would be tantamount to saying that it doesn't matter, in practical affairs, whether you are a Christian or not. But if it doesn't matter in practical affairs, how can it matter anywhere else? Faith must influence practice or else be insignificant; but if it influences practice, then practice does not remain the same when faith is absent. Christianity cannot be confined to the inner life without being stifled.

Yet for Christians to deny the universal validity of a broad Christian principle like prophetic hope clearly is impossible. To do that would undermine Christianity itself. The truths of Christianity cannot be significant unless manifest in some measure in the visible realities that make up the world around us, and those realities are not visible to Christians alone. A familiar example is the doctrine of original sin. We can see signs of sin in the observable behavior of those around us and in some of our own deepest inclinations. Even so central and mysterious a Christian idea as that of redemption through suffering receives a degree of confirmation from the common experience that unless tested by difficulties, a person's character is apt to remain weak and unformed. More will be said on this matter shortly.

One of the oldest and most basic principles of Christian theology is that Christ is the Logos incarnate—an embodiment of the order and meaning of all things. Some such concept is inevitable on Christian grounds, for if Christ were not the Logos, then, in the final analysis, he would be nothing but another human being, lacking the universal significance implied by the centering of religious faith on his life. But everyone can see glimmerings, if nothing more, of the order and meaning of things—and thus see glimmerings, albeit unconsciously, of Christ. Early in the Christian era the author of the Gospel according to John wrote of Christ that "all things were made through him and without him was not anything made that was made" (John 1:3). If that is so, then all human beings dwell amid signs and manifestations of Christ and can, in some form, know Christ.

The first great Christian thinker, Paul, explicitly drew this inference when he wrote of God that "ever since the creation of the world his invisib\, namely, his eternal power and deity, has been clearly perceived in the things that have been made" (Rom. 1:20). The word "clearly" in that statement is especially noteworthy. Moreover, Paul drew the moral consequences—consequences that might readily be construed politically too. Of Gentiles, "who have not the law," Paul wrote that "what the law requires is written on their hearts" (Rom. 2:14–15).

The issue as to what things can be known only in the light of faith neither can nor need be settled here. The answer to the question asked above is clear: the concept of the prophetic stance does have universal validity. It would be tedious, and incompatible with the space available, to consider precisely how that concept might be framed in order to be acceptable to various sorts of non-Christians—to agnostics, to pantheists, to Buddhists, to Confucians, and so forth. Nor can we consider whether an atheist could adhere to the prophetic stance. It might be claimed that Marx did, but whether that is so depends on how loosely the prophetic stance is defined. It also depends on the debatable assumption that Marx was rigorously logical in his atheism. The important point is that the prophetic stance need not be an exclusively Christian posture. The combination of detachment and attentiveness, personal independence and political responsibility, critical wariness and enduring hope—the combination our age in its confusion and disappointment seems to cry out for—is, although brought to light by Christian faith, a stance that might be held to by many beyond the bounds of that faith.

Prophetic Hope in America

That America today is not alive with prophetic hope seems evident. Hence the sadness of which Walker Percy spoke. It is perhaps in the intense emphasis placed on physical pleasures and possessions and on enjoying these with little or no delay that the absence of prophetic hope is most apparent. Life is largely concentrated within the private sphere and the present moment. This is no doubt due in large part to advertising; but advertising has the backing of vivid realities—a spectacular abundance of cars, clothes, and other material goods. Whatever the causes, the conception of human existence as properly private and momentary seems now to be deeply rooted in the American ethos. For large majorities, life seemingly consists mainly in present and imminent physical satisfactions; the distant future and the human race are dim and are easily forgotten altogether.

It may be, of course, that genuine prophetic hope in America has been weak or dead for a long time. The principal formulation of prophetic hope has been the doctrine of progress; thus was history assigned direction and meaning. But the doctrine of progress does not necessarily incorporate the idea of God, or any other transcendental reference point, and normally it is not eschatological. Even though it can bear a measure of prophetic hope, therefore, it lends itself to secular distortions. The ideal future, for example, may come to be envisioned as a state of affairs soon to be achieved within a particular nation. Thus the doctrine of progress in America is closely linked with a patriotism that, to say the least, incorporates little prophetic detachment from the established order. Further, when an outlook already deficient in prophetic content was weakened, if not demolished, by the historical catastrophes of our time, the ground was cleared for the welfare state and the consumer's capitalism through which both Left and Right support an ethos that obscures the prophetic future.

One of the major large-scale questions before us today is how to loosen the hold of this ethos and gain a prophetic sense of our times and of the possibilities before us. I believe this question has an answer, one closely linked with Christian symbols. But the answer is strange to modern ears.

It is not, in the first instance, through any sort of social movement or political activity that we will learn to look prophetically toward the future, I suggest. It is rather through something that can happen only in the deepest interior of personal life, that is, suffering. Suffering forces one to leave the confines of a hedonistic ethos and either to despair or to "hope against hope"—to look toward a future that does not consist in any worldly arrangements. Suffering draws one toward transcendence. In the background of this hypothesis, of course, is the central image of Christianity, the cross. Life arises from death, hope from suffering. Christians believe that the suffering and death of one powerless man, abandoned even by the few followers he had, is the fount of the whole human future. This faith suggests a broad principle of historical development: the dependence of true progress in history on personal suffering.

Such a principle is apt to seem strange and incomprehensible in an age that regards suffering as useless and humiliating. But here again we can see that insights of Christian faith may be understood and accepted by people who are not adherents of that faith. The realization that enjoyment of unbroken pleasure and security makes for superficiality and that tribulation may lead to wisdom is at least as old as Greek tragedy. And it is sustained even by daily experience; living through tragedy and trouble, common people often show forth uncommon qualities. Whether the cross is the ultimate revelation of God's pathway in the world is a question for faith; that it reflects a recurrent pattern of life, however, is proved by world literature and by common experience.

Admittedly, suffering, like pleasure, draws one's mind back to the immediate and private moment. One is intensely conscious of suffering *now*; and one is ordinarily conscious of this suffering as a peculiar personal burden, a burden that is uniquely one's *own*. But suffering impels one to long for relief and thus to look beyond the immediate moment, sometimes even to the most distant and ultimate possibilities. Suffering in this way gives rise to hope. And although it does not in the same way impel one to look beyond one's own private experience, it *enables* one to do so. Suffering alone creates the capacity for entering into the suffering of others, and a unique and isolating moment of personal anguish may generate a movement of attention toward the entire human race. In sum, suffering lends itself, as pleasure does not, to prophetic transfiguration. Is there another source from which hope for humankind in all its agony can come?

Today, the idea that suffering has an essential role in life offends us partly because of our technological pride and proficiency; suffering is experienced as defeat and humiliation. But the idea that suffering has an essential role not only in personal but also in political life compounds the offense. My rebuttal is implicit in the preceding paragraphs. To divide private and public experience absolutely is to fly in the face of reality. It blinds us to the repercussions of private experience on public attitudes and makes it impossible for us to understand how public attitudes can be changed. The truth is that powerful and enduring public attitudes are bound to have roots in private experience. The idea that one can be a participant in the affairs of tormented humanity without tasting personal torment is radically implausible.

The idea that personal suffering has a historical role collides not only with our technological pride and proficiency, and with our tendency to sequester personal suffering in a private realm divided categorically from the public realm, but also with the assumption, particularly among liberals, that public problems practically always have public—that is, legal and organizational—solutions. If things are not working well in the society at large, what is called for, presumably, are new laws and new arrangements. Hence the impatient demands, heard so often when someone is speaking of general principles or spiritual conditions, for attention to practical details, the "nitty-gritty." It is rare for even the most penetrating analysis of a social or political problem, when left standing alone as simply a presentation of the problem, not to call forth the complaint that no solutions—that is, no remedial legal and institutional changes—have been proposed. It may be, however, that one of the basic causes of our present historical plight is that we think too much of programs and institutions and not enough of the spirit underlying them. We are perhaps entirely too respectful of the nitty-gritty. The argument I am advancing here presupposes that spirit is prior to structure and that we are unlikely to devise better social and political structures if we fail to consider first of all the spiritual conditions on which such structures rest.

Hence, I shall take the liberty of ignoring programmatic and institutional issues and of saying only that those who learn amid suffering to stand prophetically become (to use the title of a book Ignazio Silone wrote about a small and powerless group of misfits living underground in Fascist Italy) "the seed beneath the snow." The idea is not entirely novel. Socrates sought a new society through the intellectual and spiritual awakening of individuals, and Plato argued dramatically the dependence of outward order on the inward qualities of a few human beings. Prophetic hope is readiness for the rise of a new humanity. Christianity suggests that the deepest source of such readiness, and thus the matrix of the new humanity, lies in the participation of individuals (and not necessarily just Christian individuals) in the suffering of the prophetic figure who stands at the center of their faith.

Notes

1. See Malcolm Jones, "Moralist of the South," *New York Times Magazine*, 22 March 1987, 42 ff.

2. Psalm 118:22; Matt. 21:42 (Revised Standard Version). All biblical citations are from the RSV.

3. Karl Barth, *The Doctrine of the Word of God, Church Dogmatics*, trans. G. T. Thomson and Harold Knight (Edinburgh: T. & T. Clark, 1956), 1: 2, 117.

4. Albert Schweitzer was especially important in making this clear. See *The Quest for the Historical Jesus: A Critical Study of Its Progress from Remarius to Wrede*, 3d ed., trans. W. Montgomery (London: Adam & Charles Black, 1910).

5. See Wolfhart Pannenberg, *Jesus—God and Man*, trans. Lewis L. Wilkins and Duane A. Priebe (Philadelphia: Westminster Press, l968), 235–44, for a discussion of this matter and for conclusions that support my argument.

6. For examples of other versions of the prophetic outlook see Martin Buber, *The Prophetic Faith,* trans. Carlyle Witton-Davies (New York: Harper & Row, 1949); and Neal Riemer, *Karl Marx and Prophetic Politics* (New York: Praeger, 1987). See also Neal Riemer, *The Future of the Democratic Revolution: Toward a More Prophetic Politics* (New York: Praeger, l984).

7. For a very able and balanced critique of liberation theology, see Dennis McCann, *Christian Realism and Liberation Theology: Practical Theologies in Creative Conflict* (Maryknoll, N.Y.: Orbis Books, 1981).

8. Actually, Paul contrasts love with prophecy, "tongues," and knowledge, but the contrast with faith is implied.

9. Fyodor Dostoyevsky, *The Best Short Stories of Dostoevsky*, trans. David Magarshak (New York: Modern Library, 1992), 135–36.

10. The title, of course, of a book by a noted liberal—Walter Lippmann (New York: Grosset & Dunlap, 1936).

4

Prophetic Tradition and the Liberation of Women: A Story of Promise and Betrayal

Rosemary Radford Ruether

Are women today's prophets? This theme immediately begs the question, what is a prophet? And why should women see any particular connection between feminism as a theological and social movement and the figure of the prophet? I would like to argue that there are some compelling reasons to make special links between feminism and prophecy. The prophet in the biblical tradition is a figure who stands outside the institutionalized leadership—specifically the priesthood—of the religious tradition, but within the covenant of the community. The prophet speaks a judgmental word of God in order to call the community back to faithfulness to the radical foundations of biblical faith, contextualized in the contemporary situation.

Prophecy presupposes a relationship between religion and society that conflicts profoundly with established religion. Established religion sees religion as the sacred ideology of the established social order. It is the "handmaiden" of the ruling class. It pronounces the established social order to be created by God and to be a reflection of the divine will. Words for God resemble titles for the ruling class. God and the ruling class are called by the same names and imaged as having similar lifestyles, except God is raised to the immortal level. The ruling class therefore appears godly and is seen as having special closeness to the divine and as representing the divine on earth. By contrast, those lower classes who are to be ruled do not image the divine and obey God by obeying their social superiors. This is the way most religion has functioned, including most Christian religion. A certain stratum of the Bible, particularly the laws in the Old Testament and the household codes in the New, also presupposes such a relationship between religion and society.

Prophetic faith, by contrast, sets God in tension with the ruling class by having God speak through the prophet(ess) as the advocate of the poor and the oppressed. The word of God comes through the prophet(ess) to denounce the unjust practices of the rich and powerful who grind the faces of the poor and oppress the widow and the orphan. The prophet(ess) also denounces the corruption of biblical faith itself into a religious establishment that has become purely cultic and has turned away from the social substance of faith, which is justice and mercy. Thus the prophets in Hebrew Scripture and Jesus in the Gospels are figures in conflict with religious establishments, denouncers of the use of religion to sacralize unjust privilege and to ignore the needs of the people.

The prophetic tradition goes on to imagine God active in history as a power that will overthrow an unjust social order and transform the world into a new social order where there is no more war and no more injustice, where justice between human and human and harmony between human and nonhuman nature have been restored, and all creation is in communion with God. This vision in the prophetic tradition was not equated with immortality or life after death. It was thought of as an ideal state to be established on earth as the right relation between creation and its Creator. As Jesus put it succinctly in the Lord's Prayer: "God's Kingdom come, God's will be done on earth."

Early Christianity saw itself as having a particular affinity with the prophetic tradition. Not only was Jesus the ultimate messianic prophet, but in the dispensation of the Holy Spirit that founded the church on Pentecost, the prophetic spirit had been restored, as had been predicted by the prophet Joel. For first-generation Christians, and for some Christians well into the third century, the prophet was the normative leader of the local Christian community and the one empowered to bring down the power of the Holy Spirit upon the eucharistic gifts. Unlike the priesthood, from which women were excluded in the Old Testament and again excluded as this concept of leadership developed in patristic Christianity, women were never excluded from prophecy. Miriam, Deborah, and Huldah were prophets, and prophecy was seen as restored to women, as well as men, in the Pentecostal tradition. Patriarchal Christianity excluded women from the kind of leadership exercised by bishops and presbyters, although it retained a marginal place for women in the diaconate. It also waged a battle in the second and third centuries to suppress charismatic or prophetic traditions of leadership. But it never, in principle, denied that God might send contemporary prophets and that women could exercise prophecy equally. It simply tried to discount any actual prophets that came along as being true prophets, especially if those prophets were female. And if they were female, it also tried to prove that they were witches and agents of the devil.

Prophecy also has a close relationship with the renewal of women's ministry throughout church history. The Waldensians of the twelfth century included women in public preaching, on the basis of the sect's equation of preaching and prophecy. The same connection was made among Baptists in the Puritan Civil War, who included women as preachers. In the sermon at the ordination of Antoinette Brown, the first woman to be ordained in the Congregationalist tradition, Luther Lee argued in 1853 for women's ordination by equating preaching with the prophetic office. Christ himself, according to Lee, restored the prophetic office to women, and so the church had erred throughout history in excluding women from ordained ministry. Again and again through the centuries up to the present, women who claimed the right to public ministry did so by claiming the text of Acts 2:17: "Your sons and your daughters shall prophesy."[1]

Yet despite this continual tradition of the inclusion of women in prophecy, women have been betrayed by male-led prophetic movements. Such movements represent the rebellion of oppressed males against dominant males but have no intention of including in their rebellion the overthrow of male domination. These male-led movements typically welcome the enthusiastic participation of women in the work of the revolution. But when women try to include themselves in the revolution's ideology and program, the male leaders make clear that this is not the agenda, that women are being selfish and diversionary by bringing up questions of the emancipation of women from patriarchy.

We see this betrayal of women in the Exodus tradition of Hebrew Scripture. Here women begin the rebellion against Pharaoh by being the first to disobey his orders to kill the firstborn. Moses' mother and sister and Pharaoh's daughter establish a subversive conspiracy that not only saves Moses' life but also raises the leader of the rebellion in the court of Pharaoh. In the Exodus, Moses, Miriam, and Aaron are named as leaders, but in Num. 12:12–16, when Aaron and Miriam criticize Moses for betraying the people by marrying a Cushite woman, it is Miriam who is stricken with leprosy. It is said that she had become like a daughter whose father has spit in her face, that is, repudiated her totally. Thus Miriam is marginalized from coequal leadership in the Exodus. When the "people" of Israel assemble at Sinai to receive the Law, they are told to purify themselves for three days by "not going near a woman." So it becomes clear that the "people of Israel" means the males of Israel (Exod. 19:14–15).

Similarly, in the Gospels the church is seen as a new Exodus community. It is identified in the Magnificat with a servant-class woman who has been lifted up, as the mighty are put down from their thrones. The story line of all four Gospels is one in which the messianic prophet is rejected by successive groups. First he is betrayed by his family and the hometown folks, who try to kill him after his first sermon in Nazareth, when he identifies the coming of God's liberation to the poor with the lepers and poor widows among despised social groups living around Israel. Then he is betrayed by the established religious leadership—scribes and priests—and by the crowds who turn fickle when he is arrested for subversion in Jerusalem. Finally, he is betrayed by his own male disciples, led by Peter, when the crisis of impending crucifixion reaches its climax. Only the women disciples, led by Mary Magdalene, remain faithful at the cross. They are the first to receive the news of the Resurrection, which they carry back to the unbelieving male disciples.

However, Christian tradition marginalizes Mary Magdalene's role in apostolic leadership by identifying her as a prostitute and repentant sinner (an identification found nowhere in the New Testament) rather than as a leading disciple. Although Paul establishes a close connection between apostleship and witnessing the Resurrection, making himself the last such witness, he doesn't use the tradition that women were the first witnesses, instead identifying Peter as the first witness and hence first apostle. It is not accidental that we find in alternative early Christian gospels that were not included in the canon, such as the *Gospel of Mary*, a controversy between Peter and Mary Magdalene over women's apostleship. In these gospels Mary's apostleship is confirmed, while Peter is rebuked for denying the inclusion of women in the discipleship that Christ has established.

The same pattern of promise and betrayal of women appears in the Reformation—for example, in the conflict between Radical and Magisterial Puritanism. When Puritanism was a dissenting movement in England, it encouraged women to dissent against husbands, ministers, and magistrates and to act according to their own conscience when these authorities were Anglican. Research has shown that dissenting congregations often had a predominance of women, and women often played de facto leadership roles in gathering such congregations and securing an independently paid minister. As a result, New England Puritanism in the 1640s included a significant number of strong women who had become accustomed to independent thinking as a result of decades of leadership as dissenters against established authorities in England.

However, once the Puritan ministers and magistrates made themselves the new established church of the Massachusetts Bay Colony, they reverted to a patriarchal social order, which they regarded as the reflection of the order of creation. They distinguished between the covenant of grace and the covenant of works. In the covenant of grace, all humans were equal before God and were elected without regard to merit, including social status. However, in the covenant of works, God had established a social order of husband over wife, parents over children, masters over servants. Social subordinates obeyed God by obeying their divinely ordained social superiors. For women to dissent against the male authority of husband, minister, or magistrate now became heresy, a rejection of the law of God, and probably witchcraft as well, because only the devil could empower weak women so to rebel against their rightful place in God's order. Thus the Puritan male leadership occupied itself in the seventeenth century by suppressing strong, independent women in a series of campaigns: first against women as heretics in the antinomian controversy, led by Anne Hutchinson; then against the Quakers, who had developed the equalitarian traditions of Radical Puritanism and allowed female leadership; and finally, at the end of the century, against witches.

A similar pattern of promise and betrayal of women can also be found in modern male-led reform and revolutionary movements, such as liberalism, socialism, and antiracist and anticolonialist liberation movements. For example, in the American Declaration of Independence it is said to be a "self-evident" truth that God created "all men" equal and endowed them equally with the rights of life, liberty, and the pursuit of happiness. (Property, included among natural rights in the French Declaration of the Rights of Man and the Citizen, is pointedly not included as a natural right in the American Declaration.)

Women, organized in women's support work for the American Revolution, called themselves the Daughters of Liberty. However, it soon became clear that the male revolutionary merchants and planters had no intention of including their wives or daughters, much less their slaves, in those claims to natural equality that led, self-evidently, to the rights of the citizen. Abigail Adams, herself a leading Daughter of Liberty, wrote to her husband, John Adams, at the Constitutional Convention admonishing him to "Remember the Ladies" and to include them equally in the rights of citizenship, even threatening that if he did not do so, women would foment a rebellion, just as men had done, and would not hold themselves bound by any laws that they could not participate in making. She was brushed off with a laugh. John Adams confessed that the American Revolution had raised fears that all constituted order might be overthrown; that Indians had begun to slight their guardians, slaves their owners, and servants their masters, but that "your Letter was the first Intimation that another Tribe more numerous and more powerfull than all the rest were grown discontented."[2] Clearly, Adams thinks that women are easily mollified, although his letters to his male peers show that he is worried by the inconsistency of the universalist claims of equality with the maintenance of patriarchy, a social order assumed to include not only the domination of women, but of servants and slaves as well.

Promise and betrayal are also found in the socialist movement. In the Owenite and Fourierite movements of the 1830s, socialism not only included many women but also enunciated a clear relationship between socialism and the emancipation of women. Socialism was understood to mean not only the socialization of productive labor but also the socialization of reproductive labor, of the labor of women in the family, in a communal society owned and managed at the base. One of the strongest tracts on women's liberation ever to be written by a male feminist came from the collaboration of the Owenite socialists William Thompson and Anna Wheeler in England in 1825: *The Appeal of One Half of the Human Race, Women, against the Pretensions of the Other Half, Men, to Retain Them in Civil and Domestic Slavery.*

Marxist socialism, however, dismissed these ideas as mere utopianism, in contrast to truly "scientific socialism." Engels reaffirmed feminism as a part of socialism, but socialism was defined as a political movement that would seize and redefine the power relationships in the sphere of paid labor, not of domestic labor. Feminism apart from this context was dismissed as a "bourgeois" movement. Socialist women should reject feminism and give themselves solely to the emancipation of the worker, in whose cause they were automatically included. Thus the connection between women's inequality on the job and the unpaid labor that women did in the home was covered up. In Hilda Scott's study of Eastern European socialism, *Does Socialism Liberate Women?*[3] she shows that despite all commitments to equal civil rights, equal education and jobs, and some collectivized domestic services, such as nurseries, women are at the bottom of the economic and political hierarchies of socialist societies and receive less pay than men in the same jobs. The chief reason for this, she shows, is the four to six hours of unpaid labor that women do for the family in addition to the "equal" work roles with men in the paid labor force.

The pattern of promise and betrayal of women is also found in antiracist and anticolonial liberation movements today. This is especially true of cultural nationalist movements, such as is found in Muslim nationalism in Iran and in American black nationalism, which is modeled on Muslim nationalism. Here we find a need in the male nationalist to reassert the total subjugation of women. Women should be reduced to invisibility and total obedience to men. Any assertion of women's rights is defined as the corrupt influence of the decadent West, against the purity of the culture of the nation which is throwing off the shackles of Western colonialism.

One finds acted out here, in extreme form, the conflict between the patriarchal egoism of dominant and subordinate males. Dominant males act out their superiority to subjugated males not only by insulting them as a racial group but, above all, by insulting their masculinity, by treating them and referring to them as "boys." Thus, males in rebellion typically see themselves not only as asserting the autonomy of their people but also as vindicating their injured masculinity. They often act this out by rigid insistence on the resubordination of the women of their community, who are regarded as having lost their proper respect for their men as a result of colonialism. We may have here, in the ego conflict of dominant and subordinate males based on a shared model of male domination as normative, the key to the promise and betrayal of women in male-led exodus movements.

Liberation movements based on socialism rather than on cultural nationalism are generally more generous to women. They concede those aspects of feminism traditional to socialism: civil rights, equal education, incorporation into the paid labor force, and state nurseries for working mothers. But they are generally hostile to a feminism that goes beyond these limits and that organizes women autonomously to criticize the sexual, domestic, and psychocultural dimensions of patriarchy. Such feminism is regarded as bourgeois and antisocialist.

What is to be concluded from this history of promise and betrayal of women in male-led exodus movements? One should not conclude that women have no stake in the liberation of subjugated nations, classes, and races, nor that the prophetic tradition of biblical faith is irrelevant for women. Rather, what women must conclude is that they cannot entrust the definition of such prophetic and emancipatory movements exclusively to male liberators. They cannot believe that any liberation movement that does not define itself as liberation from patriarchy will truly include women.

Moreover, they have a right to suspect that any liberation movement that is not defined as liberation from patriarchy will not truly overthrow class domination between ruling and subordinate males. A reform or revolution not defined as emancipation from patriarchy leads inevitably to a new social order in which the former male revolutionaries set themselves up as a new ruling class of priests and kings, or ministers and magistrates, or merchants and politicians, or commandos and party apparatchiks. Patriarchy is once again declared the order of nature, as defined either by God or by science. Women are thanked very much for their help in bringing about the revolution and then sent back to their homes and neighborhoods to do the unpaid and low-paid labor that supports the new society's male hierarchy.

Can feminism do better than this as a prophetic and emancipatory movement? Feminism, as renewed in the last twenty years in Western Europe and particularly in the United States, has been very creative in reestablishing the interconnections between all relations of domination and violence. First, modern feminism has clearly enunciated the personal as political in patriarchal relations. Feminists have brought crimes against women out of the invisibility of the private world. The unpaid work of women in the household; the denial to women of reproductive self-determination; physical violence against women in the home and in the streets; mugging, battery, child abuse; sexual violence against women in the home, the streets, and the workplace; incest; marital and nonmarital rape; sexual harassment and the culture and practice of pornography and prostitution—feminists have shown that all these support a social structure built on the subjugation of women as sexual objects and exploited workers.

Modern feminism has also shown the interconnections between patriarchy and class and racial hierarchy. Feminists have shown that racial and class hierarchies include sexual hierarchy within all their stratifications and thus place poor women of color at the bottom of the whole system. These hierarchies are also characterized by the sexualizing of race and class domination. Subordinate males are portrayed either as sexual brutes who represent a threat to the virtue of ruling-class women or as overgrown children who lack adult male status. In this way, white women are split from black men, black men from black women, and black women from white women. The whole system is held in place by setting subordinate groups against each other, each nursing its wounds and protecting its privileges against the others, rather than uniting against the common master of all, the ruling-class white Western male system.

Modern feminism has also established the relationship between patriarchy and the global systems of destruction that threaten the survival of everyone on the planet: militarism and destruction of nature. Both of these systems of violence and destruction have been shown to operate on the sexual imagery of male domination of women. In military violence, the male soldier is taught to identify his weapon with his sexual organ and to repress all revulsion to killing another human being as an effeminate trait that threatens to deprive him of male status, to make him a "sissy" or a "fag." The right of ruling-class males to dominate nature and to deny their own roots in natural ecology is justified by imaging nature as a "virgin" who invites "rape" and as a sensuous courtesan who entices the scientist-technocrat to "bare her secret" and "penetrate her inmost recesses."[4]

Not only does patriarchy provide the cultural, symbolic, and psychological connections between male ruling-class egoism, militarism, and ecological destruction, it also provides the social structure that allows the rapacious use of the world's resources for the profit of the few to the impoverishment of the many. And it directs that this empire of wealth and power be defended even to the death of the last man, woman, and child on earth and of the planet itself.

In that sense I would claim that feminism is a most important prophetic movement in contemporary culture. It is the prophetic movement that attempts the most comprehensive analysis of the systems of oppression and evil that dehumanize us all and reaches for the most comprehensive vision of what is necessary to save our lives and our planet from the many injustices and threats that surround us.

Moreover, I would claim that this comprehensiveness, far from making feminism utopian (in the sense of a movement characterized by excessive demands and dreams that transcend realistic possibilities of change within the human condition), provides the only account that really gets at the root of the systems of domination. Any attempt to dismiss feminism as excessive or marginal is based finally on the assumption that male domination is itself the constitutive framework of what is called "the human condition." But this is a human condition defined by males who assume that maleness is normative humanness. This definition is, and has always been, dehumanizing to women. No movement to rehumanize our life on earth will succeed in making significant changes until men, as well as women, take seriously the need to root out patriarchy with all its works and pomps.

However, the fact that feminism contains the promise of being a most comprehensive prophetic movement today, a movement that gets at the root of the system of domination, does not mean that it will succeed in realizing this promise. Feminism may fail to realize its prophetic promise. It may fail, first and most important, because males refuse to take it seriously, continue either to try to ridicule it or to coopt it into their systems of control, and disdain to imagine that they might include themselves in it, not just to liberate women, but also to liberate themselves from patriarchy. The refusal of males to include themselves in liberation from patriarchy has meant, as we have shown, that every male-led liberation movement has failed to get at the roots of social domination. As long as men continue to identify their masculinity with domination, there can be no real humanization of society.

Although male rejection is the most important reason feminism may fail as a prophetic movement and be gradually silenced with token changes, as it has been in the past, feminism may also fail because it succumbs to the internal contradictions and antagonisms that patriarchy sets up among women. A feminism that does not maintain both the radicality of its vision and compassionate outreach to all women is already providing the ammunition for its own suicide.

Feminism may commit suicide in one of several ways. First, it may remain a white, middle-class movement and fail to establish itself as a genuine interclass and interracial (interreligious, intercultural) movement. This danger was discerned in the socialist criticism of feminism as a bourgeois movement, but this criticism was used to dismiss feminism as an autonomous movement demanding its own organization and analysis of patriarchy. In order to be truly a women's liberation movement, feminism must include all women of all classes, races, and cultures. This means that black women, working-class women, Jewish women, Muslim women, Asian women, African women—all women in every social context—must form self-defined feminist movements that critique patriarchy from within their own situations. Feminism then would become a network of solidarity among all these movements, in which white and middle-class women (and we must remember that "middle class" is not synonymous with white or Western) define their own movement in solidarity with these movements of less privileged women, rather than define feminism only in terms of their own class and cultural context.

Feminism could also commit suicide by becoming merely the feminism of professional women, a more extreme version of middle-class feminism. Feminism would become primarily a vehicle for a small number of middle-class women who are seeking inclusion in male-defined, high-status professions and who bond with the few other women of their same professional group in order to win equality between themselves and their male colleagues. Feminism would mean women clergy, women lawyers, women doctors, and women politicians seeking equality with male clergy, lawyers, doctors, and politicians, while failing to establish solidarity, either in theory or practice, with other women—with women secretaries or maintenance workers in their own workplace or with housewives.

Such a feminism assures that it will remain the feminism of an elite and will achieve only token success in its own context, while awakening the animosity of the 90 percent of women who work as unpaid houseworkers and low-paid salaried workers. Very soon this feminism of the elite will become the struggle of each woman in the elite for herself, in a way that disavows any interest in women's issues either within her own profession or in relation to the vast body of other women. In other words, it ceases to be feminism at all and becomes sheer Jeane Kirkpatrick–ism.

Finally, feminism may commit suicide by distorting the radical critique of patriarchy into an in-group sectarianism of women who define their ideological purity by their disavowal of the humanity of all males and the repudiation of any women who have friendly intercourse with males in either sense of the word. Such sectarian feminism writes off the humanity not only of all males and all nonfeminist women but also of all feminist women who seek to reclaim traditions of male culture or who have social and sexual relations with males. Thus, feminists who also wish to be Christians (Jews, Muslims), feminists who are married or heterosexual, finally even feminists who are lesbian mothers raising male children, will come to feel uncomfortable in the feminist "sect." They will be made to feel guilty of crimes of ideological impurity through their social, sexual, or cultural complicity with the "enemy." Such a feminism not only fails to convert any men or any women who are not presently feminists, but manages to turn off many women who consider themselves feminists.

Thus, if feminism is to continue as a prophetic movement that can grow and attract increasing numbers of women, as well as men, into its alternative vision, it must clearly reject these ways of dividing women against each other. This does not mean muting the radicality of its criticism of patriarchy. It does mean constantly striving to communicate its criticism of patriarchy in a way that shows why it is in the self-interest of all women and most men. It does not mean pretending that there are no disagreements between feminists and nonfeminist women, much less antifeminist women. It means discussing those disagreements in ways that lead to clear insight into antifeminism as the defensive ideology of women trapped by patriarchy.[5]

It does not mean denying that women need to talk together without men and to establish autonomous groups not controlled by men. It certainly does not mean denying that lesbianism is a valid sexual and human relationship. It means not transforming lesbianism or the need for organizational autonomy into an ideological sectarianism that denies the humanity of all males and of male-friendly women. Finally, it does not mean that feminists don't dispute with each other. Rather, it means that one recognizes in differences among feminists evidence of contradictions in reality that call for clear and compassionate struggle that can lead to a new synthesis.

In short, to maintain its vision as a prophetic alternative to the historical reality of patriarchy, feminism must be comprehensive enough to embrace all women and to convince increasing numbers of males that their humanity, too, could be enhanced if they ceased to identify being a human of the male sex with social and sexual domination of others, particularly of women.

Notes

1. This and other biblical citations are from the New Revised Standard Version.

2. See *The Feminist Papers: From Adams to de Beauvoir* (New York: Bantam Books, 1974), 10, 11.

3. Hilda Scott, *Does Socialism Liberate Women?* (Boston: Beacon Press, 1974).

4. The development of this type of sexual language in modern science is explored in Brian Easlea, *Witchhunting, Magic, and the New Philosophy* (Atlantic Highlands, N.J.: Humanities Press, 1980).

5. For a model of this kind of radical, yet compassionate, insight into antifeminist women, see Andrea Dworkin, *Right Wing Women* (New York: Perigee Books, 1983).

5

Frederick Douglass, William Lloyd Garrison, and the Prophetic Tradition in Nineteenth-Century America

William B. Rogers

In this article the nineteenth-century reformers William Lloyd Garrison (1805–79) and Frederick Douglass (1817–95) will be critically compared and evaluated in light of a paradigm of prophetic politics.[1] I will be concerned with illustrating the extent to which they demonstrate the prophetic tradition in nineteenth-century America. The chosen model of prophetic politics directs our attention to four commitments grounded in the prophetic tradition: (1) to achievement for everyone in society of the great biblical prophetic values of peace, freedom, love, truth, justice, and prosperity in a superior universal order; (2) to fearless and forthright criticism of the existing order based upon these prophetic values; (3) to constitutional action to lessen the gap between prophetic values and existential reality; and (4) to ongoing prophetic scrutiny and futuristic projection. This model will permit me to assess both the strengths and weaknesses of these two key spokesmen of the American anti-slavery movement.

Garrison and Douglass were leading forces in the American abolitionist movement. Douglass began his career as an abolitionist and social reformer under Garrison's tutelage and spent nearly a decade working directly with him in the antislavery cause. These two reformers—who were sometimes close colleagues and at other times at odds—provide valuable comparisons and contrasts on a number of important issues in nineteenth-century America and within the prophetic tradition.

How valuable is the model of prophetic politics as a framework for analyzing and criticizing Garrison's and Douglass's thought? In this study, I argue that the prophetic paradigm is a helpful model for analyzing and criticizing a historical figure insofar as it encourages the critical exploration of the values of such a figure; directs our attention to such a figure's ability to illuminate the real world of politics; requires us to ask about the figure's understanding of the relation of theory to practice, of ideas to action, of knowledge to wise judgment;

and looks to the future and addresses future problems.

The model of prophetic politics seems a particularly appropriate one to employ to analyze and criticize Garrison and Douglass. This is the case, first, because both men's thought was unquestionably influenced by such prophetic values as universal human emancipation, the attainment of harmony within society, peace between nations and peoples, and the opportunity for rich human development. Second, Garrison and Douglass—like those in the prophetic tradition—were committed to investigation and radical criticism of conditions that enslave, degrade, or retard human beings. Further, both were acutely aware of the gap between their conceptions of human beings as they are capable of being and their existential reality. Third, Garrison and Douglass were indeed committed to action to break through to a new order to achieve their normative objectives for humankind. Finally, both Garrison and Douglass were very much concerned about the future.

As we will see, however, they differ on a number of key issues. Comparative analysis permits us to highlight their agreements and their differences and to determine more fully the extent to which each fits—or does not fit—into the pattern of prophetic politics.

Values

The evidence is compelling that both Douglass and Garrison strongly illustrate a commitment to a number of cardinal prophetic values. Both men endeavored throughout their lives to defend and advance the key prophetic values of freedom, justice, peace, and love. Between them, Garrison and Douglass were involved in every major reform effort of the nineteenth century—antislavery; women's rights; temperance; civil rights for freed slaves, Native Americans, Chinese, and other minorities; nonviolence; and antilynching laws. Their lifelong commitment to the values of peace, justice, and equality can scarcely be questioned. In this article I will try to articulate the similarities and differences between Garrison and Douglass with respect to the four commitments of prophetic politics. Within the commitment to prophetic values, the similarities are obvious and overwhelming. After briefly treating their prophetic commitments, I will call attention to the differences between the two men and where each falls short of a fuller illustration of prophetic values. This discussion of their ethical weaknesses is not designed to shatter their moral reputations, but to help understand the difficulties of achieving a perfect prophetic reputation.

Garrison's entire life was a testament to prophetic values. He devoted his energies for thirty-seven years to the cause of emancipation of the slaves. During all of this time (at least until the latter part of the Civil War), the reward for his efforts was calumny, hatred, public ridicule, constant personal danger, violent physical attacks, and unrelenting financial struggles. Yet he remained steadfast in his commitment to freedom for all Americans.[2] Garrison, in fact, advocated a doctrine of universal emancipation. He was a relentless defender for the "least free" in society: slaves, free blacks, women, Native Americans, and Chinese immigrants. He supported the temperance movement, the peace or nonresistance movement, and prison reform efforts.

Douglass, like Garrison, spent his life in defense of key prophetic values. He fully embraced the full range of reforms prevalent during his life: antislavery, women's rights, temperance, and the elevation of free blacks and other oppressed groups in society. Leslie Goldstein argues that Douglass's political actions were guided by a set of reasoned principles. These principles followed two fundamental concepts: the belief that all men and women have equal and inalienable rights to life and liberty, and the notion that the most complete freedom would include not only legal freedom but also the full development of one's human capabilities such as wisdom and courage.[3] Douglass's commitment to equality between the sexes demonstrated the depth and range of his humanism. All individuals were equal in natural rights and duties; all individuals possessed basic capacities and endowments, regardless of sex or race. The great social-reform goal of universal emancipation, therefore, necessitated the liberation of oppressed women as well as oppressed racial and ethnic minorities. As just one example, Douglass played a key role in supporting the resolution at the women's rights convention at Seneca Falls in 1849 demanding that women be given the right to vote and hold office. Douglass's impassioned speech in favor of the resolution helped gain its passage by a small majority.[4]

From a modern democratic perspective, however, both men were partly flawed. Garrison, for example, reflected the anti-Semitic and anti-Catholic prejudices of nineteenth-century America. Both were less understanding of the plight of white working men and their attempts to organize. Douglass, however, possibly because of his experience as a slave, was better able than most white abolitionists to take the side of the oppressed, no matter how unpopular that stand might be in the broader society. Garrison, despite his extremely strong support of abolition, elevation of free blacks, women's rights, and the rights of other oppressed groups (Native Americans, Chinese immigrants), simply could not completely overcome the prejudices of his evangelical Protestant upbringing. One might argue instead that the degree to which he did overcome his youthful beliefs was quite remarkable. His modest overcoming is revealed, for example, in his rejection of revealed theology, his willingness to consider the ideas of heretics like Thomas Paine, and his lifelong devotion to many of the most despised groups in society.[5]

Douglass recognized both Jews and Catholics as victims of oppression and discrimination in the United States and throughout the world. Douglass did not ignore or excuse the fact that many Catholics had racist attitudes toward blacks, but he did not denigrate the entire religion for the actions and beliefs of some of its adherents.

Evidence of anti-Catholicism or anti-Semitism on the part of Frederick Douglass is simply not in the current record. For example, in a speech given in 1863 entitled "The Present and Future of the Colored Race in America," Douglass discussed at length the strong prejudice against blacks among Irish Catholic Americans. While he granted that the Irish people were among the most bitter persecutors of blacks, he did not end his analysis there. He stated that "the Irishman has been persecuted for his religion about as rigorously as the black man has been for his color. The Irishman has outlived his persecution, and I believe that the Negro will survive his." He then detailed some of the laws the English passed in order to maintain Protestant control of Ireland. Again, while he deplored Irish prejudice against blacks, he displayed great sensitivity to the harsh and oppressive conditions Irish Catholics have lived under for centuries.[6]

Regarding Judaism, Douglass often compared the treatment of American blacks with the experiences of Jews throughout history (4:243). In "The Color Line," he said that blacks

> may remonstrate like Shylock—'Hath not a Jew eyes? hath not a Jew hands, organs, dimensions, senses, affections, passions? fed with the same food, hurt with the same weapons, subject to the same diseases, healed by the same means, warmed and cooled by the same summer and winter, as a Christian is?'—but such eloquence is unavailing. They are Negroes—and that is enough to justify indignity and violence. (4:343-44)

Douglass believed that blacks and Jews have much in common—"for the Negro, like the Jew, can never part with his identity and race. Color does for the one what religion does for the other and makes both distinct from the rest of mankind" (4:479). He stated: "At one time to hate and despise a Jew, simply for being a Jew, was almost a Christian virtue. The Jews were treated with every species of indignity, and not allowed to learn trades, nor to live in the same part of the city with other people. The Jew has come up, and the Negro will come up by and by" (3:327).

The one area where both Garrison and Douglass fall short of a fuller conception of prophetic values is in their attitudes towards working men and organized labor. As self-made men, they could not bring themselves to support organized labor unreservedly, and both in some sense felt themselves to be "better" (possibly "special" or "unique" would be a more accurate term) than the average laborer. They certainly sympathized with the difficult conditions faced by the working class, but their sympathy was tempered by their belief in hard work, clean living, and moral rectitude as the route to an improved standard of living. Neither man saw that the economic system was often fundamentally stacked against the average laborer, farmer, or factory worker, making it less likely that he would be able to advance through his (or her) own efforts alone.

Despite their normative shortcomings, Douglass and Garrison expressed many of the values of the prophetic tradition. Their concern for the least free in society—slaves, women, free blacks and other oppressed groups—is impressive. Although we have identified several minor, yet still meaningful, differences in the value systems of Garrison and Douglass, the preponderance of evidence demonstrates clearly that the two men shared a dramatic commitment to most key prophetic values. Their moral blind spots underscore the difficulties any merely human being has in reflecting a total commitment to prophetic values. Garrison's anti-Semitism and anti-Catholicism raise disturbing questions about his full-fledged devotion to what we, in twentieth-century democratic America, call authentically prophetic values. In the next section I shall explore Garrison's and Douglass's record in light of the second commitment of prophetic politics, prophetic criticism.

Criticism

Here the evidence supports the thesis that both Garrison and Douglass strongly illustrate the prophetic commitment to fearless criticism of the status quo on almost all issues where the existing order falls short of fulfilling prophetic values. Douglass and Garrison took on, at various times, the institutionalized churches, the entire federal government, slaveholders and the entire South, the clergy, newspaper editors, their Northern neighbors, all political parties, state and local governments, railroad and shipyard companies, Congress, presidents, and even the Constitution.

The key characteristic of prophetic criticism is fearless empirical examination of the existing order. Empty moral indictments of the dominant order are not enough. Criticism of the past, present, and future must rest upon persuasive empirical evidence and upon sound theoretical explanation.[7] In their general devotion to fearless criticism of the existing order, Garrison and Douglass are largely in accord and display a similar level of commitment. However, key differences between Garrison and Douglass appear when we examine their views on empirical evidence and theoretical explanation.

The criticism expressed by both Garrison and Douglass was passionate, unrelenting, and, for the most part, firmly grounded in prophetic values. However, Douglass's criticism was more solidly empirical, fuller, and more comprehensive than Garrison's.

Garrison's indictment of slavery, especially slavery's effects on whites and on slave families, was quite cogent and a strong addition to the criticism of slavery. His critique of the American Colonization Society and colonization schemes was Garrison's greatest contribution to empirical study and criticism of slavery as an institution. His book *Thoughts on African Colonization* effectively ended the influence of the American Colonization Society and recruited hundreds, if not thousands, to the antislavery crusade. His accurate identification of the fact that slaveowners and Southern society generally were ready and willing to abrogate the civil rights of any who opposed them in order to maintain property rights in their slaves was also a significant addition to the abolitionist critique of slavery. Further, Garrison correctly warned the South as early as 1831, only seven months before Nat Turner's rebellion, and three decades before the outbreak of the Civil War, that its choice was to free the slaves peacefully of its own volition or to have the same end accomplished through violence and horrible bloodshed.[8] Although he overestimated the slaves' ability to revolt, Nat Turner's rebellion, other smaller slave uprisings, Kansas, John Brown's raid, and, ultimately, the Civil War, proved Garrison to be correct in essence if not in all details. As armed opposition to slavery grew, the South was forced to adopt ever harsher laws enforcing slavery and punishing those who opposed the slave system or sought to ameliorate its worst effects. As Garrison foresaw, the Civil War cost the lives of over 200,000 Southerners and caused the utter ruin of many cities, towns, farms, and families throughout the South (and North). Also altered forever was the social and economic system supported by slavery.

Garrison, like Douglass, recognized the evil effects of the slaveholding system on master as well as slave, and on the nonslaveholder as well as the slaveowner. His critique of this aspect of slavery, although important, is nonetheless overshadowed by Douglass's much fuller, more detailed, and more developed analysis of this issue. This points to the fundamental difference between the criticism of Garrison and that of Douglass. Douglass was endlessly searching for explanations for the actions people took and the beliefs they held. He needed to understand why blacks were so discriminated against in order to formulate a proper remedy for the problem. Garrison, in contrast, merely knew that slavery and discrimination were sins and should be eradicated from the face of the earth. An excellent example of Garrison's attitude can be found in his book, *The New "Reign of Terror" in the Slaveholding States,* published in 1860. All 144 pages of the book are devoted to reprinting newspaper articles and editorials demonstrating the violation of individuals' civil rights by slaveholders, Southern state and local governments, and other pro-slavery forces. There is, however, not one word from Garrison on how to end slavery, only a seemingly endless documentation of its enormous evil, including its ability to corrupt otherwise honest men.

Once Garrison established his basic philosophy of reform—that of moral suasion of individuals—his criticism never went much deeper than the identification and exposure of "sins" and calls for changed behavior on the part of the "sinners." His criticism was always based on the higher law of God's word. It should be noted, however, that pro-slavery interpretations of the Bible convinced him that every individual must use his or her own mind and heart to know the deeper truths of God's laws.[9]

Douglass, despite a kinship with the Christian sentimentality of Garrison, believed that a fuller critique of slavery and discrimination was necessary if large numbers of Americans were ever to actively oppose these evils. Douglass developed a fairly sophisticated theory of government to buttress his criticism of slavery, discrimination, and race prejudice. In a very real sense, Douglass took the critiques formulated by Garrison and provided them with deeper meaning and a broader context.

Douglass's critique of slavery and its effects drew upon the work of Garrison, Theodore Weld, Wendell Phillips, and others, but Douglass also went beyond these men as he incorporated into his critique knowledge gained from his personal experience with slavery. Additionally, Douglass provided compelling and cogent critiques of race prejudice, discrimination against women, blacks, and other oppressed groups, and reform activity versus revolution, all within a quite fully developed theory of government.[10]

Douglass pointed out that slaves live under the constant threat of cruel and arbitrary punishment, are forced to live with all whites as their masters, and have no hope of defense or exoneration. He argued that slavery debases whites, including nonslaveholders, since the absolute power whites have over slaves inevitably leads to the abuse of that power. Douglass persuasively made the case that slavery debases religion and ministers, since they are forced to rationalize brutality, promiscuity, and murder as appropriate behavior for Christians. In his later years he blasted the South for lynching black men at the mere suggestion of an impropriety toward a white woman, when for hundreds of years white men had had black women, including his own mother, as their sexual slaves. (Interestingly, a recent study shows that African Americans on average have about 30 percent "white" DNA.) Douglass also provided a compelling refutation of the defenses of slavery. Because he used examples from his own slave experience, it is difficult to ignore Douglass's criticism. This brief summary provides but a glimpse of the breadth and depth of his critique of slavery and race prejudice.[11]

For Garrison, "the politics of a people, will always be shaped by its morals, as the vane on the steeple is ever indicating in what direction the wind blows."[12] Thus, Garrison concentrated the force of his criticism on changing the hearts and minds of men rather than on instituting laws or structures that would mandate certain reforms. It was only after three decades of antislavery agitation and the violence in Kansas and John Brown's raid at Harper's Ferry that Garrison's faith in moral suasion faltered even a little. And, as did many abolitionists, he saw the Civil War as divine retribution for the failure to eradicate the evil of slavery.

Douglass and Garrison emerge as powerful, fearless, and illuminating critics who are substantially within the tradition of prophetic politics. By focusing on the key prophetic values of freedom, justice, and individual fulfillment, they emphasized the gap between these ideals and the existing reality. Douglass goes beyond Garrison in that he provides a fuller explanation for the gap and more clearly identifies some possible remedies to help narrow the gap.

Constitutional Action

There is no doubt that fundamental differences exist between these two men with regard to the third commitment of prophetic politics. A comparison of the two men reveals that Garrison was sometimes foolishly utopian, while Douglass was more realistically prophetic. It is clear from the evidence that Garrison's overall plan for the improvement of American society exhibited many traits of the "foolishly utopian" paradigm of politics.[13] As Nelson says, "The true, sad splendor of Garrison's vision of man was that he felt that every revolutionary program he offered had an excellent chance of being adopted by the millions; by everyone who called himself a Christian. He asked no more of anyone than that they accept the moral system of the prophet Jesus."[14] Garrison's answer to the question What must be done? only a few months into his antislavery campaign was: "The work of reform must commence with ourselves. Until we are purified, it will be fruitless and intrusive for us to cleanse others. I say, then, that the entire abstinence from the products of slavery is the duty of every individual."[15] While his faith in the ability of moral suasion to persuade slaveowners voluntarily to emancipate their slaves waned over time, he never gave up hope for the moral regeneration of those in the North and, through them, the entire nation.

Certainly, Douglass was more practical and pragmatic than Garrison in his outlook and philosophy. Early on, Douglass called for changes in the Constitution to bring that document into accord with the ideals of the Declaration of Independence, the Preamble, and, he argued, the American people themselves.

The status of the oppressed in society was his primary concern, and plans for their relief and advancement were always a foremost part of his calls to action. Douglass was a leader in the political movement to have the Thirteenth, Fourteenth, and Fifteenth Amendments to the Constitution adopted. Further, the evidence demonstrates that Douglass formulated cogent proposals that he believed would greatly improve the condition of blacks and others in America after emancipation. These included land reform, voting rights, a national association of African Americans, and antilynching laws, among other proposals. Douglass was also a strong supporter of an amendment to provide women suffrage rights.

An effective way to explore their differences on constitutional action (or on bridging the gap between prophetic values and existential reality) is to take a closer look at their contrasting views of the American Constitution and political action as a means to achieve social reform. Up until the time of Douglass's change of mind in the early 1850s, both men believed that if Americans could be shown the true picture of slavery, they would gladly work toward its extinction. For Garrison, public opinion was not only a means toward the end of abolishing slavery, it was his ultimate concern. According to his principles, it would not be enough to convince a majority of Americans that they should use their legal power to prevent some Americans from enslaving other Americans. In the tradition of Christian perfectionism, Garrison condemned not only the American Constitution, but all constitutions that allowed any use of physical coercion, whether for national defense or for the enforcement of a penal code (although he recognized the necessity of a penal code and prisons, given the current nature of mankind).

Garrison believed that it is wrong to do evil so that good may come, and he viewed all use of physical force, even the force of the legally constituted majority, as evil, if necessary, acts (121–22). Garrison recognized that this philosophy might "seem, to many, absurd, paradoxical, impossible." His trust was that although men of goodwill would not be able to attain the high standard of Christian perfection, they would move closer to it, and so would take political action to soften wicked laws and elect better leaders (159–69). He, however, refused to lower his standards against his own personal involvement in politics simply in order to adhere to the standards of ordinary people.

Garrison's argument was that the Constitution supports slavery and therefore must be rejected. The argument that the Constitution might be either changed or interpreted differently so that it could be used to enforce freedom rather than slavery did not appeal to Garrison, for he had no grounds on which to distinguish legal force from lawless force. More important, for most of his reform career he had been witness to the full weight of local, state, and federal governments being brought to bear time and again on behalf of pro-slavery interests. Having been rejected by those he thought most likely to support his reforms—the churches, their ministers, and their congregations—Garrison reacted by rejecting all the forms and institutions of American society. Garrison lost faith in constitutional and political action to end slavery, and therefore turned completely to the radical doctrines of Christian perfectionism as a solution to his problem. Garrison's view was illogical, as he himself recognized, unless one is willing to believe, with him, that humans are capable of achieving moral perfection. His extreme positions cut him off from the American mainstream but provided him with a small but tremendously loyal and supportive following.

Douglass, even when a "Garrisonian," never went as far along the path to nonresistance (Douglass was not a pacifist and would defend himself if attacked, as often happened) and Christian perfectionism as did Garrison and the most extreme of his followers. During the time when he continued to believe the Constitution to be pro-slavery, Douglass was still deeply troubled by the kind of thinking displayed by the political abolitionist Gerrit Smith in his suggestion that if a government "have a Constitution under which it cannot abolish slavery, then it must override the Constitution and abolish slavery." Douglass replied that this would make "the government superior to and independent of the constitution, which is the very charter of government, and without which the government is nothing better than a lawless mob, acting without any other or higher authority than its own convictions or impulses as to what is right or wrong."[16]

Even before he decided the Constitution was actually an antislavery document, Douglass saw the necessity of constitutional action based upon a higher authority than the whims of individual politicians. Once he decided that the Constitution was indeed an antislavery document, Douglass began to work within the existing political system for the implementation of measures that would lead to the abolition of slavery. Thus, for example, he called for the abolition of slavery in the District of Columbia and the halt of the interstate slave trade by the federal government, as Garrison had done over twenty years previously. During and after the Civil War, Douglass pushed hard for amendments to the Constitution outlawing slavery and providing black males the right to vote.

Yet Garrison also supported these measures. So the question must be asked, What is the difference, if any, between the two men with respect to constitutional action? The answer, I contend, can be found in the temperament of each man. Garrison and Douglass responded in opposite ways to being "rejected of men." Garrison believed that political, social, and legal change could result only from the moral improvement of individuals. Douglass agreed that individual moral progress was vital but argued that laws and institutions could be changed for the better and that people could to some degree be "forced" to live more moral lives under the threat of punishment or censure. Douglass wanted whites to like and respect blacks, but it was more important to him that whites allow blacks to vote and to exercise all their other innate civil rights. If it took the might of the federal government to achieve this goal, then Douglass was willing to use that power and to be disliked by whites. One way of expressing the difference between them may be to see it as a question of more or less. Douglass saw the need for more than moral suasion and was willing to accept the less than perfect world of political measures. In addition, Douglass had more faith in political measures than did Garrison.

Throughout his life, Douglass agreed with Garrison that the basic problem blacks faced was a moral one and that the abolition of slavery and the advancement of free blacks depended upon a moral rebirth. He eventually concluded, however, that the Garrisonians had no comprehensive answer to the question of how this moral rebirth and the accompanying abolition of slavery were to be accomplished. Herbert Storing argues that Douglass felt the Garrisonians needed to learn morality in the politics of a free, although imperfect, republic. "As a mere expression of abhorrence of slavery," Douglass wrote, the Garrisonian theory of no union with slaveholders was a good one, "but it expresses no intelligible principle of action, and throws no light on the pathway to duty. Defined, as its authors define it, it leads to false doctrines, and mischievous results."[17]

Garrison reveals himself to be foolishly utopian in his belief that meaningful social reform can be accomplished primarily through the moral regeneration of individuals. However, he did not consistently practice what he preached. Garrison criticized governments, government officials, and elected representatives as much as he did the actions of individual slaveowners. Early in his reform career Garrison had turned to government and institutions such as the churches and newspapers for help in implementing reform, but he was sorely disappointed by their rejection of his views. During the latter part of the 1830s, he turned away from political and constitutional action in favor of moral suasion and Christian perfectionism. Garrison's perhaps simplistic preference for Christian perfectionism and individual moral suasion, as contrasted with political action by often immoral men, led him to denigrate political action even as he, sometimes inconsistently, supported certain political measures. Garrison, it seems, lacked a creative understanding of constitutional politics.

In contrast to Garrison, Douglass did attempt to formulate a series of recommendations regarding slavery and its aftereffects in order to achieve what would be called in the prophetic paradigm a prophetic constitutional breakthrough. Regrettably, almost none of his proposals, which included low-interest federal loans to ex-slaves to purchase land, a national association of black Americans, and strict enforcement of voting rights, were implemented in his lifetime; and certain of them, such as a first-class education for all children, are still not a complete reality today. What is reasonably clear is that Douglass illustrates the prophetic commitment to wise and effective constitutional action to a significant extent and to a far greater degree than does Garrison.

Continuous Prophetic Scrutiny and Futuristic Projection

Another requirement of the prophetic paradigm is continuous prophetic scrutiny and futuristic projection. Here, too, Douglass better illustrates the prophetic tradition than does Garrison. Although he was far more open to compromise than most historians have portrayed him to be, Garrision was less willing than Douglass to examine and reexamine his basic principles.[18] Garrison engaged in tortuous twists of logic to justify both his withdrawal from political action and his call for others to engage in political action if that was what their conscience bade them do. He experienced a similar problem with his defense of nonviolence while granting to the oppressed the right to violent revolution.[19]

Douglass, upon reflection, rejected much of Garrison's platform (though not the whole of it) in order to develop a more practical and meaningful approach to reform, especially the abolition of slavery. It is significant that Douglass never repudiated Garrison or the importance of his work even while criticizing Garrison's reliance on moral suasion and his policy of disunionism. Rather, once Douglass came to believe moral suasion would be insufficient to secure freedom for the slaves, he went beyond this theory, retaining the best of its points and incorporating them into his broader philosophy of political reform action.

Historians commonly accuse Garrison of abandoning his position as a leading social reformer once slavery had been abolished. He is seen as being naive about racism in both the South and the North and complacent about the ongoing oppression of blacks and others in society.[20] Some writers have made similar claims about Douglass. While Garrison is said to have sold out for public acclamation and respect as an elder statesman, Douglass is accused of ignoring the plight of blacks after the Civil War in order to maintain his patronage positions with the Republican Party.

I contend that these charges are for the most part false and, where valid, much exaggerated. Garrison continued for the remainder of his life to speak out against injustices committed against blacks, women, Chinese immigrants, and other persecuted groups.[21] Despite a few lapses, such as briefly supporting the deal Rutherford B. Hayes made in 1876 abandoning blacks in the South in order to be elected president, Douglass in the main was remarkably steadfast in his ideals, criticizing Republican presidents and their policies even while holding appointive government positions.[22] It appears that the source of at least some of the criticism of Garrison's and Douglass's post–Civil War activities is their shared faith in America as a chosen nation and a sustaining optimism about the possibility that America and Americans might achieve their full potential. Many Americans lost this faith after the Civil War, but neither Douglass nor Garrison ever did.

What, then, is the key difference between the two men with regard to the final prophetic commitment of ongoing scrutiny and futuristic projection? Garrison remained convinced to the end of his life that progress was both inevitable and the result of the perfectibility of individual human beings. If sinners will mend their evil ways, then human progress towards God's kingdom on earth must surely follow. Douglass, although sharing a good deal of Garrison's faith in progress, believed that progress was achieved as much by the hand of man as by the hand of God.

Unlike Garrison, Douglass proposed a wide range of specific reforms to improve the condition of the former slaves as a whole. These included land reform, compulsory education, suffrage, and a national association of black Americans. Douglass was more keenly aware than Garrison that the abolition of slavery and even the granting of the vote to blacks were not sufficient in and of themselves to ensure the protection and advancement of blacks in American society. At the final meeting of the American Anti-Slavery Society he reminded the members that the work of the movement had not been completed:

> I am glad to know that we are to unite in other works, and that though the form of this association shall be dissolved, the spirit which animates it . . . is to continue its activity through new instrumentalities, for the Indian whose condition today is the saddest chapter of our history . . . and to the interests of suffering humanity everywhere; and of woman, too, for whose cause we can now labor upon a common platform.[23]

Douglass also remained a formidable critic of Reconstruction as it progressed and as conditions gradually worsened for blacks in the South.[24] He openly criticized his patrons in the Republican Party and provided compelling criticism, as well as condemnations, of the lynching epidemic that plagued black men in the South during the 1890s.

The most basic difference between Garrison and Douglass is that Garrison simply was not concerned with the long-range details of reform. To him, the overriding priority was the need to call attention to the obvious existing evils so that they might be eradicated. How exactly they might be eradicated and what should follow in their stead were not questions which overly troubled William Lloyd Garrison.[25] While he supported the franchise for blacks and women, schools for free blacks, and an end to discriminatory laws and treatment, he never made comprehensive proposals to implement his reform agenda.

Douglass, with his broader theoretical and philosophical outlook, was better prepared to offer concrete proposals to achieve his objectives. In this, as with constitutional action, Douglass was more illustrative of the prophetic tradition with regard to continuous prophetic scrutiny and futuristic projection.

Conclusion

The model of prophetic politics—admittedly an exacting standard in politics—serves to underscore the strengths and weaknesses of an individual's commitment to prophetic values, criticism, constitutional action, and the future. Given their commitments to the least free—especially to slaves and all African Americans—both Garrison and Douglass could eloquently articulate most prophetic values and criticize an American society that failed to honor such values. However, bridging the gap between prophetic values and existential reality proves more difficult, as does speaking to future problems.

Our discussion points up a critical issue regarding the four commitments of prophetic politics: the relative ease of supporting the first two commitments compared with the third and fourth. It is comparatively easy to espouse prophetic values and to criticize the existing order for falling short of those values. Many antebellum reformers, such as Garrison, excelled in these two characteristics of the prophetic paradigm. Formulating and implementing solutions that will reduce the gap between prophetic values and existential reality are far more difficult tasks. This is clearly exemplified by the experience of both Garrison and Douglass. Garrison had difficulty in conceptualizing concrete practical proposals, while Douglass, although he developed many specific suggestions, was unable to have many of them put into practice. Several of Douglass's favored proposals, such as the Thirteenth, Fourteenth, and Fifteenth Amendments to the Constitution and the civil rights bills, were reversed, overturned, or effectively circumvented mere years after their adoption.

Even more problematic is the commitment to continuous scrutiny and futuristic projection. Of the four commitments of the model of prophetic politics, this is clearly the most difficult to fulfill. Many reformers ardently believed that their key reform was all that was needed to bring America to the fulfillment of her promise as God's chosen nation. Few, if any, of the reform movements spent much effort in attempting to discern the long–term implications of their particular proposals, or their impact once adopted. This remains a major problem in liberal democratic politics—witness the mode of formulation of most social policy in the United States over the past several decades.

In this study the model of prophetic politics has helped to identify the weakness of a major ante- and postbellum reformer—William Lloyd Garrison—regarding constitutional and prudential action to effect change. Many other reformers had, like Garrison, a preference for individual action and individual reform and perfectibility. These tendencies exhibited a naive understanding of the process of social change. The model of prophetic politics aids us in classifying these beliefs as foolishly utopian. In the prophetic tradition, only God is perfect. Garrison's faith in the perfectibility of human beings caused him to have unreasonable expectations for the reform tactic of moral suasion. The failure of his expectations to be realized led him to develop ever more radical views of society and government that made it increasingly difficult for him to put forward any practical (constitutional) solutions to the problems facing America. The prophetic mode calls for social and political action as well as individual action and reformation.

The model of prophetic politics also highlights the failure of the more politically active reformers to engage in continuous scrutiny and futuristic projection. Few had developed long-term proposals to improve the condition of the ex-slaves, and even fewer foresaw the relatively rapid abandonment of the commitment to the freedmen once the war was over.

This examination of Frederick Douglass and William Lloyd Garrison has underscored the enormous difficulty of translating the prophetic stance into concrete action in the real world of politics. We have seen the intellectual gyrations Garrison engaged in to reconcile his radical beliefs with the political realities of his time. Remarkably enlightened for his day, and keenly aware of the many failings of nineteenth-century American society, Garrison was never able to put concrete proposals for reform into words, much less into action. Garrison could not even cogently and consistently define a basic concept such as "immediate emancipation" or the role of freed blacks in society after the abolition of slavery.

Douglass was far more politically astute than Garrison, and he was also more pragmatic, developing a set of reform proposals that, taken together, might have resulted in a modest, yet significant, prophetic breakthrough. Despite his national prominence and his influence with the Republican Party as its leading black spokesperson, Douglass was not able to achieve his full agenda. Further, much of what was accomplished was watered down or nullified by reactionary forces in both the South and the North.

Slavery was the central focus in the lives of both Garrison and Douglass, as well as the ultimate cause of the Civil War. It is important to ask whether a prophetic breakthrough might have averted the war. Looking at the various schemes proposed in the antebellum period—colonization, gradual emancipation, gradual emancipation with compensation to the owners, and immediate emancipation with or without compensation—it seems hard to reconcile any but immediate emancipation with the key prophetic values.

A related issue is the fact that both Garrison and Douglass, along with almost all other nineteenth-century reformers, viewed the Civil War as a just war, especially after the release of the Emancipation Proclamation. Yet Southerners argued that theirs was a just revolution in accordance with the standards set out in the Declaration of Independence. These are difficult questions for those exploring the relationships between the prophetic tradition and real-world politics, but they are issues that must be fully grappled with.

With regard to the twentieth century, the prophetic paradigm helps us in our critical understanding of issues that were important in the last century and remain so today. For example, the exploration of Garrison's ambiguous philosophy of nonresistance highlights the continuing problem of nonviolence and the controversies surrounding the idea of the just war or just revolution. The prophetic mode's criteria for a just war or just revolution might prove quite useful in analyzing and criticizing varying models of nonviolence, such as Garrison's, Tolstoy's, Ghandi's, and Martin Luther King Jr.'s, and such philosophies as Marxism and liberation theology.[26]

Similarly, the model of prophetic politics could provide important insights into modern African-American leadership through a comparison of Douglass and modern black leaders such as Marcus Garvey, Malcolm X, and Martin Luther King Jr. As Howard-Pitney has shown, each of these leaders engaged in a form of the jeremiad, which has many affinities with the prophetic tradition. Clearly, this type of analysis (using the model of prophetic politics) should be helpful in determining how relevant is the social and political thought of Frederick Douglass. Such analysis may also be helpful in demonstrating key linkages between Douglass and modern African-American leadership.

The model of prophetic politics helps to illuminate our understanding of two important historical figures in nineteenth-century America. Critically employed, it may be equally helpful in illuminating our understanding of modern American society.

Notes

1. Neal Riemer, *The Future of the Democratic Revolution: Toward a More Prophetic Politics* (New York: Praeger, 1984), 93–119.

2. Walter Merrill, *Against Wind and Tide* (Cambridge: Harvard University Press, 1963), 258; Louis Filler, *Crusade against Slavery* (Algonac, Mich.: Reference Publication, 1986), 99–101; John L. Thomas, *The Liberator* (Boston: Little, Brown, 1963), 190–93, 345–50.

3. Leslie Goldstein, "The Political Thought of Frederick Douglass" (Ph.D. Diss., Cornell University, 1974), 280.

4. Philip S. Foner, *Frederick Douglass* (New York: Citadel Press, 1950), 104–5; Nathan Huggins, *Slave and Citizen: The Life of Frederick Douglass* (Boston: Little, Brown, 1980), 48.

5. Although Garrison was not as free of prejudices as Douglass and the most enlightened of white Protestant Americans, he was far less strident in his religious prejudices than most Protestant Americans. Although Garrison was critical of the "Romish" church, his criticism of Catholicism paled in comparison to his denunciations of the Protestant churches for supporting slavery. See, for example, "Garrison Blasts Lyman Beecher," (23 July 1836), in *Documents of Upheaval,* ed. Truman Nelson (New York: Hill & Wang, 1966), 96–110.

6. Philip S. Foner, *The Life and Writings of Frederick Douglass* (New York: International Publishers, 1955), 3:356–59.

7. Riemer, *Future of the Democratic Revolution,* 120.

8. Nelson, *Documents of Upheaval,* 28–36.

9. William Lloyd Garrison, *Thoughts on African Colonization* (Boston: Garrison & Knapp, 1832), 6.

10. Goldstein, "Political Thought," 221. See also Waldo Martin, *The Mind of Frederick Douglass* (Chapel Hill: University of North Carolina Press, 1984); David Blight, *Frederick Douglass' Civil War* (Baton Rouge: Louisiana State University Press, 1989); and David Mac Howard-Pitney, *Afro-American Jeremiahs: Appeals for Justice in America* (Philadelphia: Temple University Press, 1990).

11. William B. Rogers, *"We Are All Together Now": Frederick Douglass, William Lloyd Garrison, and the Prophetic Tradition* (New York: Garland, 1995), 98–105. This work expands on the ideas and arguments presented in this chapter.

12. *Liberator,* 12 March 1847; quoted in Rogers, *"We Are All Together Now,"* 140.

13. Riemer, *Future of the Democratic Revolution,* 31–41.

14. Nelson, *Documents of Upheaval,* xvii.

15. Ibid., 10.

16. Frederick Douglass, *Life and Times of Frederick Douglass: Written by Himself* (New York: Pathway Press, 1941), 375–76.

17. Douglass's words are from Foner, *Life and Writings,* 2:351, quoted in Herbert J. Storing, "Frederick Douglass," in *American Political Thought,* eds. Morton J. Frisch and Richard G. Stevens (New York: Scribners, 1971), 147–48.

18. Aileen Kraditor, *Means and Ends in American Abolitionism: Garrison and His Critics on Strategy and Tactics, 1834–1850* (New York: Greenwood Press, 1969), ix.

19. Merrill, *Against Wind and Tide,* 50–53, 145–46; Thomas, *Liberator,* 260–62; Nelson, *Documents of Upheaval,* xxiii–xxx; Gerald Sorin, *Abolitionism* (New York: Praeger, 1972), 89–93; Merton Dillon, *The Abolitionists: Growth of a Dissenting*

Minority (New York: W. W. Norton, 1979), 118–25.

20. C. Vann Woodward, "The Antislavery Myth," *American Scholar* 31, no. 2 (Spring 1962): 181–82; Filler, *Crusade against Slavery,* 342; Goldstein, "Political Thought," 94.

21. Nelson, *Documents of Upheaval,* 276–82. See, for example, the passage Nelson quotes (276) from Garrison's final editorial, published on 24 April 1879, only a month before his death.

22. Foner, *Frederick Douglass,* 324–26; *Life and Writings,* 4:101–5.

23. Foner, *Frederick Douglass,* 267.

24. Ibid., 317–18.

25. Nelson, *Documents of Upheaval,* 279–81.

26. Neal Riemer, *Karl Marx and Prophetic Politics* (New York: Praeger, 1987), 109.

6

The Prophetic Tradition in Afro-America

Cornel West

Prophetic modes of thought and action are dotted across the landscape of Afro-American history. I understand these modes to consist of protracted and principled struggles against forms of personal despair, intellectual dogmatism, and socioeconomic oppression that foster communities of hope. Therefore, the distinctive features of prophetic activity are Pascalian leaps of faith in the capacity of human beings to transform their circumstances, engage in relentless criticism and self-criticism, and project visions, analyses, and practices of social freedom. In this essay, I shall attempt to characterize and criticize—hence to reactivate—the prophetic tradition in Afro-America.

The American Terrain

It is impossible to characterize adequately prophetic activity among Afro-Americans without understanding the specific circumstances under which these practices occur. So it is necessary to sketch briefly the specificity of American society and culture, highlighting the ideological, political, and economic spheres.

The most crucial, brute fact about the American terrain is that the United States began as a liberal capitalist nation permeated with patriarchal oppression and based, in large part, upon a slave economy. The country was born modern, born liberal, and born bourgeois. Its relative absence of a feudal past gave way in the Northern states to an agrarian utopia of free independent farmers on "free" land. In the Southern states, the thriving economy of slavery underscored an aristocratic ethos and entrepreneurial ethic. These beginnings facilitated the ideological dominance of an American-style liberalism that, on the one hand, promoted the sanctity of private property, the virtue of capital accumulation, and the subordination of women and, on the other hand, encouraged the flowering of a slave-based society founded principally upon the ideological pillar of the inferiority of non-Europeans, especially Africans.

This native form of liberalism was engendered not by opposition to feudalism as in Europe, but rather by securing the consensus of property-owning white males in order to maintain social stability. Motivated by notions of new beginnings, Edenic innocence, and exemplary performance, the anticolonial sentiments of the nation entailed an abiding distrust of institutional power, bureaucracy, and, above all, the state. Despite an unprecedented proliferation of voluntary associations, American political discourse placed great emphasis on the welfare of propertied persons as atomistic individuals, rather than as community dwellers or citizens of a republic.

This liberal ideology of Americanism embodied the ideals of bourgeois freedom (such as the freedom to own property, accumulate capital, speak one's mind, and organize to worship) and formal equality (equal treatment under the law)—circumscribed by racist, sexist, and class constraints. These ideological viewpoints indeed have undergone change over time, yet their traces strongly persist in contemporary American life. To put it crudely, most Americans even now—be they of the Right or the Left—are highly individualistic, libertarian, and antistatist, as well as racist and sexist.

The ideals of bourgeois freedom and formal equality became a beacon to oppressed social classes and ethnic groups around the world. Widespread immigration to the United States contributed to the first ecumenical, multiethnic, and multiracial working class in the world and the most complex, heterogeneous population in modernity. In addition, the boomtown character of American industrialization—urban centers appeared virtually overnight—set the context for the flourishing of nativism, jingoism, anti-Semitism, the already entrenched sexism, and, above all, racism.

In the political sphere, the infamous "gift of suffrage" to the white male component of the working class without the need for an organized proletarian movement—in fact prior to widespread industrialization, hence substantive modern class formation—yielded deep allegiance of the white male populace to the existing political order. The political arrangement of coalitional politics and political machines within the framework of a two-party system channeled organizational efforts of class, race, and gender into practical interest-group struggles and thereby relegated oppositional movements to either ill-fated third parties or political oblivion. Furthermore, harsh state repression has been exercised against perceived extremists who threaten the tenuous consensus that the liberal ideology of Americanism reinforces.

This ingenious political setup encourages diverse modes of interest-group articulation and permits incremental social change; it also domesticates oppositional movements, dilutes credible wholesale programs of social change, and encourages sustained organizational efforts to undermine the liberal consensus. The political predicament of all prophetic practices in the United States has been, and remains, the choice between ideological purity and political irrelevance, and ideological compromise and political marginality.

Extraordinary American productivity, principally owing to tremendous technological innovation—motivated, in part, by labor shortage, abundant natural resources (secured by imperialist domination of indigenous and Mexican peoples), and cheap labor (usually imported from various parts of the globe)—has enabled social upward mobility unknown elsewhere in the modern world. The availability of goods, luxuries, and conveniences—which has made comfort an American obsession—to significant segments of the population gives the appearance of a widely fluid social structure. This perception provides credence to the Horatio Alger dimension of the liberal ideology of Americanism: the possibility of rags-to-riches success for all. Even the lower classes remain enchanted by this seductive ideological drama.

High levels of productivity, with uneven expressions across various regions of the country, have made the commitment to economic growth an unquestioned national dogma. From the far Right (for whom growth is a symptom of liberty) to the sophisticated Left (for whom growth makes easier redistribution), Americans remain captive to the notion of economic expansion. This dogma undergirds the consensus of American-style liberalism and thereby views *as natural necessity* the close partnership of the state, banks, and large corporations and their coordinated expansionist activities abroad—often with repressive consequences for native populations. This partnership, along with its imperialist extension, is the bedrock of the American terrain.

On Black Prophetic Politics

These distinctively American circumstances have produced *truncated* prophetic practices, especially among Afro-Americans. Such practices—be they populist, feminist, trade-unionist, socialist, or red, green, or black politics—are truncated in that they are rendered relatively impotent if they fall outside the liberal consensus, and irrepararably innocuous if they function within this consensus. In other words, if prophetic practices radically call into question the orthodoxy of American-style liberalism, they are either repudiated or repressed; and if they accept the parameters of this orthodoxy, they are effectively domesticated and absorbed by the powers that be. This clever American way of dealing with prophetic critiques has produced a marvelously stable society; it also has reduced the capacity of this society to grow and develop. In fact, it can be said with confidence that American society is one of the few to move from innocence to corruption without a mediating stage of maturity. In short, American society has been and remains unable to face its systemic and structural problems.

A major problem perennially facing black prophetic practices is that only in brief historical moments have basic black concerns, such as institutional racism, gained a foothold in American public discourse. Hence, most black prophetic practices have had minimal impact on American society and culture. This is ironic in that a strong case can be made that black Americans are the most American of all Americans; that is, they not only cling most deeply to the ideals of Americanism as enunciated in the Declaration of Independence and the Constitution, but they also are the most hybrid of Americans in blood, colors, and cultural creations.

Black prophetic practices best exemplify the truncated content and character of American prophetic practices; they reveal the strengths and shortcomings, the importance and impotence, of prophetic activities in recalcitrant America. Black prophetic practices can be generally characterized by three basic features: *a deep-seated moralism, an inescapable opportunism,* and *an aggressive pessimism.*

This deep-seated moralism flows from the pervasive influence of Protestant Christianity—a pervasiveness unmatched in other modern industrial and postindustrial nations. Afro-American prophetic practices have been and, for the most part, remain ensconced in a moralistic mood; that is, they are grounded in a moralistic conception of the world in which the rightness or wrongness of human actions, whether individually or collectively understood, is measured by ethical ideals or moral standards. Like the Puritans, the first European Americans, black prophetic Americans have tended to assume that such ideals and standards ought to make a difference in how individuals act and how institutions operate. In short, black prophetic practices assume that, after the most intense scrutiny, some ultimate morally grounded sense of justice ought to prevail in personal and societal affairs.

The inescapable opportunism—or the unprincipled scrambling for crumbs—of black prophetic practices is largely a function of both the unmet needs of black Americans and, more important, the design and operation of the American social system. The needs of black Americans are similar to those of most Americans: they need more control over their lives and destinies; better living conditions, health care, and education; and the extension of liberties for the effective exercise of their unique capacities and potentialities. The satisfaction of these needs is rooted in the quest for more democratic arrangements—in the political, economic, and cultural spheres—to facilitate more self-realization.

The design and operation of the American social system require that this quest for democracy and self-realization be channeled into unfair competitive circumstances so that opportunistic results are unavoidable. In fact, in an ironic way, opportunistic practices become requisite to sustain the very sense of prophetic sensibilities and values in the United States. This is so primarily because deliverance is the common denominator in American society and culture—and a set of practices of whatever sort cannot be sustained or legitimated over time and space without some kind of delivery system or some way of showing that crucial consequences and effects (such as goods and services) flow from one's project. This "delivery prerequisite" usually forces even prophetic critiques and actions to adopt opportunistic strategies and tactics in order to justify themselves to a disadvantaged and downtrodden constituency.

This situation often results in a profound pessimism among prophetic black Americans regarding the possibilities of fundamental transformation of American society and culture. The odds seem so overwhelming, the incorporative strategies of the status quo so effective—and the racism so deeply entrenched in American life. Yet most prophetic practices among black Americans have given this pessimism an aggressiveness so that it becomes sobering rather than disabling, a stumbling block rather than a dead end, a challenge to meet rather than a conclusion to accept.

In the remainder of this essay, I shall try to defend my general characterization of black prophetic practices by presenting persuasive interpretations of three central sets of these practices in Afro-America: prophetic black Christian practices, prophetic black womanist practices, and prophetic black socialist practices. Although I may highlight certain individuals within each set of practices, I intend to view these individuals as but embodiments of the set they best represent.

Prophetic Black Christian Practices

The institutional roots of the prophetic tradition in Afro-America lie in black churches. Although never acquiring a majority of black people within their walls, black churches have had a disproportionate amount of influence in Afro-America. These institutions were the unique products of a courageous and creative people who struggled under excruciating conditions of economic exploitation, political oppression, and cultural degradation. In comparison to Latin America and the Caribbean, the United States had a lower ratio of African to European Americans. In addition, the Afro-Americans worked on smaller plantations, with much less absentee ownership. As a result, black people in the United States interacted more intensely and frequently with white

Americans. And with an inhumane stress on slave *reproduction* in the United States—as opposed to slave *importation* in the Caribbean and Latin America—it was more difficult for younger generations of Afro-Americans to preserve their ties to African customs and rituals. It is important to keep in mind that only 4.5 percent of all Africans imported to the New World—427,000 out of 9.5 million—came to North America. In stark contrast, 3.7 million Africans were imported to Brazil, 748,000 to Jamaica, and 702,000 to Cuba.

The African appropriation of Euro-American Christianity was, in part, the result of the black encounter with the absurd; that is, it was an attempt to make sense out of a meaningless predicament. With the generational distancing from African culture—hence the waning of African traditional religions among the progeny of slaves—Afro-Americans became more and more attracted to religious dissenters in American culture. White Methodists, and especially white Baptists, seized the imagination of many black slaves for a variety of reasons. First, black people found themselves locked into what Orlando Patterson has coined "natal alienation"; that is, the loss of ties at birth in both ascending and descending generations. Hence, they suffered a form of social death as dishonored persons with no public worth, only economic value. Dissenting Protestant Christianity provided many black slaves with a sense of "somebodiness" by introducing the idea of a personal and egalitarian God who gave them an identity and dignity not found in American society. It also yielded a deep sense of the tragic—not accented in West African religions—while holding out the possibility of ultimate triumph.

The Baptist polity, adopted by a majority of black Christian slaves, provided a precious historical possession not found among other groups of oppressed black people in the New World: control over their own ecclesiastical institutions. The uncomplicated requirements for membership, open and easy access to the clergy, and the congregation-centered mode of church governance set the cultural context for the flowering of Africanisms, invaluable fellowship, and political discourse. In fact, this setting served as the crucible not simply for distinctive Afro-American cultural products, but also for many of the uniquely American cultural contributions to the world, including spirituals, blues, and jazz.

Black churches permitted and promoted the kinetic orality of Afro-Americans—the fluid and protean power of the word in speech and song, along with rich Africanisms such as antiphonality (call-and-response), polyrhythms, syncopation, and repetition; the passionate physicality, including the bodily participation in liturgical and everyday expressions; and the combative spirituality that accents a supernatural and subversive joy, an oppositional perseverance and patience. Some of these churches served as the places where slave insurrections were planned, including those of Gabriel Prosser, Denmark Vesey, and Nat Turner. And legal sanctions against black people worshiping God without white supervision pervaded the Southern states. In short, black churches were the major public spheres in Afro-America where strategies of survival and visions of liberation, tactics of reform, and dreams of emancipation were put forward. Black Christian discourse became the predominant language in which Afro-Americans' subversive desires and utopian energies were garnered, cultivated, and expressed.

Yet, as has been noted, Afro-American Christianity did not produce a militant millennialist tradition. This does not mean that there was no prophetic tradition among Afro-American Christians, only that this prophetic tradition did not promote explicitly revolutionary action on a broad scale. This was so for three basic reasons. First, the American status quo, especially in the South, was too entrenched, too solid. A black Christian millennialist revolt would only result in communal or personal suicide, as evidenced by the executions of Prosser, Vesey, Turner, and those who followed them. Second, the Afro-American Christian accent on the tragic sense of life and history precluded perfectionistic conceptions of the kingdom of God on earth—conceptions that often fuel millennial movements. Third, militant millennial movements usually result from the complex tension generated from a clash of two distinct ways of life in which an exemplary prophet calls for a return to, and recovery of, pristine origins that yield ascetic sensibilities and revolutionary action. Afro-American Christian slaves—despite harsh domination—had too much culture and civilization in common with Euro-American slaveholders. Although there were deep dissimilarities, these differences were not deep enough to give cultural credence and existential authenticity to claims that Afro-Americans and Euro-Americans inhabited two distinct and different ways of life. Subsequent black nationalist movements have attempted to authenticate such claims, but usually without inciting revolutionary action. In fact, most black nationalist movements have been Zionist, as with Chief Sam and Marcus Garvey; or explicitly apolitical, as with Elijah Muhammad's Nation of Islam. Owing to Maulana Karenga's creative leadership and openness to criticism, the exception among black nationalist organizations is US.

The inability of Afro-American Christianity to produce a millennialist tradition is a tribute to black Christians, for as great and heroic as such a tradition may sound in books, it would have resulted, more than likely, in either wholesale black genocide or disabling despair and overwhelming self-destruction among black people. In fact, the latter result has been in process since the sixties among young poor black people brought up on the high, almost millennial, expectations generated by the civil rights and Black Power movements and frustrated by the inadequate response of the American powers that be. In stark contrast, the Afro-American prophetic tradition has remained more pessimistic—and realistic—regarding America's will to justice, and it has thereby preserved a more tempered disposition toward quick change. Such a disposition may indeed buttress the status quo, yet it also resists suicidal efforts to revolt prematurely against it.

Martin Luther King Jr. is a unique figure in Afro-American Christianity in that he represents both a heroic effort to reform, and a suicidal effort to revolutionize, American society and culture. In the early years of his prophetic Christian leadership of the civil rights movement, King attempted to bring oppressed black southerners into the mainstream of American life. In a crypto-fascist, underindustrialized, racist American South, even these efforts at minimal reform could cost one's life. Yet as King moved into the urban North and reassessed the U.S. presence in the Dominican Republic, South Africa, and South Vietnam, he concluded that only a fundamental transformation of American society and culture—a democratic socialist United States that promoted nonracist lifestyles—could provide black freedom. This latter conclusion moved King far out of the mainstream of Afro-American Christianity and of American public discourse. Such a prophetic vision of America proved too threatening to America from one whose prophecy was not simply words but, more important, action. In this regard, King, with his ability to mobilize people of different races and groups, was far more dangerous than a library full of black liberation theology or a room full of black liberation theologians who remain distant from people's resistance movements. Yet King's deep moralism, rooted in his black Christian convictions; his inescapable opportunism, as enacted in his deal with President Johnson to exclude Fannie Lou Hamer and the black Mississippi Democrats at the 1964 Democratic National Convention in Atlantic City; and his aggressive pessimism, as seen in his later depiction of American society as "sicker" than he ever imagined, bear out the predicament of black prophetic practices in the United States.

Prophetic Black Womanist Practices

The first national articulation of black prophetic practices in the United States came from black women. The first nationwide protest organization among Afro-Americans was created by black women. Predating the National Urban League (1900) and the National Association for the Advancement of Colored People (1909), the National Federation of Afro-American Women (1895) brought together black women across denominational, ideological, and political lines. Inspired by militant antilynching and womanist spokeswoman Ida

Wells-Barnett, black women's club movements around the country came together in order to focus on two major issues: the humiliating conditions of black women's work, especially the sexual abuse and degrading images of black women in domestic service (in which a majority of black women were employed); and the debilitating effects of Jim Crow–ism, especially the unique American institution (literally invented here) of lynching, which victimized two black persons a week from 1885 to 1922. Furthermore, the black women accented the subtle connection between black sexuality and white violence by acknowledging that lynching was often justified by the white community as a way of protecting white women against rape by black men.

Building upon the heroic action of Underground Railroad revolutionary Harriet Tubman, the outspoken abolitionist Marie W. Stuart, the exemplary nineteenth-century womanist Sojourner Truth, and the Sorbonne-educated teacher and writer Anna Cooper, the national organizations of black women raised their voices in unison against institutional racism in the country, as well as institutional sexism in the country and the black community. In her texts *Southern Horrors* (1892) and *A Red Record* (1895), Ida Wells-Barnett delineated, in excruciating detail, the figures and facts of southern lynchings— including the white male and female victims. The books also put forward a broad account of why the lynchings systematically occurred—an account that acknowledged the sexual and economic motivations for lynching. And in Anna Cooper's important, yet neglected, book, *A Voice from the South* (1892), a sophisticated case was made again linking racism in American society and sexism in Afro-America.

The long and winding career of Ida Wells-Barnett is illuminating for the understanding it offers of the power and pitfalls of black prophetic practices. Beginning as editor of *Free Speech and Headlight,* a Baptist weekly in Memphis, Tennessee, Wells-Barnett was run out of town by racist whites after one of her articles presented a scathing critique of the city's silence concerning the lynching of three of her close friends. She served briefly as a columnist for T. Thomas Fortune's renowned *New York Age* and then moved to Chicago, where she founded and edited (along with her militant lawyer-husband, Ferdinand Barnett) the *Chicago Conservator.* Famous for her devastating criticisms of accommodationist black clergy and her bold support of black self-defense, Wells-Barnett engaged in a lifelong battle with Booker T. Washington and his ubiquitous machine. Recent works on Washington have disclosed the extent to which he controlled, connived with, spied on, and manipulated the major black institutions and movements of his day. His opposition to Wells-Barnett—principally owing to her militancy—exemplifies such behavior. For example, Washington's wife, Margaret, not only headed the first national black women's organization, she also joined the other major leader, Mary Church

Terrell, in blocking Wells-Barnett from holding high office. Furthermore, Washington's control of the Chicago NAACP branch cut off valuable funding for Wells-Barnett's settlement house. Even W. E. B. Du Bois curtailed Wells-Barnett's presence on the national level of the NAACP—an organization she, along with Du Bois and others (mostly white liberals and socialists), founded—by excluding her from the board of directors. In short, Wells-Barnett employed a moral standard and found the black male clergy wanting. She fell victim many times to Booker T. Washington's rapacious opportunism and was abandoned by the very organizations she helped found and build. Her career ended with an aggressive pessimism similar to that of Martin Luther King Jr., but her pessimism is directed not only at the "sickness" of American society but also at the sexism of Afro-America.

This sense of aggressive pessimism can be seen in subsequent prophetic practices of black women. It is apparent in the efforts of Bonita Williams and Eloise and Audley Moore, all black women members of the Communist Party USA in the thirties, who, in the midst of the least racist organization in the nation during the depression, still objected to its subtle racism. In their attempt to promote a ban on the rampant interracial marriages in the party, they were forced to ask a black male comrade from Kansas City, Abner Berry, to make the motion at the Central Committee meeting—only to discover later that he was married to a white woman. Similar experiences of marginality in the labor movement can be seen in the gallant struggles of Victoria Garvin, who as vice president of the Distributing, Processing and Office Workers (DPOWA-CIO) was the first black woman to hold a high elected office in American trade-unionism, and Octavia Hawkins, the leader of UAW Local 453 in Chicago. Both were major figures in the National Negro Labor Council, the foremost black protest group in the early fifties, which was soon crushed by McCarthyism.

In the recent black freedom struggle, the list goes on and on, from the legendary Fanny Lou Hamer of the National Welfare Rights Organization, Miranda Smith of the Tobacco Workers Union, Frances Beale of the Student Nonviolent Coordinating Committee (now of Line of March), and Ericka Huggins of the Black Panther Party, to Angela Davis of the Communist Party USA. Although each case is quite different, the common denominator is protracted struggle against the effects of race, class, and gender oppression in the United States and those of class and gender discrimination in Afro-America. The contemporary writings of Gayl Jones, Toni Cade Bambara, Alice Walker, Toni Morrison, Sonia Sanchez, Lucille Clifton, and Audre Lorde, though constituting both a grand literary upsurge and a dim hope for black women's enhancement, repeat the cycle of black prophetic practices: initial moralism, inescapable opportunism, and combative pessimism.

Black Prophetic Socialist Practices and the Future

Black prophetic practices as manifest in black socialist thought and action, though in my view the most important set for political purposes, require less attention than the black prophetic church and black womanism. This is so, in part, because socialism as a modern tradition is less indigenous to black prophetic practices than the other two. Socialism—different from African communalism or agrarian cooperativism—is preeminently European and remains far removed from both Afro-American and American life. Unlike Euro-American Christianity and white feminism, socialism has not been seriously appropriated by black people and rearticulated within an Afro-American context and language. This does not mean that there have been no noteworthy black socialists; yet none has had the will, vision, and imagination to *Afro-Americanize* socialist thought and practice. Yet, recently, rudimentary efforts have been made—efforts such as Manning Marable's *Blackwater,* Maulana Karenga's *Kawaida Theory,* my own *Prophesy Deliverance!* and Cedric Robinson's *Black Marxism.*

The cultural distance from socialist thought and action has forced most black socialists to shun the very riches and resources of Afro-American culture, especially its deep moralism, combative spirituality, and aggressive pessimism. The results have been mere bland imitations of Euro-American socialists, who themselves possess a weak tradition of theory and practice. It is no accident that the disproportionate number of black socialist intellectuals in the United States since World War II has yet to produce a major black socialist theorist. (I consider neither Du Bois nor Oliver Cox a major theoretical thinker.) Nor is it an accident that there has been but one serious black socialist leader in this century—a Baptist preacher during the Debsian phase of American socialism, Rev. George Washington Woodbey.

The Major Challenge

The major challenge of the prophetic tradition in Afro-America in the last decades of this century is to build upon the best of the black prophetic church, promote the further flowering of black womanist practices, and indigenize socialist thought and practice in conjunction with ecological concerns. This latter endeavor consists of reinscribing and rearticulating within the Afro-American context the specific forms of class exploitation, imperialist oppression, and violent destruction of the biosphere, nature, and potentially the planet.

This challenge is both intellectual and practical. It is intellectual in that it requires new forms of theoretical activity from black thinkers who are in close dialogue with European, Asian, African, Latin American, and Native American intellectuals, yet rooted in the best of the Afro-American intellectual past. These new forms of theoretical activity must learn from Marxism (class and imperialist oppression), populism (local peoples' empowerment), civic republicanism (decentralized democratic control), liberalism (individual liberties, due process of law, separation of church and state, and checks and balances), and womanism (women's control of their bodies and destinies), as well as ecologism (communion with, rather than domination of, nature), and elements of Garveyism (dignity of African peoples). It is a practical challenge in that it must be feasible and credible to a majority of the populace; that is, it must have organizational expressions with enough support, potency, and power to transform fundamentally the present order. In this regard, black prophetic practices are not simply inseparable from prophetic practices of other peoples; they also hold a crucial key to the widespread impact of prophetic practices upon prevailing retarding influences.

Therefore, black prophetic practices will remain truncated, as will all other American prophetic practices, unless the struggles against forms of despair, dogmatisms, and oppressions are cast on a new plane—a higher moral plane, a more sophisticated and open-ended theoretical plane, and a more culturally grounded political plane. The higher moral standard must make the all-inclusive ideals of individuality and democracy the center of a prophetic vision. The more sophisticated and open-ended theoretical activity must reject unidimensional analyses and master discourses yet preserve intellectual rigor and complexity. And the more culturally grounded political plane must be deeply rooted in the everyday lives of ordinary people—people who have the ability and capacity to change the world and govern themselves under circumstances not of their own choosing.

7

The Prophetic Mode and Challenge in Literature

J. Mitchell Morse

No prophet has ever had an acquiescent mind. The essence of the prophetic vision is that it does not acquiesce in sin. Whether or not anybody agrees, it sets high moral standards: it insists that there must be justice in public life and in private life; it defines justice as a recognition, in living practice, that all human beings are equally human, and that we are required by that fact to treat each other with equal consideration.

We are not so required by nonhuman nature, nor by our own surviving prehuman instincts. Everybody who watches nature films on TV knows that nonhuman nature is conservative: that in its constant struggle for survival it doesn't think beyond its fighting instincts. It has no ethical sense. We like to think that we have evolved beyond the other animals, and to some extent we have; but everybody who reads the economic and political news knows that *Homo economicus* and *Homo politicus* are so fully dominated by the unevolved elements of our nature that they think we are too. I am not reading them out of the human family; I *am* suggesting that their unevolved conception of our more developed human nature is a delusion. It is what Plato called "the lie in the soul" (*Republic* 382 a-b): a fundamental ignorance (habitual but not incurable) of our humane possibilities.

The vital civilizing function of the prophetic vision is to disabuse them: to cure their souls.

That is the chief value of good writing and of great literature. It exalts us. It raises our perception of humanity to higher levels and new intensities. It clarifies our vision. It shows us better human possibilities. In this sense it is prophetic, and this fact, which I propose to demonstrate with examples, gives us a standard by which to judge literary quality: an ethical standard.

It shows us, for example, that technical excellence, though necessary, is not enough. Consider two technically excellent autobiographical novels of

World War I: E. E. Cummings's *The Enormous Room*[1] and Louis-Ferdinand Céline's *Voyage au bout de la nuit.*[2] Both authors viewed the war with loathing and contempt, but Cummings's treatment is prophetic and Céline's is antiprophetic. The difference lies entirely in their attitudes toward human beings. Cummings, for all his snobberies and prejudices, and for all the verbal improprieties that thickly sprinkle *The Enormous Room,* appreciated the virtues of many ordinary and even infraordinary people; sympathized with them in their troubles and griefs; resented the injustices to which they were subjected; and, within the limits of his opportunities, tried to help them. The technical verve with which he describes his experiences enhances our understanding of them and of our own experiences. But Céline apparently never met a human being he didn't despise and, within the limits of his opportunities, abuse. Therefore the technical verve with which he describes his experiences only redoubles our regret for his aggressive lack of human sympathy, his missionary zeal for all forms of cruelty, and his moral stupidity.

The principles of morality have nothing to do with the rules of propriety. Céline was improper as well as immoral; but before and during the Nazi occupation of France his pro-Nazi immorality caused many conservative and reactionary readers to ignore their proper distaste for his improprieties—a little polite hypocrisy in the interest of the greater good of Pétain's Call to Order. Céline's predecessor in impropriety, Emile Zola, had quite different effects. He wrote about coal miners, railroad workers, and market porters with full sympathy for them in their hard lives, but without prettying up their language or behavior. As a result, not only did genteel conservative critics attack him for writing about people one doesn't know, but the Socialist Party also attacked him as an enemy of the working class. How's that for political correctness?

The prophetic tradition in literature encourages a Zola-like sympathy without regard for politics. It always seeks to counteract the influence of the coarse and mean-spirited in our common life and to stimulate in readers the liveliest possible sympathy. For social injustice is always and everywhere due to a deficiency of sympathy in individuals: a moral numbness in the souls of those who make or execute policy, such as is revealed by their racist, sexist, and homophobic sneers, and in the souls of those who defend their behavior.

Hard as it is for us to understand such moral numbness, we must investigate its nature in order to know how to counteract it. As we have just seen, literature offers us examples that enable us to proceed by contrasting it with its opposite, the liveliest moral sympathy. Doing so will also help us to work out ethical standards for judging literary quality.

Three Poems

The first fact we encounter in our investigation is that the lack of a moral sense is not due to any lack of IQ—of innate or acquired brainpower—or of the particular kind of brainpower known as literary talent.

This fact makes our investigation difficult, for human feelings and motives are not easily classifiable. They are full of nuances and shades and tints and blendings and mixtures and compounds and inconsistencies and contradictions. The same writer may be both sensitive and insensitive, both intelligent and stupid, even when writing about the same subject. Consider two poems of T. S. Eliot about drowned men, and their common source in Shakespeare.

In act 1, scene 2 of *The Tempest,* the invisible Ariel sings:

Full fathom five thy father lies;
   Of his bones are coral made;
Those are pearls that were his eyes:
   Nothing of him that doth fade,
But doth suffer a sea-change
Into something rich and strange.
Sea-nymphs hourly ring his knell:
          Ding-dong.
Hark! now I hear them,—Ding-dong, bell.

This is pure, singing lyricism of the most artful and artificial seventeenth-century kind. Its high value is purely formal. It is not an expression of prophetic vision. Neither is it antiprophetic. It is nonprophetic.

Our next example is from Eliot's *The Waste Land.* As a brief transition between the squalid scenes of London life in "The Fire Sermon" and the surreal nightmare of "What the Thunder Said" comes the calm, pure lyricism of "Death by Water":

Phlebas the Phoenician, a fortnight dead,
Forgot the cry of gulls, and the deep sea swell
And the profit and loss.
          A current under sea
Picked his bones in whispers. As he rose and fell
He passed the stages of his age and youth
Entering the whirlpool.
          Gentile or Jew
O you who turn the wheel and look to windward,
Consider Phlebas, who was once handsome and tall as you.

On our first reading, this seems to be English lyric poetry at its finest, with resonances of classic Greek lyricism at its finest. It is not prophetic in any obvious sense, but its perfection of form and the seemingly unsentimental purity with which, on our first unwary reading, it evokes our deepest feelings of human community seem to give it a unique and absolute value. To some extent its value seems to be that of prophetic utterance, even though its chief and most obvious value seems to be that of a work of art. But our experience of poems changes with rereading, and I shall have more to say about this one presently. As you may perhaps have begun to suspect, it will turn out to be a fake.

Our third example is a poem Eliot had written earlier, "Dirge," which remained unpublished during his lifetime. His friend Ezra Pound had suggested that he omit it from a proposed collection, along with two other poems, simply because it wasn't good enough. "One test," he wrote to Eliot, "is whether anything would be lacking, if the last three were omitted. I don't think it would." In the upper right corner of the sheet bearing "Dirge" he had written two question marks, and under them the word "doubtful."[3]

This is what Pound called "doubtful":

Full fathom five your Bleistein lies
Under the flatfish and the squids.
Graves' disease in a dead Jew's eyes!
   When the crabs have eat the lids.
   Lower than the wharf rats dive
   Though he suffer a sea change
   Still expensive rich and strange
That is lace that was his nose
   See upon his back he lies
   (Bones peep through the ragged toes)
With a stare of dull surprise
   Flood tide and ebb tide
   Roll him gently side to side
   See the lips unfold unfold
   From the teeth, gold in gold
Lobsters hourly keep close watch
Hark! now I hear them   scratch scratch scratch.

The tone of this poem is so radically different from that of "Phlebas the Phoenician" that Pound, who was if possible even more anti-Semitic than Eliot, can only have rejected it because of its inferior quality as verse. One of Pound's criteria for good verse was natural rhythm, "the rhythm of the phrase, not of a metronome"; and by that criterion "Phlebas the Phoenician" is good verse and "Bleistein" is bad verse. But when we reread "Phlebas the Phoenician" for this examination, we see that there is more in it than we saw on any of our earlier, unwary readings. On our earlier readings we assumed that the cry of gulls and the deep sea swell evoked in Phlebas much the same feelings that they do in us when we read about them—that he had the sensibility of a poet or at least of a reader of poetry, as well as the skills of a sailor and a merchant. But now, not renouncing but adding to our earlier readings, we recall some of the methods of navigation before the invention of the compass and the astrolabe and the chronometer and the establishment of the Greenwich Observatory. We recall that navigators judged the distance and direction of land by the numbers and behavior of gulls, and that on the deep sea beyond the range of gulls they navigated not only by the sun and stars but also by the direction of swells. This recollection changes our view of Phlebas. We know now that his observations of gulls and swells were integrated with his calculations of profit and loss; and that although he may indeed have had the sensibility of a poet it had little or no relation to his skill as a navigator or his success as a merchant.

This realization gives the poem, technically, more unity—more validity as a work of art—than it seemed to have on our first reading. But our new reading also intensifies our awareness of its artificiality. It reads like a fine translation of an ancient Greek poem; it is a bit of literary antiquarianism, on a par with the early Pound's *Personae*. "Make it new," Pound had said, but he usually made it old. He was a mad antiquarian; and Eliot was by comparison an amateur antiquarian.

Has a poet no right to be an antiquarian? Of course he or she has; but antiquarianism is socially suspect. It is usually—not always, but usually—associated with nostalgia for old ways in politics and social institutions (which presumed a hereditary hierarchical gradation of classes) as well as in furniture and architecture. Somewhere in *A la recherche du temps perdu* Proust says that if the people who lament that Paris is not what it was a hundred years ago had lived a hundred years ago, they would have raised the same lament. In my South Carolina childhood I knew a number of old ladies and gentlemen who thought the American Revolution was a mistake, and the outcome of the War Between the States (as they called it) an unmitigated social disaster. A few of my contemporaries shared that view with their parents and grandparents, and their present avatars, as I write, constitute a majority of both houses of Congress. They are trying to revive what the old ladies and gentlemen of my youth called the Lost Cause. Such people are antiprophetic personalities.

So was Eliot, only more so. His message for this world was one of despair. "Phlebas the Phoenician" belongs to the broad genre of *ubi sunt* poems: where are the snows of yesteryear, where is the beauty of Helen, where is the glory of Constantinople, where are all our profits and losses and endeavors and hopes, and what difference do they make? What does the human world amount to? What does human justice amount to? Vanity, vanity! We can only hope for undeserved redemption after death. Repent! Repent!

Two Paintings

The prophets also urged us to repent, but not because they thought life wasn't worth living. They urged us rather to establish human justice and decency, and even went so far as to point out that doing so would bring rewards in this world: political independence and even economic prosperity. Eliot's negative view flourished chiefly in the Middle Ages, and was largely superseded in the Renaissance. Two paintings of the same subject, in the Rijksmuseum in Amsterdam, give striking evidence of the supersession, gradual though it was. Let us recall that after Jesus raised Lazarus from the dead, Lazarus's sisters, Martha and Mary, invited Jesus to the house for dinner. While Martha was busy cooking the dinner and setting the table, Mary sat on the floor at Jesus' feet, drinking in his words, and when Martha asked Mary to lend a hand, Jesus said, "Martha, Martha, thou art careful and troubled about many things: But one thing is needful: and Mary hath chosen that good part, which shall not be taken away from her" (Luke 10:41–42 Authorized [King James] Version). As in most serious literature, there is obviously justice on both sides, reason to sympathize with both women. When God comes into your house, can you think of nothing but eating? Jesus is evidently on Mary's side. It is not recorded, however, that he was so ungracious as to refuse to eat Martha's dinner. And if she too had sat at his feet and neglected to feed him, or if she had indifferently fed him with whatever happened to be in the kitchen at the time, taking no special pains for the man who had restored her brother to life, would that have been better?

This theological dilemma has exercised Christian theologians for quite a while. Our two paintings in the Rijksmuseum indicate a clash of values and the difference between the lingering medieval view and the emerging Renaissance view of life. Cornelis Engebrechtsz (1468–1533) and Joachim Bueckelaer (ca. 1530–73), though their lives overlapped by about three years, lived in largely different worlds of feeling. They painted the same joyful occasion from opposite points of view, literally as well as symbolically. In Engebrechtsz' painting, "Christ teaching in the house of Lazarus," the foreground is filled with Jesus and Mary, and through the open door in the far back wall we have a distant view of Martha in the kitchen. In Bueckelaer's painting, "Christ in the house of Martha and Mary," the foreground is filled with Martha in her kitchen full of good things—fish, fowl, bread, meat, vegetables, fruits, cakes, pies, cheeses, wines, etc.—and through the open door in the far back wall we have a distant view of Jesus and Mary.

The Renaissance joie de vivre could on occasion evoke even from death by drowning images of coral and pearls rather than of the picking of our bones, whether by a current or by crabs and lobsters; but Eliot had the medieval melancholy. In a letter he called it "an aboulie and emotional derangement which has been a lifelong affliction."[4] In view of the energy with which he managed his life amid many difficulties, this may be only the familiar affectation of laziness that is a minor vanity of many writers; but he certainly had a sense of despair, which was no doubt a serious difficulty. Medieval moralists called it acedia: spiritual "unlustihood," listlessness. Baudelaire called it "a disease of monks."[5] That Eliot was intensely religious is well known; that he was a bitter antihumanist is quite evident, not only in the poems about the cliché Jew Bleistein and the cliché simian Irishman Sweeney (in a period when want ads said "Christians only" and "No Irish need apply") but also in the poems about the Phoenician Phlebas and about all other unsaved human beings, however handsome and tall. Staying in the Phoenician age, he doesn't say "Christian or Jew," but "Gentile or Jew," quite possibly intending the biblical sense of the word "Gentile": "pagan." However that may be, he gratuitously invites us all, Gentile, Jew, and Christian, not only into the natural human community of death but also into the not necessarily necessary human community of despair.

So we are quite right to call Eliot an antiprophetic writer, in his poetry as well as in his social and literary criticism. As Stanley Edgar Hyman pointed out sometime ago (in *The Armed Vision*), all the poets and dramatists Eliot praised, with the exception of Virgil, whom he praised as a proto-Christian, were orthodox Anglicans and Roman Catholics; all those he dispraised were atheists like Shelley or dissenters like Milton. All those he praised, moreover, were social conservatives or reactionaries; all those he dispraised were liberals or radicals. Nor did he shrink from using religious orthodoxy and social conservatism as standards of literary value. So much was his literary judgment vitiated by this practice that he actually preferred Kipling to Milton. His embarrassed second essay on Milton, grudgingly recognizing genius, was as much a tactical retreat as his statement after the defeat of Nazism, "I am a Christian, and therefore I am not an anti-Semite."[6] That was either a remarkably naive or a remarkably disingenuous exercise in stipulative definition. As intellectual attainments, racism and anti-Semitism are on a par with cheating at cards. They cannot be explained away.

The Written Word

But whether a writer is prophetic or antiprophetic or nonprophetic is another question than that of his literary talent: his mastery of language: his skill in using its resources to direct the thoughts and feelings of readers, both naive and sophisticated. The prophetic Joyce, reviewing a book of thumping patriotic verse with the rhythm of a metronome by a fervent Fenian, said, "A man who writes a book is not excused by his good intentions, or by his moral character; he enters into a region in which there is question of the written word." But skillful use of the written word is inextricably involved with respect for the readers. If good intentions and high moral character were the only conditions for writing great literature, *Uncle Tom's Cabin* would be a great novel and the fervent Fenian's metronomic verse would be great poetry. But incompetent writing cannot be prophetic, because its technical absurdity evokes amusement rather than moral zeal in readers of any sophistication at all. This fact takes us a long way toward a defensible definition of prophetic literature: that it must evoke moral zeal in its readers and that it must have enough literary validity to be taken seriously by readers who can see the many demonstrable differences between competent and incompetent writing.

Respect for the Readers

But there are two remaining difficulties. One is that this definition leaves naive readers—that is, most readers—out of account. The other is that there are evil geniuses—for example, Eliot, Pound, Céline, Jouhandeau—whose highly competent writing arouses zeal for evil causes.

   We must recognize that a great deal of technically absurd verse like that of Joyce's Fenian did in fact do a great deal to keep the Irish independence movement alive among many readers who had no literary sense at all, and that *Uncle Tom's Cabin* did in fact arouse moral zeal against slavery in many equally naive readers.

   Would *Uncle Tom's Cabin* have been more effective as antislavery propaganda if it had had more literary validity and fewer readers? Obviously not. But would it necessarily have had fewer readers? That does not follow. To be sure, if it had been written in an extremely precious literary style—say, that of Euphues—it would have had precious few readers and precious little effect. But if it had been written in the style of Stowe's contemporary Dickens, or the style of one of their older contemporaries Balzac and Hugo or their younger contemporaries Zola, Dostoyevsky, and Tolstoy, all of whom were both popular and great, it would have had at least as many readers, more effect, and better effect.[7]

The effect would have been better because propaganda based on respect is better in every way than propaganda based on condescension. That Stowe's attitude toward the slaves was one of pitying condescension there can be no doubt. Among all the possible models for her hero, she chose not one of the contemporary bold fighters against slavery (such as William Wells Brown, Martin Delaney, Frederick Douglass, Henry Highland Garnet, John Russworm, Nat Turner, Denmark Vesey, or Samuel Ringgold Ward) and not one of the earlier bold fighters (such as Benjamin Banneker, Lemuel Haynes, David Walker, or Peter Williams). But rather than one of those strong men, she chose the weak and servile Josiah Henson, who rebelled reluctantly and was despised by the others. The name she gave him, Uncle Tom, has become an eponym of servility, and her own attitude toward African Americans, disseminated through her novel, has infected many white liberals ever since.[8] In purely literary terms, her attitude cheapened her performance as a novelist; we can thus unequivocally assert that *Uncle Tom's Cabin*, its immediate good effect notwithstanding, has also had long-term bad effects that are due to its literary absurdity. In any case, its good effcts have been exaggerated: the causes of the Civil War were economic and political, not literary, and the causes of its outcome were economic and military, not literary. Abraham Lincoln's alleged statement to Stowe, "I've always wanted to meet the lady who started the war," if he made it, was a condescending pleasantry, not a statement of fact.

Prophetic writing must therefore be technically good writing, for it will be good in prophetic terms only to the extent that it is good in literary terms. In the long run, bad art does not make good propaganda; the notion that it does is a delusion, and to act on it is a mistake. A writer who writes down to his readers, or offers them oversimplified fantasies of reality reduced to physical adventure and nothing more, because he fears that the complex and subtle truths of human life would baffle or bore them, has no respect for them—or for himself. I am thinking of the likes of Stephen King and Robert Ludlum. If such writers are not conscious of their disrespect, it is only because they have no valid conception of themselves as thinkers or writers. Since the means always influence and often determine the end—since, for example, we cannot establish democracy by undemocratic means—bad writing cannot have good social results.

Much good writing is not prophetic, because the moral atmosphere doesn't always lend itself to prophetic utterance. Just as rebellion and revolution occur not when conditions are at their worst but when they have improved enough for the oppressed to have the energy and self-confidence that revolt requires, or when conditions have not yet deteriorated far enough to deprive the oppressed of the necessary energy and self-confidence—just so, when the moral atmosphere is at its worst, when insensitivity and complacency are at their most abject and are most widespread, prophetic utterance rarely occurs. Rather, it occurs chiefly when the atmosphere has improved enough to produce both an utterer here and there and an audience.

Prophecy and Popularity

In the long ascending period of the bourgeois revolutions—1688, 1776, 1789, 1848, 1865—Europe and America resounded with prophetic voices. The defeats and retreats of 1815 and 1852 in Europe and the post–Civil War reaction in the United States had no lasting effects; and though much of that progress has been undone by the ensuing decades of Hitlerism and Stalinism and the current Radovichism, there continue to be major as well as minor prophetic voices among twentieth-century writers.

But when we consider them, a curious fact emerges: The great prophetic writers of the nineteenth century, unlike those of the twentieth, were widely popular. Dostoyevsky's poverty was due to his gambling and to his noble assumption of his dead brother's debts, not to any lack of readers. When he said, "My name is worth a million," he was not idly boasting; and each of the others I have mentioned—Tolstoy, Balzac, Hugo, Zola, Dickens—might have said something similar. They were all international best-sellers. On this side of the Atlantic, Confederate soldiers called themselves "Lee's Miserables." Crowds awaited each new installment of Dickens's latest serial novel from London, and the author himself twice toured the United States in triumph, his readings from his works filling all the biggest theaters from coast to coast. The twentieth century has equally great and greater writers, but they have not had a comparably wide appeal: certainly not Joyce, Proust, Kafka, Broch, or Rolland; certainly not Beckett; certainly not Camus. Their books do, to be sure, sell well, but chiefly among professors of literature and their students. Günter Grass and Gabriel García Marquez have even achieved bestsellerdom, but not on a scale at all comparable to that of John Le Carré, John Gardner, Tom Clancy, Harold Robbins, Danielle Steel, Judith Krantz, Erica Jong, the late Jacqueline Susann, the late Ian Fleming, or the late Ayn Rand. Too many bestselling authors whose names are now worth millions are chiefly purveyors of soft porn. Moreover, by all accounts, many of these writers consider themselves great writers and dismiss their critics with contemptuous shrugs. Their attitudes indicate the aggressively antiprophetic stance of much current writing. Nonetheless, the prevalence of airport-gift-shop schlock does not prevent the publication of prophetic books, for which there is also a market, and which do leaven our culture.

Some Conditions for Prophetic Utterance

The first major novel of the twentieth century was Thomas Mann's *Budden-brooks* (1901). It was a masterful study of the decline and fall of a family of rich grain traders whose scale of business was large enough for them to own their own ships and whose last head was a thoughtful man with a sense of social responsibility, a taste for philosophy, and a sternly repressed artistic inclination. But *Buddenbrooks* is not a prophetic novel in the sense of being a call to redeem ourselves from sin. That is because it is full of Gobineauvian pessimism, the bankruptcy of the dynasty being ineluctably due to the insidious influence of "inferior" racial strains that at one time and another in the past had "tainted" its otherwise pure German "blood."

The obsessive racism that tainted Mann's work from first to last has damaged him in our esteem for many years now, and rightly so; but there is a new biography by Donald Prater (Oxford University Press, 1995) that attempts to redeem him. His own works, however, testify against him. The anti-Semitism of "Tristan" and "Blood of the Walsungs" (1903) is unmistakable; so is the Gobineauvian fear of "mixing, mixing, always mixing," in "Tonio Kröger" (1921). Racism was an acquired automatism that Mann could not control. It appeared even in the generally liberal *Magic Mountain* (1924) and *Doktor Faustus* (1947), and even in the deliberately philo-Semitic *Joseph* quartet (1934–44), which he wrote to dissociate himself unequivocally from the Nazis, who he saw had acted on his racist ideas with unmannerly unrestraint. For all his purely literary brilliance, a miasma of invalidity sickened all his work. With that foul disease of the spirit, he could not be a prophetic writer.[9]

Perhaps the first major work of literary art in the twentieth century that was unmistakably prophetic was the first volume of Proust's *A la recherche du temps perdu: Du côté de chez Swann* (1913). Because of the wartime shortages of paper and printers' time, to say nothing of Proust's own endless revisions, the remaining six volumes appeared at irregular intervals from 1918 through 1927. Death overtook Proust in 1922, but he had already begun to be rightly recognized as a great writer and a major prophetic voice. That was because, like Thomas Mann, he had seen already in the belle époque the beginning of the decline of European civilization that was to become unmistakable in World War I. But whereas Mann observed the decline with an ironic smile, Proust protested that it was not irreversible. He correctly saw its causes not in biology but in the social evolution of thought and feeling; not in "racial degeneracy" but in the contagious spread of hedonism and opportunism. The biblical title he gave to the central novel in his series, *Sodome et Gomorrhe*, was a condemnation not only sexual but social. Mann's pessimism was due to his ironic recognition that the only cure for "racial degeneracy" is genocide—a nonsolution, unworkable and in any case destructive to the perpetrators, from which he recoiled in fastidious horror when he saw it being practiced. Proust's more valid humanism consisted in his belief that we as individuals can with great effort sometimes overcome our bad habits and redeem ourselves from sin: that we can reverse our social decline, not by killing others, but by redirecting ourselves. On his deathbed he was still revising his work and his soul.

In 1913, the year Proust published *Du côté de chez Swann,* Kafka abandoned, unfinished, his first novel, *Amerika.* Thanks chiefly to the efforts of his devoted friend Max Brod, he did publish five small volumes of short stories and meditations and a few other pieces during his lifetime. Their high quality was immediately recognized by a few perceptive readers such as Rilke and Musil, but his novels remained unknown until Brod, against Kafka's equivocally stated wish, began publishing them in 1924, soon after Kafka's death. Simone de Beauvoir testified eloquently to the enthusiasm of those of her generation who could read German.[10] But although Kafka wrote with meticulous purity, his works were translated into other languages carelessly and inaccurately. Even so, much of their power comes through in English. During the Nazi period all known copies of his works in Germany were destroyed, but after World War II a number of exiled German writers began pointing out, in German literary magazines, his unique value as a prophet in all senses, and there began to be a demand for his works. Piratical German publishers, unable to find copies from which to set their type, imported copies of inaccurate French and English translations, had them hastily retranslated into German by anonymous hack translators, and sold the resulting lifeless and sloppy prose as Kafka's work. Readers with any literary sense at all concluded that his reputation as a good writer was unjustified. Not until a decade after the war did S. Fischer Verlag begin to publish accurate texts under license from Kafka's exiled publisher, Zalman Schocken, founder of Schocken Books. In Kafka's native Czechoslovakia, as in the other countries of then-Communist Eastern Europe, except for a brief period during the Khrushchev administration, his works were, and until quite recently remained, banned.

That history is itself a Kafka story: a story of the insensitivity that he saw as the source of all the evil in the world, and against which he fought in the only way he could, as an artist, revealing its devious ways—among them those of its indwelling in ourselves, the authoritarian within.

But there is objective evidence that it is possible to redeem oneself. Günter Grass is an outstanding example. His father, a small neighborhood grocer, was an enthusiastic early Nazi, always glad of any occasion to put on his storm trooper's uniform, even before Hitler came to power. At the age of five Günter joined the Hitler Youth, and in his adolescence moved up through the labor service and into the army at age seventeen. After the war, amid many difficulties, he had some minor successes as a painter, poet, and playwright. At age 31, while living in Bremen, he published a major novel, *The Tin Drum,* which portrays with complex art and prophetic fury the base lives of small-time Nazis. The Bremen city council had the pleasant custom of awarding an annual prize, on the recommendation of an independent committee, for the best work of literature by one of its citizens. That small local prize normally attracted little attention outside of Bremen. But when in 1959 the committee unanimously recommended *The Tin Drum* for the award, the council indignantly refused to award the prize to Grass. The council's action produced an international brouhaha, and Grass's great prophetic novel became an instant and long-term best-seller. That fact, though gratifying, tells us nothing about *The Tin Drum*'s quality, but I believe it is a permanent major addition to world literature.

Having lived Nazism all through his childhood and youth, having seen it from the inside, Grass saw his own madness. All his heroes are insane in one way or another. Thus his works are acts of repentance, if not actually of self-healing (though repentance is the first step toward self-healing). Like Jeremiah, Grass preached self-knowledge and called on his fellow citizens to reform their lives. He even recommended asceticism; he said repeatedly, and only half ironically, that Germans should refrain from eating foods they enjoy and eat only those that nauseated them; that every recipe should contain large quantities of guilt and remorse; that Germans should not only renounce any intention of regaining any of the territories they had lost in the war but should also acknowledge their personal guilt and their complicity in the sins of their leaders. In *Dog Years* (1963) he parodied the unrepentant Heidegger in prose as resoundingly flatulent as Heidegger's own. All Grass's novels are confessions. But their great prophetic value is due to their high quality as works of art. As he said of *The Tin Drum,* it is "a political novel, but a novel, not politics."

Let us honor him and all our prophets by paying more heed to them. The essence of prophecy is that it does not acquiesce in sin.[11]

Notes

1. E. E. Cummings, *The Enormous Room* (New York: Horace Liveright, 1922, 1950). The first, corrupt, edition was irresponsibly genteelized by an anonymous editor. The second edition, edited with scholarly responsibility by George James Firmage and supplied with an enlightening foreword by Richard S. Kennedy and an editorial afterword by Firmage, restores the text as Cummings wrote it.

2. Louis-Ferdinand Céline, *Voyage au bout de la nuit* (Paris: Denoël & Steele, 1932.)

3. Valerie Eliot, ed., T. S. Eliot, *The Waste Land: A Facsimile and Transcript of the Original Drafts including the Annotations of Ezra Pound* (New York: Harcourt Brace Jovanovich, 1971), 121.

4. Ibid., xxii.

5. Charles Baudelaire, *Fusées,* IX. See the Pléïade edition of the *Oeuvres complètes* (Paris: Gallimard, 1961), 1254.

6. Robert Giroux, "A Personal Memoir," *Sewanee Review* 74, no. 1 (January–March 1966): 335

7. For your convenience, the respective dates are: Harriet Beecher Stowe, 1811–96; Charles Dickens, 1812–70; Honoré de Balzac, 1799–1850; Victor Hugo, 1802–85; Emile Zola, 1840–1902; Fyodor Dostoyevsky, 1821–81; Leo Tolstoy, 1828–1910.

8. For a brief biography of Henson, see Brion Gysin, *To Master, A Long Good Night* (New York: Creative Age Press, 1957).

9. For illustrative quotations from his works, see my "Gobineau and Thomas Mann," in *Helen Adolf Festschrift,* eds. Sheema Z. Buehne, James L. Hodge, and Lucille B. Pinto (New York: Frederick Ungar, 1968), 252–67.

10. Simone de Beauvoir, *La force de l'age,* 193. Translated and quoted by Ernst Pawel in *The Nightmare of Reason: A Life of Franz Kafka* (New York: Farrar, Straus, Giroux, 1984), 276, 351.

11. Sander Gilman has shown, however, that although Grass consciously despised anti-Semitism and anti-Semites, he unconsciously used the anti-Semitic assumptions with which he had grown up. (See Gilman's *Inscribing the Other* [Lincoln: University of Nebraska Press, 1991], chap. 11.) In so doing, Grass was like Mark Twain, whose naive refutation of anti-Semitism, "Concerning the Jews," in *Harper's New Monthly Magazine* for March 1898, was unconsciously full of the nineteenth-century assumptions about Jews that were used by anti-Semites.

8

The American Catholic Bishops and Prophetic Politics

Jo Renée Formicola

The paradigm offered by Neal Riemer in *The Future of the Democratic Revolution: Toward a More Prophetic Politics*[1] serves as a valid prism through which to view the religiously inspired politics of the American Catholic bishops. Based on a concern for transcendent values, a willingness to critique and continuously scrutinize society, and a commitment to take constitutional action to bring religious insights to bear on contemporary political and social problems, the prophetic paradigm can also serve as the framework for understanding the bishops' increased participation in the U.S. public policy debate.

Their energized prophetic position, however, also underscores the difficulties involved when religious leaders in a democratic and pluralistic society attempt to bring their perspective to bear on concrete political problems. Having to deal with opposition from members of the laity and clergy, oversight from the Vatican, and potential divisions within their own hierarchical ranks, the American Catholic bishops have often found themselves standing alone on significant political, social, and economic matters. This paper will explore the prophetic stance of the American Catholic bishops and articulate the problems that arise from it, in order to shed light on their unique response to the political world that challenges them.

The American Catholic Bishops: Their Prophetic Stance

The modern commitment of the American Catholic bishops to prophetic values can be traced to Vatican II and the General Council's mandates to advance peace, social justice, and human rights. *Christus Dominus,* one of the major documents that emanated from the synod, reinforced the notion that bishops had been designated by the Holy Spirit to "take the place of the apostles as pastors of souls" and that they were to be "teachers of the faith."[2]

The declaration also specifically encouraged them to "comment on events" that would promulgate the gospel of Christ[3] and to join with other bishops collectively to formulate a program "for the common good of the Church."[4]

Within the confines of church doctrine and the magisterium, then, the bishops were expected to foster the advancement of the human person, life, the family, procreation, and education. They were also encouraged to examine questions regarding the progress of society, the redistribution of wealth, poverty, and peace.[5] The means by which to pursue such principles, however, were clearly expected to be pastoral, as the council decreed: "Christ, to be sure, gave his Church no proper mission in the political, economic, or social order. The purpose he set before her is a religious one."[6]

Thus, bishops' conferences throughout the world had to find their own innovative ways to implement the religiously mandated challenges of Vatican II. In the United States, the American Catholic bishops responded by reorganizing the long-standing National Catholic Welfare Council in 1966. This resulted in the establishment of the National Conference of Catholic Bishops and its administrative arm, the United States Catholic Conference, to deal with matters of pastoral and political import.[7]

During the latter 1960s, then, impelled mainly by their pastoral responsibilities, the American Catholic bishops played a largely evangelical role. Speaking out principally on matters of peace and human rights, they began by voicing concern about the proportionality of the U.S. involvement in Vietnam in 1966, seeing it as their duty to "magnify the moral voice of [the] nation"[8] and to be advocates for peace.

Growing stronger during the decade, however, the American Catholic bishops reinforced their commitment to peace by officially articulating stronger stands against war at their annual meetings.[9] They condemned "without qualification" wars of aggression and nuclear warfare, and questioned the "policy of maintaining nuclear superiority . . . for security."[10] By the 1970s, the bishops pledged themselves to form a climate of public opinion for peace. They followed their statements and pastoral letters with clarifications on conscientious objection, continued their opposition to the war in Southeast Asia,[11] and decried conflagrations in other areas of the world as well.[12]

These early peace activities, however, were merely prologue to the NCCB's 1983 benchmark pastoral entitled "The Challenge of Peace: God's Promise and Our Response." Motivated by their belief that nuclear war threatened the very existence of the planet, the bishops contended that they had "grave human, moral and political responsibilities to see to it that a 'conscious choice' [would be] made to save humanity."[13] They believed that "religious leaders have a task in concert with public officials, analysts, private organizations, and the media to set the limits beyond which our military policy should not move in word or action."[14]

To that end, then, the American bishops reappraised the prevailing Catholic "just war" theory in the context of the nuclear dilemma. In essence, they opposed the deliberate initiation of nuclear warfare, no matter how limited, and tightly circumscribed, as well, the notion of a justified nuclear deterrent force. Further, they came out in support of (1) "immediate, bilateral, verifiable agreements to halt the testing, production and deployment of new nuclear weapons systems";[15] (2) cuts in the existing arsenals of nuclear weapons; (3) negotiations for a test-ban treaty; (4) ratification of existing arms limitations agreements; (5) the removal of all short-range nuclear weapons; (6) the development of nonviolent alternatives to war; and (7) means to strengthen the control and command of nuclear weapons.

These positions on behalf of peace were reinforced by hierarchical actions to implement the bishops' continuing critique of existing American nuclear policy. In 1984, Joseph Cardinal Bernardin and John Cardinal O'Connor testified before the House Foreign Relations Committee in support of arms control, specifically encouraging the resumption of the Mutual Balanced Force Reduction Talks and the government's initiatives on chemical warfare. They urged a reconsideration of funding for the development of the MX missile and the space-based Strategic Defense Initiative.[16] Within the year, Bishop James W. Malone, the president of the NCCB, also wrote to all the members of Congress urging them to vote against the funding of the MX because of its potentially destabilizing impact on the arms race,[17] a stance that was again supported by both Bernardin and O'Connor. The latter had, in fact, questioned both the "necessity" and "efficacy" of such a "dubious" weapons system,[18] while Bernardin had challenged the government's proposed development of the MX because of the burden that would be placed on the poor to advance the arms race.[19]

Thus, in the thirty years since Vatican II, the American Catholic bishops have led a religiously inspired movement for peace, openly opposing the U.S. involvement in Vietnam, the use of nuclear weapons under any circumstances, and the development of a nuclear deterrent force. Their prophetic stance, carried out through pastoral letters, official statements, and congressional testimony, served to shed light on morally questionable aspects of U.S. military policy and to create a climate for peace within American society, government, and the international community.

This growing and continued commitment to peace was simultaneously complemented by the evolution of the American hierarchical concern for human rights. In this instance, however, the NCCB took its cues from a radicalized Latin American hierarchy, one committed to the transformation of society through the establishment of communities based on Christian social teachings.

Originally serving as a clearinghouse for missionary reports on repression in the Southern Hemisphere, the NCCB simply provided solidarity and witness at first,[20] but very quickly thereafter established a system of advocacy and intervention for those individuals or their families who sought redress for governmental torture, kidnapping, or murder.[21] In 1970, the USCC's Office of Justice and Peace was even successful in bringing an indictment against the government of Brazil before the Inter-American Human Rights Commission of the Organization of American States. Three years later, the Brazilian leadership was found guilty of systematic human rights violations.[22]

Buoyed by such success, but still concerned with increasing reports of human rights violations, specifically in the Southern Hemisphere, the NCCB itself began to work more actively in the political sphere. Functioning as an embryonic religious lobby, the bishops' organization used its international resources to monitor human rights violations abroad and to provide credible data about growing global repression at the hearings of the Subcommittee on International Movements and Organizations of the House Committee on Foreign Affairs in 1973. The NCCB was instrumental in encouraging the Congress, ultimately, to enact twenty-nine pieces of legislation that tied reception of foreign aid, security/technical assistance, and loans from international monetary institutions (of which the United States was a member) to respect for human rights.[23]

These hierarchical activities on behalf of human rights were supported politically in the 1970s by coincidental American presidential attempts to promote civil, political, and personal rights abroad. The Ford administration had moved the United States toward an energized commitment to human rights in the East-West context as a result of the signing of the Helsinki Accords; while Ford's successor, Jimmy Carter, formed a well-received ideological détente with the NCCB. Pressing for strategic arms limitation talks, "open diplomacy," and a foreign policy that refused to do business as usual with those nations whose domestic priorities were predicated on repression, the American Catholic bishops found themselves philosophically and politically in favor with the White House on the matter of human rights.

During the remainder of the decade, then, members of the Catholic hierarchy emerged as players in the formulation of a U.S. foreign policy grounded in transcendent values. Individual members of the Office of International Justice and Peace, now ubiquitous voices on Capitol Hill, testified regularly about human rights violations in Central and South America, as well as in Eastern Europe and Africa.

This close working relationship between the NCCB and the U.S. government on human rights began to erode by the end of the decade. State-sponsored violence against Catholic religious activists working to democratize

Central American society increasingly resulted in heinous acts such as the assassination of Archbishop Oscar Romero and the murder/rape of five churchwomen in El Salvador. But it was rarely met with American reprisals beyond rhetoric or restricted U.S. military or security assistance. As a result, U.S. foreign policy in Central America was challenged by stronger and more frequent episcopal criticism of American complacency toward escalating human rights violations.[24] Viewing the growing repression in Central America as a consequence of social injustice, rather than as a result of communist political activity, as the incoming Reagan administration maintained, the bishops concluded in their 1987 "Statement on Central America" that neither policymakers nor citizens grasped the totality of the crisis in that region. They highlighted the problems of El Salvador and Nicaragua, to be sure, but argued that the situations in Guatemala, Honduras, Costa Rica, and Panama still were part of an unfinished U.S. responsibility to Central America.[25]

This hierarchical concern for human rights in Latin America and the Caribbean resurfaced again in the 1990s with the controversy surrounding Haitian and American attempts to democratize that Caribbean nation. The NCCB broke ranks once more with the White House, opposing the stands of both Presidents Bush and Clinton as to how best create a viable, responsive government after the downfall of "Baby Doc" Duvalier. The Bush administration had given its cautious support first to the transitional government of General Prosper Avril and then, in December of 1990, to the freely elected government of Father Jean Bertrand Aristide. Later, it provided both an asylum and a platform to the ousted priest-leader after a military coup led by General Raul Cedras toppled Aristide in 1991. But beyond rhetorical solidarity with the Governors' Island Accords, nothing in the Bush foreign policy agenda had even hinted at a long-term American strategy to advance the economic, social, and political transformation of Haiti. President Clinton, on the other hand, had promised more. In campaign pledges, the Democratic candidate had assured the voters that he would both restore democracy to Haiti and allow more Haitian immigrants into the United States. After winning the 1992 election, Clinton acted to reinstall Aristide to the Haitian presidency with the help of American troops; but he continued the policy of restricting the entrance of the Haitian boat people into the United States.

The American Catholic bishops remain critical of current U.S. policy toward Haiti and Aristide. They highlight the moral importance of the need for a solid constitutional democracy in Haiti, one based on human rights and social justice. They question the personalization of democracy with Aristide, a defrocked Salesian priest, expelled because of his affinity to liberation theology. They oppose Aristide's Marxist-Christian criticism of the Haitian religious hierarchy and his support for mob violence that has already resulted in the humiliation of the papal nuncio, Lorenzo Baltezari, and the beating of his assistant. The American bishops believe that the solution to Haiti's problems cannot be achieved simply by the return of a political novice. They challenge the United States to a broader commitment to social justice: to meet the needs of Haiti's refugees, the marginalized, and the poor.[26] Until a long-term strategy can be worked out, the Catholic bishops, because of their moral perspective, will continue to question American foreign policy with regard to Haiti and other Third World states in similar circumstances.

This sustained hierarchical commitment to peace and human rights since Vatican II has also grown into a pervasive American episcopal concern for all life. The 1973 Supreme Court decision in *Roe v. Wade* served as a powerful catalyst, moving the American Catholic bishops to respond to yet another moral challenge: the perceived threat to unborn life.

In accord with a traditional moral opposition to abortion,[27] the bishops quickly moved from evangelization to political involvement after *Roe v. Wade*. Their defense of unborn life was based on the need to support the Catholic doctrinal stance that a fetus is a human being from the moment of conception.[28] As a result, the bishops issued their 1973 "Pastoral Message on Abortion," mobilizing the Catholic constituency in the United States to oppose abortion as an immoral act. Further, they urged the legal profession to articulate and safeguard the rights of fathers of unborn children, challenged the public to provide positive alternatives to abortion, offered support to hospitals and other institutions that refused to perform abortions, and pledged to work to reverse the Supreme Court decision in *Roe v. Wade*.[29]

In 1983, in a speech at Fordham University in New York City, Joseph Cardinal Bernardin philosophically tied together the bishops' views on war, peace, human rights, and abortion, claiming that the commitment to life should be conceived as a coherent and seamless whole. The "seamless life ethic," as it has become known, emerged as the rationale for both the creation of a broad Catholic hierarchical commitment to life and the foundation for continued episcopal political involvement on behalf of a pro-life agenda.

By 1984, in fact, the NCCB had actively lobbied for many antiabortion measures. Supporting the Hatch Act in 1981, the bishops for the first time endorsed a specific piece of legislation, one that would empower Congress and individual states, rather than the courts, to enact laws to regulate and ban abortion. Soon after, they became involved in several funding debates; in the fight over the passage of the Hyde Amendment, which would deny federal aid for abortions to the indigent; and in battles on the use of public moneys to advance a pro-choice social policy.[30] The NCCB had encouraged grassroots lobbying organizations, participated in mass demonstrations, and committed episcopal resources to act as an amicus curiae in virtually every abortion case heard by the Supreme Court after *Roe v. Wade*. It was no surprise, then, that a prominent member of the hierarchy, John Cardinal O'Connor, would openly criticize Catholic political candidates who tolerated or supported abortion in the 1984 presidential, state, and local elections.

To clarify its position, the NCCB, right before the 1984 election, hastily issued a statement declaring that "the Church does not take positions for or against particular parties or individual candidates. . . . We are constitutionally committed to the separation of Church and State, but not to the separation of religious and moral values from public life."[31]

The bishops' concern for religious and moral values—for peace, human rights, and pro-life matters—took a distinctly political and economic turn by the 1980s. Earlier, the bishops had been concerned with the costly human consequences of nuclear weapons, with a Cold War posture blind to its impact on human rights, with defense spending out of reasonable relation to national security. Now, the American episcopate had to face the possibility that the implementation of a conservative economic policy—especially President Reagan's supply-side economics—could stifle the ability of individuals to be active and productive participants in the life of society. Therefore, the NCCB felt responsible to become officially more involved in a renewed area of concern: social justice.

In 1986, in another prophetic high-water mark, the American Catholic bishops issued "Economic Justice for All," a pastoral letter that applied Catholic social teaching to the U.S. economy. The bishops' purpose in writing the letter, "to lift up the human and ethical dimensions of economic life,"[32] was predicated on six moral principles: first, that every economic decision and institution be judged in light of whether it protects or undermines the dignity of the human person; second, that human dignity be realized and protected within the community; third, that all people be allowed to participate in the economic life of society; fourth, that all members of society be obliged to help the poor and vulnerable; fifth, that human rights be the minimum condition for life in community; and sixth, that society as a whole, acting through public and private institutions, enhance human dignity and protect human rights.[33]

The bishops supported unions, private ownership, initiative, and work. But they also challenged the government and the private sector to think differently about social justice and capitalism, as well as to act differently to implement social justice. They called on their audience to find creative breakthroughs to ensure full employment; to alleviate poverty, particularly among women, children, and minorities; and to bring about the reform of agriculture and the production and distribution of food. Most important, they challenged the United States to play a global role that would help the nations of the Third World to develop economically and participate in the creation of their own financial futures.

Through all of this, the bishops maintained that "the poor have the single most urgent economic claim on the conscience of the nation."[34] They supported, then, a modified communitarian, rather than a strict capitalistic, economic theory, one predicated on a "preferential option for the poor." Promulgated by the Latin American Episcopal Conference at Puebla, Mexico, in 1979, that commitment was supported by the NCCB as the valid, central priority for U.S. policy choices. Rejecting national security as the principal factor in the foreign policy equation, the bishops now encouraged, instead, a consistent ideology that placed social justice and human rights at the center of U.S. international relations.

By the 1990s, then, the American Catholic bishops had taken many public positions and articulated their defense of transcendent values such as peace, human rights, and social justice. Their scrutiny and continued criticism of society after Vatican II, coupled with a commitment to take action, both pastoral and political, to bring ethical and prudential insights to bear on contemporary political and social problems, have clearly revealed them to be a prophetic force in politics and society.

But do all agree that the bishops' stance is fully or always prophetic? And what are the problems that a prophetic commitment encounters?

The Catholic Bishops' Prophetic Stance: Its Problems

Clearly, the problems that have emerged from the American Catholic bishops' prophetic stance underscore the difficulties involved in relating a religiously inspired perspective and strategy to the reality of politics. These quandaries—which often create dilemmas for the bishops—stem from troublesome problems about the role of the NCCB, its agenda, and the church's internal cohesion. They highlight questions about institutional priorities and diversity, as well as the church's relationship to its adherents and the U.S. government.

Initially, the American hierarchy had to decide what part, if any, the renewed Catholic Church should play in U.S. politics after Vatican II. The General Council had prescribed only an evangelical role for the newly formed episcopal conferences, but in one of its statements, *Gaudium et Spes,* it had also called on the bishops to "read the signs of the times" and apply the lessons of the gospel to their communities. The American Catholic bishops functioned in a pastoral way in the early aftermath of Vatican II. But as they became accustomed to their new canonical powers, and as the political events of the 1970s unfolded, they responded increasingly by participating vigorously in the public debate on peace, escalating human rights violations in Latin America, abortion, and economic justice. Their criticism and scrutiny—negative and positive—soon evolved into the development of moral guidelines, and then into initiatives for public policy measures on behalf of transcendent values. Presented to members of Congress and its relevant committees, as well as to key advisers in various presidential administrations, the bishops' actions increasingly took on the forms of testimony and lobbying, as well as official discussions and interactions with members of the government.

By the 1980s, these and other mounting nonpastoral actions found the bishops firmly involved in the political process, almost to the point of partisanship. Members of the hierarchy—such as Bishop Leroy Matthiesen of Amarillo and Archbishop John Quinn of San Francisco—used their religious offices to urge job actions in the name of peace against weapons factories and the Defense Department. Bishop Thomas Daily of Brooklyn rescinded Governor Mario Cuomo's invitation to speak at a Catholic church, and Bishop Leo T. Maher of San Diego barred assembly candidate Lucy Killea from receiving Communion, both sanctions the result of the Catholic politicians' pro-choice stances. It was John Cardinal O'Connor of New York, however, who openly spoke out against Geraldine Ferraro in her 1984 bid for the vice presidency, castigating her for contending that the Catholic pro-life stance was not a monolithic one. Supported by Bernard Cardinal Law of Boston, the New York prelate seemed vindicated by Law's designation of abortion as the critical issue of the election.

These sporadic, yet multiplying, political challenges led to an official response clarifying the pastoral role of the bishops before the 1984 election. Bishop James Malone, president of the NCCB, spoke for the collective American hierarchy when he issued an official statement rejecting partisanship and the formation of voting blocs. Calling instead for all bishops to act as teachers, he reaffirmed the notion that their primary responsibilities were evangelical ones, requiring dialogue, debate, and communication about "the content of Catholic moral teaching . . . [and] its relevance to social and political issues."[35]

The publication of Malone's statement also shed public light on a second problem involving the implementation of the Catholic bishops' prophetic values: the growing division within the hierarchy itself over the agenda of the NCCB and its priorities. Immediately after the 1984 election, Malone made a strong plea for episcopal cohesion, citing the conference's moral positions on a broad spectrum of issues beyond abortion. Attempting to bring all of the bishops together, Malone maintained that the NCCB was not a substitute for the voice of individual bishops, but that "it provide[d] a framework within which a coherent theological, moral and social vision [could] be articulated."[36] Shortly thereafter, Joseph Cardinal Bernardin also attempted to heal the divisions, through the articulation of his umbrella notion of a "seamless life ethic."

While these statements clarified the official position of the American Catholic hierarchy with regard to politics and officially broadened the agenda, some more politicized members of the hierarchy continued to take action on behalf of their own visions of a "Catholic moral agenda." In New York, specifically, John Cardinal O'Connor, accompanied by the state's seven other bishops and a number of nuns, priests, and lay people, went to every legislator's office in Albany in 1987. They called for tuition tax credits, better health care, affordable housing, day care, and increased welfare benefits for the poor; they also opposed abortion and "death with dignity" legislation.

In 1990, members of the Catholic hierarchy, who wanted the pro-life issue to play the central role in the NCCB's agenda, convinced the conference to take a new tack. Hiring the public relations firm of Hill and Knowlton and a polling firm, The Wirthlin Group, the bishops approved the expenditure of between three and five million dollars over a five-year period to carry out a nationwide campaign against abortion.[37] In the same year, Cardinal O'Connor pressed his interpretation of the Catholic moral agenda even further, warning Catholic pro-choice politicians that they were "at risk of excommunication."[38]

This continued hierarchical challenge within the Catholic bishops' organization over its appropriate role and agenda also reflected a third problem in attempts to advance religiously inspired perspectives in the political sphere. That is, many members of both the laity and the clergy began to oppose the moral stands taken by the American Catholic hierarchy. The bulk of their criticism stemmed from the bishops' postures on abortion, nuclear deterrence, human rights, and capitalism. Various Catholic "dissidents," on both the political Left and the Right, have written petitions, published counterpastorals, and challenged the authority of the bishops as signs of their dissatisfaction with the hierarchy. Their actions have resulted in the proliferation of new lobbying organizations to advance views that are more radical or "modern" than those of the bishops.

Thomas O'Hara, who has done a most extensive, systematic study of Catholic-based lobbying groups in Washington, D.C., has empirically shown a vast diversity and pluralism within over thirty-five such activist organizations on the same basic issues: peace, human rights, abortion, and social justice. For example, the latest statistical data gathered by the General Social Survey (National Opinion Research Center) in 1993 clearly showed that Catholics opposed the hierarchy's stand on abortion when (1) there was a strong chance of delivering a defective baby, (2) the health of the woman might be compromised by a pregnancy, or (3) the pregnancy was the result of rape.[39] Clearly, O'Hara's conclusion rings true: although the bishops speak powerfully, they no longer speak "solely."[40]

Catholic-based lobbying organizations have also been supplemented, as situations have warranted, by petitions and writings to counter the views of the American Catholic bishops. For example, in 1982, in response to the draft pastoral of the "Challenge of Peace," twenty-four Catholic legislators serving in Congress opposed the bishops' stance. They argued that the ideological abuse of human freedom and dignity that would occur if the United States were to surrender its strategically superior nuclear position would virtually destroy the moral character of any potential peace that might follow. The legislators confronted the bishops by maintaining that "peace without justice is moral violence."[41]

The most widely criticized hierarchical stance, however, has been the bishops' pastoral on the economy. Interpreting the pastoral as "prophetic, or . . . just out of step,"[42] Timothy Byrnes contends that the bishops' 1986 document "rang decidedly hollow" and had only "a marginal effect on the bishops' role in American politics."[43] Further, he maintains that the many American episcopal postures, including the letter on the economy, reflect cracks in the once-solid foundation of the New Deal, Democratic-Catholic, liberal political coalition. These fractures have, in fact, resulted in Catholics' emerging as swing voters at the national level. Byrnes argues that the bishops, who may have access to the Catholic vote, can no longer deliver it: the bishops cannot always assure the compliance of the faithful on political matters. For example, a self-selected commission of lay people, headed by William E. Simon, former secretary of the treasury, interpreted the bishops' economic critique as an attack on capitalism itself. Other prominent Catholics, such as Alexander M. Haig Jr., Clare Booth Luce, and J. Peter Grace, joined William Novak of the conservative American Enterprise Institute in issuing—five days prior to the release of the hierarchy's pastoral—an eighty-page counterstatement. Some have claimed that its publication was an attempt to "undercut"[44] the bishops' stance by arguing that American capitalism was the most effective means to eliminate both tyranny and poverty.

Those who have opposed the bishops' prophetic stances have also challenged their authority to speak out politically. Citing pastoral letters and statements as guidelines for moral actions, rather than as infallible, conscience-enjoining doctrine, many Catholics have resented the attempts of some bishops to place sanctions on individuals who, in good political conscience, have challenged their stands. For example, New York politicians such as Governor Mario Cuomo and Congressman José Serrano have called Cardinal O'Connor's threats of excommunication "upsetting," while admitting that they were "saddened"[45] by the fact that the church has focused politically on the issue of abortion and that issue alone.

The National Conference of Catholic Bishops has also found itself at odds with the Vatican over the American hierarchy's application of moral principles to the concrete world of politics. In general, a basic distrust of the power of national episcopacies has developed since Vatican II, a fear of the loss of centralized papal control over the political activities of a radicalized hierarchy and clergy. In 1979, Pope John Paul II in Puebla, Mexico, reminded his religious audience that they had come together, "not as a symposium of experts or a parliament of politicians, but rather as a fraternal gathering of church pastors."[46] Further, he reasserted the bishops' traditional role, reminding them that "your chief duty is to be teachers of the truth." The pope declared unequivocally that the "essential mission, the specific vocation, the innermost identity of the Church" is one of evangelization.[47]

The pope soon followed his words by strong actions, issuing a directive disallowing members of the clergy from serving in political office and tightening control over various episcopal organizations. With regard to the United States, specifically, John Paul summoned members of the NCCB to the Vatican in 1983 to facilitate a U.S.-European dialogue on the "transnational reference"[48] of the bishops' letter on peace. Acting almost as a mediator between the Reagan administration and the national episcopacies, the pope took a position that emerged as "more general than and distinct from, all the local letters, but . . . established the moral framework for them all."[49]

John Paul II also developed a new working relationship with President Reagan, who from the early days of his election in 1980 had sought closer ties with the Holy See. In effect, the president and the pope had formed what some have called a "secret alliance"[50] to destabilize Poland after the government's internal crackdown against Solidarity in December 1981. Three years later, in 1984, Reagan proposed full diplomatic relations with the Holy See, his opposition to the "evil empire" being ideologically similar to the moral concern of the Polish pope with regard to communism. Some have also maintained, however, that this new relationship could have served as an expedient means by which to bypass a hostile American Catholic hierarchy,[51] which during the Reagan presidency challenged the White House on nuclear policy, the economy, and funding for the MX missile and the Strategic Defense Initiative. In fact, officials at the NCCB during that eight-year period reported to the author that the White House preferred to do "an end run around the conference"[52] and work instead with individual, prominent members of the hierarchy on mutual ad hoc issues.

This was clearly a step back from an emergent closer relationship between the White House and the NCCB. While Presidents Nixon and Ford had had a cautious, limited involvement with the Catholic hierarchy, members of the USCC reported to the author that relations between the bishops and the Carter administration had been "increasing and improving."[53] Now, the NCCB's political clout with the Reagan White House was compromised. In a significant sense, the NCCB was superseded also by the Moral Majority, which registered over a million voters per year. The conservative religious right supported the president's agenda and helped to render the more liberal NCCB politically impotent. Officials at the Reagan White House summed up the role of the NCCB at the time when they told this author that the Catholic Church, which had the body of a lion, had the political voice of a mouse.[54]

This pattern of minimal interaction with the White House continues to the present. President Clinton has even actively challenged the bishops' stances on two critical domestic and foreign policies. Supporting a pro-choice posture and the return of defrocked Salesian priest Jean Bertrand Aristide to Haiti, the president continues to relegate the NCCB to the political shadows. The NCCB now seems to stand in the twilight of its political and moral power in the United States.

Conclusion

This article argues that in their positions on peace, human rights, and poverty, the American Catholic bishops illustrate the reality and power of the prophetic tradition in religion, politics, and society. However, it is also clear that the public policy stances of the bishops are often challenged by those within and those outside the Catholic Church. These objections highlight the difficulties encountered by those who attempt to relate religiously inspired values to the concrete issues of public policy. They also lead to a dual question: Can the pastoral and political problems of the American Catholic bishops be overcome?

As far as the pastoral difficulties are concerned, the American Catholic bishops, theologically, do not expect to achieve total acceptance of their moral views of politics. Instead, they philosophically subscribe to the notion that individuals are called "to live the tension between the vision of the reign of God and its concrete realization in history."[55] Therefore, the hierarchy abstractly envisions itself existing in an incomplete world: one marked by conflict and injustice, and one in which love, peace, social justice, and respect for human rights are possible, but not assured. The bishops affirm their evangelical responsibility to point out correct moral choices rooted in transcendent values; they understand that continued moral opposition is part of their pastoral challenge to maintain prophetic political choices.

Nevertheless, in their 1984 statement on the role of the church in politics, the bishops underscored their need to continue to work for a more religiously inspired society. They argued: "The search for political and public policy solutions to such problems as war and peace and abortion may well be long and difficult, but a prudential judgment that political solutions are not feasible does not justify failure to undertake the effort."[56]

Thus, the bishops themselves lead us to the second part of the dual question: Can they overcome the political difficulties inherent in their sometimes futile attempts to inject the moral factor into the American political equation? The internal debates over the political role and agenda of the Catholic Church within the American democratic process will eventually be resolved through episcopal dialogue, compromise, and the inevitable changes in hierarchical personnel that come with time.

However, the bishops will have greater difficulty accommodating to those external political and social factors over which they ostensibly have no control. The movement toward social and economic conservatism, for example, threatens many of the church's traditional postures. For the first time in American history, the Catholic hierarchy must deal with an educated, increasingly diverse, and vocal membership, one characterized by dissident women, gays, liberals, charismatics, and staunch conservatives. While the bishops attempt both to respect and to protect differences among their adherents, which reflect all aspects of the political spectrum, the bishops are faced with important questions. How can they contend with the growing political influence of the conservative religious Christian Right? Can the Catholic hierarchy be politically effective in implementing a prophetic agenda of its own? Might the bishops have to succumb to partisanship in order to maintain their political relevance in the future?

Already the New Jersey Catholic Conference, mimicking the religious Right and portending a potential national strategy, has announced that it will begin to sponsor statewide voter-registration drives. The announced purpose of the action is to deliver votes to candidates who will respond to the concerns of Catholics about legalized abortion, private school vouchers, and other issues. Spokesmen within the NJCC are quick to point out that there is no political Catholic voting bloc, only "conscientiousness and concern." [57] Still, the potential for Catholic partisanship in opposition to, or even in coalition with, the religious Right could possibly alter the meaning of the separation of church and state in America. Such action should give pause even to those who would support religiously inspired political action for prophetic reasons.

Other scenarios also present future political problems. Will the traditional Catholic political affinity to the Democratic Party continue to be viable if the party continues to espouse a pro-choice posture? Or will the bishops increasingly lose the ability to support issues related to peace, human rights, and poverty and be forced to pursue a political relationship with the Republican Party in order to assure support for a social agenda that promotes pro-life, traditional family values? Will the bishops therefore become increasingly wed to

Republican candidates and programs?

Further, how will the bishops be able to deal in the future with a political milieu marked by isolationism, hostility to immigrants, and budgetary constraints? Will they still be able to support a policy of awarding increased foreign aid and Third World development funds on the basis of human rights and social justice, or will they have to move more realistically and support a foreign policy based on national security concerns? Will the bishops, then, have to narrow their prophetic focus and place their emphasis only on domestic concerns?

Such questions only serve to raise awareness about the potential problems of partisanship in the Catholic hierarchy's emerging, evolving approach to American politics. Clearly, these questions reflect a prophetic challenge for the future and can serve as a focus for the bishops as they search for religiously inspired ways to deal with the new political realities posed by a United States moving in conservative, isolationist, budget-conscious directions.

Notes

1. Neal Riemer, *The Future of the Democratic Revolution: Toward a More Prophetic Politics* (New York: Praeger, 1984).

2. Walter M. Abbott, gen. ed., *The Documents of Vatican II* (New York, Herder & Herder, 1966), *Christus Dominus,* Preface, para. 2, p. 397.

3. Ibid., chap. II, para. 13, p. 405.

4. Ibid., chap. III, para. 37, p. 425.

5. Ibid., chap. II, para. 12, p. 405.

6. Ibid., *Gaudium et Spes,* chap. IV, sec. 42, p. 241.

7. The National Conference of Catholic Bishops is a canonical and voluntary organization. It speaks for the American bishops collectively and has a membership of 375 bishops. It deals with moral issues as they affect the economic, social, and political order. While the organization may set moral guidelines for action, it may not participate in partisan political behavior to advance its doctrinal views. On the other hand, the role of the United States Catholic Conference is to advise, review, and implement policies of the bishops' conference. Technically, it has no policymaking authority of its own. However, of necessity, the USCC's daily decisions often become part of official "Catholic policy" in the economic, educational, social, and political spheres.

8. National Conference of Catholic Bishops, "Peace and Vietnam," 18 November 1966, in *Pastoral Letters of the United States Catholic Bishops,* ed. Hugh J. Nolan (Washington, D.C.: United States Catholic Conference, 1983), 3:74.

9. See "The Resolution on Peace," April 1968, p. 161; "The Resolution on Southeast Asia," November 1971, pp. 289–91; and "The Resolution on Peace," 16 November 1967, p. 90, in NCCB, *Pastoral Letters,* vol. 3.

10. Ibid. See "Human Life in Our Day," 15 November1968, paras. 98, 113–14, pp. 183–86.

11. Ibid., "Declaration on Conscientious Objection and Selective Conscientious Objection," 21 October 1971, pp. 283–86; and the "Resolution on Southeast Asia," November 1971, pp. 289–91.

12. Ibid. See for example, "Resolution towards Peace in the Middle East," November 1973, pp. 388–89. In vol. 4, see, for example, "To Live in Christ Jesus," 11 November 1976, pp. 170–95; "The Gospel of Peace and the Danger of War," 15 February 1978, pp. 38–40; and "Statement on Registration and Conscription for Military Service," 14 February 1980, pp. 360–63.

13. "The Challenge of Peace: God's Promise and Our Response," 3 May 1983, para. 4, in NCCB, *Pastoral Letters,* 4:494.

14. Ibid., para. 141, p. 530.

15. Ibid., para. 190, p. 544.

16. Richard Halloran, "Bishops Challenge MX in Testimony," *New York Times,* 27 June 1984, sec. A, p. 10.

17. "Text of Bishops' Letter to Congress on MX," *New York Times,* 16 March 1985, sec. A, p. 4.

18. "O'Connor Urges Congress to Bar MX Funds," *New York Times,* 17 March 1984, sec. A, p. 10.

19. Ibid.

20. NCCB, *Pastoral Letters,* vol. 3. See for example "Statement of Solidarity on Rights: Chile and Brazil," 4 February 1974, pp. 453–55. In vol. 4, see for example "Statement on the United Nations and the Republic of South Africa," 9 October 1975, pp. 74–77; "Resolution on Haitian Refugees," 2 May 1977, pp. 198–99; "Religious Liberty in Eastern Europe: A Test Case for Human Rights," 4 May 1977, pp. 211–14; "Statement on Small Boat Refugees in Southeast Asia," 16 February 1978, pp. 241–42; "Resolution on Cambodia," November 1979, p. 356; and "Resolution on Iran," November 1979, p. 357.

21. For a fuller explanation and a description of the activities of the NCCB with regard to human rights during the 1970s as well, see Jo Renée Formicola, *The Catholic Church and Human Rights: Its Role in the Formulation of U.S. Policy, 1945–1980* (New York: Garland, 1988).

22. Organization of American States, *Annual Report of the Inter-American Commission on Human Rights for the Year 1973* (Atlanta: Organization of American States, 1974), 72.

23. Formicola, *Catholic Church and Human Rights.*

24. NCCB, *Pastoral Letters,* vol 4. See for example "The Resolution on El Salvador," March 1981, pp. 436–37; "The Statement on Central America," 17 November 1983, pp. 65–66; "Statement on U.S. Policy in Central America," 22 July 1983, pp. 582–83. In vol. 5, see for example "Resolution of the U.S. Catholic Conference on Central America," 17 November 1983, pp. 582–83.

25. "Statement on Central America," 19 November 1987, in NCCB, *Pastoral Letters,* 5:614–28.

26. Archbishop Theodore McCarrick, Catholic archbishop of Newark, N.J., interview by author, 15 June 1994.

27. NCCB, *Pastoral Letters,* vol. 3. For early examples see statements such as "Human Life in Our Day," 5 November 1968, pp. 164–94; "Statement on Abortion," 17 April 1969, pp. 198–99; "Statement on Abortion," 22 April 1970, pp. 254–55; and "Declaration on Abortion," 18 November 1970, p. 2711. For a reaction to the court decision see "Statement on Abortion," 22 January 1973, p. 366.

28. "Pastoral Message on Abortion," 13 February 1973, in NCCB, *Pastoral Letters,* 3:367.

29. Ibid., 367–69. This plan for action was reaffirmed and further refined in "Pastoral Plan for Pro-Life Activities," 20 November 1975. See NCCB, *Pastoral Letters,* 4:81–91.

30. The NCCB came out in favor of limiting federal funds for abortion counseling, restricting payment of abortions for federal workers, and eliminating family planning centers abroad.

31. "Text for Statement by Bishops on Church Role in Politics," *New York Times,* 14 October 1984, sec. A, p. 30.

32. "Economic Justice for All," 13 November 1986, para. 7, in NCCB, *Pastoral Letters,* 5:372.

33. Ibid., paras. 12–18, pp. 373–455.

34. Ibid., para. 86, p. 405.

35. "Text for Statement by Bishops," *New York Times.*

36. "Excerpts from Speech to Bishops over Their Role in Public Policy Areas," *New York Times,* 13 November 1984, sec. A, p. 22.

37. Ari I. Goldman, "Catholic Bishops Hire Firms to Market Abortion Attack," *New York Times,* 4 April 1990, sec. A, p.1.

38. Ari I. Goldman, "O'Connor Warns Politicians Risk Excommunication over Abortion," *New York Times,* 15 June 1990, sec. A, p. 1.

39. *General Social Survey* (Chicago: NORC, 1993). With regard to a defective baby, approximately 76 percent of self-described Catholics approved of abortion; in the matter of the health of the mother, approximately 84 percent approved; and in the case of rape, 78 percent approved.

40. Thomas O'Hara, C.S.C., "The Catholic Lobby in Washington: Pluralism and Diversity among U.S. Catholics," in Mary Segers, ed., *Church Polity and American Politics* (New York: Garland, 1990), 155.

41. "Twenty-Four Catholics in House Oppose Bishops on A-Arms," *New York Times,* 23 December 1982, sec. A, p. 11. Interestingly, Henry Hyde, the NCCB's point man on abortion, broke ranks with the bishops and opposed their strategic military stance.

42. Timothy A. Byrnes, *Catholic Bishops in American Politics* (Princeton, N.J.: Princeton University Press, 1991), 131.

43. Ibid., 130–31.

44. Kenneth Briggs, "Lay Catholic Group Offers Report Praising Capitalism," *New York Times,* 7 November 1984, sec. A, p. 16.

45. Goldman, "O'Connor Warns Politicians," sec. B, p. 2.

46. Pope John Paul II, "Opening Address at Puebla," reprinted in Quentin Quade, *The Pope and Revolution* (Washington, D.C.: Ethics and Policy Center, 1982), sec. I, p. 56.

47. Ibid., 59.

48. J. Bryan Hehir, "There's No Deterring the Bishops," *Ethics and International Affairs,* 3(1989): 282.

49. Ibid.

50. See Carl Bernstein, "The Holy Alliance," *Time,* 139, no. 8 (24 February 1992): 28.

51. See for example Peter Hebblethwaite, "The End of the Vatican's *Ostpolitik,*" in Peter C. Kent and John F. Pollard, *Vatican Diplomacy in the Modern Age* (Westport, Conn.: Praeger, 1994), 238.

52. Mr. Russell Shaw, of the Public Relations Office of USCC, telephone conversation with author, 10 January 1986.

53. Mr. Thomas Quigley, of the Office of International Justice and Peace, interview by author, 6 December 1980.

54. Ms. Linda Chavez, then director of the Office of Public Liaison, Reagan White House, interview by author, 14 January 1986.

55. "The Challenge of Peace," para. 58, in NCCB, *Pastoral Letters,* 4:508.

56. "Text for Statement by Bishops," (see n. 31).

57. "Catholic Voter-Registration Push," *New York Times,* 22 September 1995, sec. B, p. 1.

9

Liberation Theology, Prophetic Politics, and Radical Social Critique: *Quo Vadis?*

John R. Pottenger

Liberation Theology and Politics

On 1 January 1994, a little-known but simmering cauldron of social discontent finally reached the boiling point. In the Mexican state of Chiapas, the *Ejército Zapatista de Liberación Nacional* (Zapatista Army of National Liberation, EZLN) used force of arms to bring to public attention the social misery of the indigenous population. Shaking the financial and economic world, and to a lesser extent the political world, with its radical action, the EZLN demanded remedies for the "lack of land, food, homes, education, health care, justice, liberty, democracy, independence and peace."[1] The Mexican army's rapid deployment of troops to the region and its harsh tactics quickly brought a cease-fire that appeared to end the insurrection.[2] Yet less than twelve months later, with little progress achieved in meeting political demands and economic needs, the EZLN demonstrated its endurance, strength, and organizational capabilities by once again occupying dozens of towns. Both sides then agreed to talks mediated by local officials of the Catholic Church to resolve the dispute.

Although scarce, some reports have suggested that the EZLN's behavior was guided by religious convictions based on a particular interpretation of Christianity. According to one account, the leaders of the EZLN called themselves "catechists," a term generally reserved for lay religious teachers.[3] In another account, the Mexican government claimed that some of the leaders were "radical Catholics" with connections to other Mexican and Central American rebel groups.[4] At the very least, the EZLN's religious and ideological commitments suggest the presence of prophetic politics, such as that found in liberation theology. Certainly, the critical perspectives of radical religious groups, especially those attuned to liberation theology, have been exceedingly influential throughout Latin America in recent decades.

133

In 1971 the Peruvian priest Gustavo Gutiérrez wrote *Teología de la liberación*,[5] the path-breaking treatise that launched the intellectual dimension of liberation theology as a movement. Referring to the traditional social teachings of the Church, Gutiérrez criticized as morally unacceptable the sufferings of the majority of Latin Americans under the weight of corrupt political regimes and massive economic poverty.[6] The public pronouncements and writings of Gutiérrez and subsequently of other like-minded Latin American theologians, both Catholic and Protestant, had an epidemic impact on religious teachings and practices. By the late 1970s and into the 1980s an explosion occurred in the number of publications dealing with themes of social justice and liberation, the radical transformation of local liturgies and rituals, and the political activities of religiously motivated individuals.[7] These publications laid the foundation for further reflections on various theological and social themes.

While liberation theology's prophetic outlook involves a vast array of religious concerns and conflicting arguments, a central issue of the primary literature supports popular involvement in politics as a means of improving social and economic conditions.[8] To understand better the origins and dynamics of poverty and oppression, liberation theologians have frequently argued for the incorporation of Marxist analysis into the methodology of their political theologies. In addition to their criticisms of capitalism, which seem to reveal the underlying causes of poverty in Latin America, Marxist critiques have also appealed to those who favor revolutionary social change.[9] Indeed, during the Central American wars of the 1980s, liberation theology was blamed or given credit for developing a political ethic that provided religious justification for social change, resulting in political activism by peasants, merchants, lay religious, and priests alike. It was charged that this intervention, influenced by Marxism and liberation theology together, frequently contributed to the destabilization of political regimes friendly to Western political establishments and economic interests.[10] Thus, liberation theology, apparently with its own political theory relying to an important extent on Marxist analysis, had indeed emerged as a major prophetic movement of the 1980s.

Yet in the 1990s new questions have arisen regarding the prudence of relying on Marxism to explain contemporary economic conditions. The apparent triumph of capitalism and the renewal of tribal, ethnic, and nationalist conflicts in many areas of the former Soviet Union and its Eastern European allies suggest the social irrelevance, and thus moral impotence, of relying on Marxist theoretical claims about economy, state, and society.[11] These recent historic changes support an increasingly common belief that a necessarily causal connection exists between Marxist theory and the failure of communist regimes.

With regard to religious preoccupation with state and politics, the triumph of capitalism over Marxism would also appear to vindicate the Catholic Church's and other denominations' long-standing denunciation of, and resistance to, Marxist movements and socialist practices throughout the world. In particular, the Vatican's Congregation for the Doctrine of the Faith has repeatedly denounced any attempt by liberation theology to incorporate aspects of orthodox Marxism.[12] The congregation warns that Marxism's emphasis on atheism and materialism will ultimately result in the denial of transcendental religion, with its consequential loss of individual faith and personal salvation. In support of these warnings, the acknowledged failure of communism and Marxist theory would seem to suggest that liberation theology can no longer employ Marxist analysis as a viable social scientific perspective.

Many critics have now come to fault liberation theology for its inclusion of Marxist social science in its prophetic denunciation of capitalism, thus also calling into question its effectiveness as a genuine prophetic movement.[13] Pointing out liberation theology's moral defense of socialism in principle and, by implication, of the disastrous consequences of communist regimes, some critics have even demanded that liberation theologians "offer apologies and public repentance" for their errant ways.[14] They argue that liberation theology has traveled down the wrong path and, as shown by recent events, must retrace its roots and rethink its priorities for social change. If it ignores the historic demise of Marxism and continues as usual, liberation theology will only prolong the despair it claims to want to alleviate.[15]

One major debate on the future of liberation theology, then, centers on the viability, and thus the advisability, of using Marxist analysis at a time when Marxism has lost currency in a rapidly changing, post–Cold War world. Is Marxism irrelevant today? To what extent has Marxism been essential to liberation theology's social message? Should liberation theology now reconsider its use of Marxism?

Contemporary Criticisms

Paul E. Sigmund has presented a critical review in which he traces the evolution in the political economic thinking of liberation theologians since their emergence nearly two and a half decades earlier.[16] According to Sigmund, liberation theologians originally naively extolled the virtues of the Cuban revolution and the promise of socialism to end the obvious abuses of capitalism and imperialism in Latin America. With their initial assessments of developmental practices in Latin America in the 1960s based on the empirical findings of dependency and Marxist theories of imperialism, the theologians chastised First World capitalism for failing to fulfill its promise to eradicate

Third World poverty.[17] They continued to praise the potential of other social-ist revolutions, such as that in Nicaragua, in the late 1970s and early 1980s to effect liberation from poverty and oppression and to establish social jus-tice.[18]

But in the 1980s, critics began to warn that continued incorporation of Marxist analytical techniques in liberation theology's methodology would undermine its prophetic politics and thus doom any prospects for success in attempting to bring about social justice.[19] More specifically, liberation theol-ogy's reliance on Marxist critiques of present economic conditions in Latin America demonstrated a fundamental misunderstanding of the proper approach to the production and distribution of national wealth.[20] And it was this fundamental misunderstanding that would perpetuate, not alleviate, the suffering of the poor. Consequently, by the late 1980s, liberation theologians began to develop a sober realization of, and appreciation for, the complexity of economics and politics and their interrelationship. Nevertheless, Sigmund notes, they had not clearly repudiated reliance on Marxist analysis.

Today, forced to consider more seriously the failings and limitations of recent and extant socialist regimes, as well as the intricacies of international and domestic economic and political development, liberation theologians, Sigmund maintains, are in a position to reaffirm their moral and spiritual concerns and to leave analyses of economics and politics to the secular world.[21] The near-worldwide failure of communist political regimes with their state-socialist economies and Marxist ideologies in the late 1980s, argues Sigmund, has placed liberation theology at an ethical crossroads: For the 1990s and beyond, theologians must choose whether to continue to guide their prophetic movement down a tortuous path poorly illuminated by Marx-ist social analysis with its attendant and requisite calls for class conflict, rev-olution, and authoritarianism; or to abandon reliance on any aspect of Marxism and thus embark on the moral high road toward cooperative democracy.[22]

Sigmund's review, however, evokes two crucial questions with regard to liberation theology and Marxism. First, does his contemporary critique of lib-eration theology adequately portray its use of Marxist analysis? That is, has Sigmund accurately depicted the understanding liberation theologians have of Marxism's limits and possibilities? And second, does such an either/or cross-roads really exist? In other words, are there in fact only two paths along which liberation theologians may choose to journey into the future? The answer to the second question is clearly connected with, and dependent upon, the answer to the first. And responsible answers to both questions are crucial for broader considerations of liberation theology, prophetic politics, and radical social-science critique.

Marxist Theory

The debate on the viability of Marxist theory and socialism has indeed had an effect on liberation theology. For example, the defeat of the Sandinistas for control of the presidency in Nicaragua in 1990 provoked an identity crisis in the party over its incorporation of Marxist critiques. This crisis has in turn induced a similar reaction in one of the Sandinistas' most prominent allies, the popular church influenced by liberation theology.[23] Yet the debates now raging focus less on the credibility of their normative commitments and the adoption of Marxist analysis and more on the most appropriate application of those commitments and analysis in a world whose geopolitics has changed considerably from that of the 1970s and 1980s. Furthermore, liberation theology's "preferential option for the poor" and its radical critique of society continue. For instance, liberation theologians increasingly refer to contemporary capitalist conditions worldwide as "neoliberalism." Under neoliberalism, capitalism emphasizes the restructuring of debt-payment schedules of Third World countries over the creation of national wealth through economic development; either way, say liberation theologians, the poor continue to suffer.[24]

With regard to the first question, however, liberation theology's experience in Nicaragua would suggest that Sigmund's portrayal of its use of Marxist analysis is woefully inadequate. In fact, Sigmund altogether avoids treatment of the diverse intellectual orientations, often only with strains of family resemblances, found in the Marxist intellectual tradition itself. Yet this diversity has not been lost on liberation theology. David McLellan has recently discussed the three orientations or types of Marxism to which liberation theologians have generally referred when defending their adoption of Marxist analysis.[25] In the first type, they understand Marxism as a particular "sociology" or social science that has produced an empirical, yet critical, explanation of the dynamics of modern society. For liberation theologians, the use of Marxism as social science offers reasonable and relevant explanations of contemporary economic and political problems. They understand the second type of Marxism as "a form of socialism" oriented toward the coercive imposition of an alternative and seemingly "just" society. Marxism as socialism is less attractive to liberation theologians, especially given the spotted history of communist-led, socialist regimes in contrast with the theologians' own vision of genuine democratic socialism. And they understand the third type of Marxism as "an overall philosophy" or cosmology. McLellan points out that Marxist cosmology finds virtually no support among liberation theologians, primarily because of its emphasis on atheism and materialism.[26]

With these distinct types and variations within each type, the number of potential combinations significantly increases the probability of achieving compatibility between some version of Marxism and religion, in terms of both a priori assumptions and consequences.[27] In principle, then, liberation theologians can accept, and frequently incorporate into their political theologies, a particular form of the first type of Marxism, understood as a critical social science. They reject forms of Marxism that propose a regimented social system or cosmology open to only one strict interpretation with a narrowly defined application. Unfortunately, Sigmund's overly generalized account of Marxism fails to take into account these distinctions and their diverse implications.

A Crossroads?

With regard to the second question, concerning the tendentious claim that a moral crossroads exists between peaceful, cooperative capitalism and violent, Marxist authoritarianism, again Sigmund stumbles. His terms belie the potential of vague and yet-to-be-carved-out paths in rather foggy moral terrain. For example, the rush to replace command economies with market economies in the former Soviet Union and other communist countries is having mixed results, as official market reforms alongside bureaucratic corruption steer economic changes in unintended directions.[28] The triumphant victory of capitalism may in fact be more political than economic. Particularly in Latin America, economic stagnation and poverty continue, despite a long history of Western developmental policies. Indeed, after billions of U.S. dollars were spent in recent decades in an attempt to achieve certain political and military objectives in Central America, some observers argue that the region is worse off both economically and politically than before U.S. intervention.[29] Social conflict may not have ceased at all with the abatement of the wars of the 1980s; it may have merely shifted more emphatically to the economic front. Nevertheless, the negative effects of decades of authoritarian regimes of the Right and the present identity crises among the Left have created a political vacuum in these countries.[30]

Furthermore, the complexity and inexactness of contemporary politics and economics, as well as the variety of Marxist analytical approaches, suggest a far richer range of options from which any political theology, including liberation theology, may develop and incorporate radical social-science critiques. Hence Sigmund's image of a clearly delineated moral crossroads appears to be an illusion. Nevertheless, his critique inadvertently, but usefully, calls attention to more serious questions surrounding liberation theology's adoption of Marxist analysis. In general, how can any aspect of Marxism find compatibility with religion and theological discourse? What kind of political theory is necessary to fuse two historically diverse traditions? More specifically, can it be said that liberation theology has, in fact, a genuine theory of politics? And what does this have to do with prophetic politics?

Political observers have long debated the legitimacy of religion's role in developing an effective political movement that can call attention to, and change, the moral failings of current economic and political arrangements and practices.[31] According to Michael Dodson, an analysis of liberation theology's social critiques reveals the presence of a solid political theoretical framework.[32] He maintains that liberation theology evinces a real political theory in the classic sense: it brings normative values to the fore of its social observations to criticize existing political regimes. That is, liberation theology attempts to realize its moral commitment to social justice by investigating the modern dynamics of economic and political development; it plays an active role in politics by supporting the mobilization of the poor to struggle for social change; and it offers a vision of a new, moral social order. Consequently, argues Dodson, liberation theology with its political theory is an authentic form of political theology, unique to Latin America.

Otto Maduro further maintains that liberation theology's political theory is integrally connected to its political activism.[33] Maduro argues that certain social conditions are necessary for any religious movement guided by a political theology to retain its autonomy in the face of a powerful state guided by the ethos of capitalist rationalization. It is possible, he says, for religious thought, practices, and institutions to develop a sense of activism in politics, or a "prophetic movement," that can seriously resist and even threaten the legitimacy and hegemony of oppressive states and develop into a catalyst for revolutionary change. Maduro argues that Latin American liberation theology, with its incorporation of Marxist analysis, is an example of such a prophetic movement.

A prophetic movement, then, would seem to consist of certain essential components, including radical criticism, a commitment to political activism, and propagation of certain moral values. But for the components of such a movement to be internally coherent and intellectually compelling, a framework or model must exist to provide the context for their proper definitions and the justification for their interrelationships. Specifically, liberation theology must have a model of prophetic politics that includes the necessity of radical social critique. The demands of such a critique may then be used to justify incorporation of Marxist analysis into its political theology.

Prophetic Politics

In the modern era, models, like ideologies, have come to supplant the overarching and unifying myths or belief systems of antiquity.[34] But unlike antiquity, modernity's pluralism tolerates, even at times encourages, the presence and proliferation of explanatory and normative models of politics. At present, according to Neal Riemer, there exist three prominent competing models of politics: Machiavellian politics, utopian politics, and liberal democratic politics.[35] Riemer describes the model of Machiavellian politics as dominated by an ethos that claims that policymakers must accept the human condition as a series of never-ending power struggles and hence must attempt to protect the vital interests of the nation-state by any means available. The model of utopian politics is inspired by a belief in the real possibility of perfecting human society and thus supports policies toward that end. And the model of liberal democratic politics is driven by a pragmatic blend of realism about untoward power in the world and the idealism of democracy, constitutionalism, and pluralism. However, these models and their attempts to explain contemporary political institutions and economic arrangements are increasingly coming under greater critical scrutiny. Alternative models, claims Riemer, such as models of prophetic politics, are emerging and struggling to replace them.

Riemer has in fact developed and proposed a model of prophetic politics as an alternative to the three dominant models of politics. He argues that his model is influenced by an ethos that is realistic about power in the world, while guided by an idealism unwilling to acquiesce in the face of abuse by power; that is, his model has "ethical, empirical, and prudential components of politics."[36] Specifically, Riemer's model rests upon a foundation of four commitments: "prophetic values," "fearless criticism," "constitutional breakthroughs," and "prophetic scrutiny." A brief description of these commitments in contrast to the commitments of the other, more prominent, models of politics will clarify the relevance of a model of prophetic politics to contemporary social criticism. This basic clarification of the relevance of Riemer's model in turn will provide an evaluative context for understanding and assessing liberation theology's own model of prophetic politics, including its justification for the inclusion of radical social science critiques.

First, Riemer's model of prophetic politics is committed to striving to attain a "superior ethical vision." This vision is based on the prophetic values of "life, peace, human rights and social justice, economic well-being, ecological health, and human excellence" (223). These values are used as a standard by which to measure the acceptability of current public policies and objectives. According to Riemer:

> Unlike Machiavellian politics, prophetic politics does not stop with the protection of the vital interests of the sovereign nation-state. Unlike utopian politics, the model of prophetic politics is not premised on earthly perfection, harmony, and salvation. Unlike liberal democratic politics, moreover, prophetic politics

does not use its understanding of human and social limitations as an excuse for not continuing the battle on behalf of peace, freedom, justice, prosperity, and excellence. (224)

Second, the model of prophetic politics is committed to "fearless criticism" of existing social orders. Guided by the model's prophetic values, this criticism relies on a social scientific understanding of the nature of political society (120, 133–35). Fearless criticism uses social science to criticize all existing social policies and institutions by determining and evaluating the gap between the prophetic vision and actual policy and practice. Crucial to the challenge of a model of prophetic politics, this second commitment relies on the necessity for "ethical criticism to link up with modern social science." Empirical research must reveal not only *how* liberal democratic regimes behave, but also *why* they do so in morally unacceptable ways. Consequently, critical research, including the possible use of Marxist analysis, will investigate "a host of empirical questions about the functioning of liberal democratic political institutions, of capitalist economics, of social systems in the predominantly white, rich, and male social world."[37] In this way, the model avoids the complacency of liberal democracy.

Third, armed with a critical understanding of the dynamics of social development, the model of prophetic politics is committed to "constitutional breakthroughs" with regard to what is ethical, empirical, and prudential. According to Riemer, "It will usually involve superior ideas as to what we ought to do; a superior understanding of political phenomena (what has been, is, and will be); and a superior judgment of what is feasible—of what is wise public policy" (137). Possessing a more farsighted approach than the other three models, prophetic politics demands that creative and prudent action be taken to change the world according to its prophetic vision and within the limits of its prophetic values. Riemer maintains that this orientation moves prophetic politics beyond the timidity of liberal democracy while remaining within the tradition of covenantal or constitutional restraints.

Fourth, prophetic politics is committed to "continuous prophetic scrutiny and futuristic projection" (195). That is, it encourages ongoing evaluation of present social conditions with an eye on the extent to which they contribute to the fulfillment of prophetic values. Furthermore, Riemer argues that his model also encourages the use of futuristic scenarios, both positive and negative, in order to anticipate an ever-changing world. The model carefully emphasizes the importance of handling present conflicts and overcoming obstacles to future objectives "in a democratic and constitutional way" (203).

The four commitments that characterize Riemer's model of prophetic politics—prophetic values, fearless criticism, constitutional breakthroughs, and prophetic scrutiny—correspond closely to the four commitments or steps that characterize the methodology underlying liberation theology's own prophetic movement. Comparing and contrasting both sets of characteristics will reveal liberation theology's model of prophetic politics, including its argument to justify the incorporation of Marxist analysis.

Liberation Theology's Model of Prophetic Politics

Liberation theology's model of prophetic politics emerges from its methodology for criticizing existing political and economic arrangements. The methodology consists of a "hermeneutic circle" that emphasizes the relationship between interpretation of Holy Scripture and political action according to a particular understanding of social justice. Often referred to as a "hermeneutics of liberation," this methodology has been defined by José Severino Croatto as "the science of understanding the meaning that human beings inscribe in their practices, as well as in their interpretation by word, text, or other practices."[38] Thus, any adequate methodology of interpretation, according to Croatto, must recognize the crucial link between text and context, theory and practice, ethics and politics, language and event.[39]

Influenced by this methodology, Juan Luís Segundo demonstrates the steps of the hermeneutic circle essential to liberation theology's model of prophetic politics.[40] A religious individual who is morally disturbed by the presence of poverty and oppression and wishes to improve current social conditions may take the following four steps to complete the circle's dynamics: "an act of will," "ideological suspicion," "exegetical suspicion," and "a new hermeneutic."

In the first step of Segundo's hermeneutic circle, an act of will, the morally concerned individual makes a commitment to the liberation of his or her fellow citizens from economic poverty and political oppression. This commitment derives from the individual's own religious upbringing that traditionally has stressed the importance of showing respect for other human beings, as well as from personal experience with social deprivation.[41] This commitment to respect for the dignity and rights of others in the face of massive poverty and human rights violations motivates the individual to search for explanations of, and solutions to, problems of social injustice.[42]

Segundo's first step, act of will, is nearly identical to Riemer's first commitment, prophetic values. Both models of prophetic politics assume that a quest for a social order morally superior to any that presently exists is the primary motivating factor for engaging in social critique, political activism, and, if successful, democratic participation.[43] Segundo's hermeneutic circle assumes a dialectical relationship between theory and practice, thus preventing the attainment of perfection, although presumably always coming nearer to the just society. Riemer's model also maintains a vision of justice based on superior values, although a vision never completely attainable. Both approaches, too, eschew the moral complacency of Machiavellian and liberal democratic models of politics, while recognizing the appeal of individual and national self-interest as a powerful psychological motivation of human and state behavior.

Following the act of will in liberation theology's model of prophetic politics, the individual has now arrived at the second step of Segundo's hermeneutic circle, ideological suspicion. In the role of critical observer with a commitment to human liberation, the religious individual assesses the ideological arguments offered by the elites of the political and economic establishment who attempt to justify oppression and poverty. These justifications will make extensive claims about the nature of contemporary politics, proper economic arrangements, and general societal objectives. Thus, to be in any position to evaluate critically the merit of the arguments in favor of the status quo, the individual must understand the structure and dynamics of current social conditions. In the search for appropriate explanations, he or she discovers that certain modern social sciences can both explain present social conditions and consciously assist in the eradication of social injustice. For many liberation theologians, Marxist social analyses often offer appropriate insights into Latin American social conditions, as well as moral condemnation of structures and institutions that perpetuate the pernicious aspects of those conditions.[44]

With regard to the second step of the hermeneutic circle, ideological suspicion, Segundo requires the incorporation of contemporary social scientific analyses as necessary for grasping the patterns of modern economic development and political arrangements, as well as the dynamics of, and the possibility for, social change. In Riemer's model of prophetic politics, the second commitment, to fearless criticism, also requires "a more ethically sophisticated and scientific theory of criticism" of contemporary society.[45] In this way, to balance the overreaching claims of utopianism, with its naïveté regarding political possibilities, the realistic appraisals of society typically found in Machiavellian and liberal democratic models are also preserved in both liberation theology's and Riemer's models of prophetic politics.

With the commitment to liberate the poor and oppressed, and with analytical tools that provide penetrating critiques of the ideological arguments attempting to legitimate present conditions of social injustice, the religious individual as critical observer is now in a strong position to invalidate prevailing political ideologies and hence unmask unjust political and economic practices. Furthermore, any comprehensive assessment of society necessarily leads the critical observer to evaluate the role of all social institutions participating in the unjust society, including the role of the Church and its supporting theologies. Consequently, the individual now moves to the third step of the hermeneutic circle, exegetical suspicion.

Unfortunately, argues Segundo, seminaries and universities have generally understood, written, and taught theology as consisting of a specific set of timeless truths located in, and hence to be extracted from, biblical scripture.[46] This typical academic approach to scriptural interpretation assumes that revelation is a matter of divine communication, wherein God dispenses information to humankind, with the Bible serving as a repository of timeless truths collected over the centuries. By using various scientific techniques and disciplines borrowed from history, language, culture, and literary criticism, careful exegesis of ancient documents will reveal the author's intent and the truths to be communicated. And, of course, these truths, once discovered and understood, may be applied in any social context.

Segundo argues that this assumption of academic theology—divine communication is simply an act of revealing timeless truths—results in interpretations that fail to recognize the authentic intent of the communication itself. The Scriptures, after all, contain diverse stories with apparently conflicting teachings on a variety of subjects; such conflict in turn invites the reader to search for the true purpose behind the communication. Revelation, he maintains, "is not a deposit of true information, but a *true pedagogy.*"[47] Consequently, the important legacy of Scripture, with its myriad stories and historical examples, is its revelation of a process of *how* to learn, not of *what* to learn. And as with unmasking prevailing political ideologies, to understand this revelatory process the exegete must also rely on technical sciences to unmask false exegetical claims.[48]

In the critique of political arguments justifying poverty and oppression, the religious individual assesses the arguments set forth by the Church in defense of society's status quo.[49] These arguments are scrutinized as to their credibility given the individual's moral commitments and the new social scientific understanding of contemporary economic, political, and sociological dynamics. Critical analyses of the dominant exegetical interpretations of Christian social dogma influenced by academic theology reveal the ideological infiltration of those interpretations by the norms of a corrupt and unjust society. Furthermore, these analyses reveal the great disparity between the original commitment of early Christianity to human liberation and the ideological arguments supported by the contemporary Church's exegetical interpretations defending conditions of social injustice.

As to the two models of prophetic politics, the descriptions appear to diverge with regard to the third step of Segundo's hermeneutic circle—exegetical suspicion—and the third commitment of Riemer's prophetic politics—

constitutional breakthroughs. Segundo's third step builds upon insights gained from the second step. That is, the focus of suspicion on ideological justifications defending economic poverty and political oppression has shifted to related exegetical claims made by theologians and ecclesiastical officials, as they, too, attempt to justify the Church's role in supporting the state's oppressive activities. But under Riemer's third commitment, the model shifts its focus to related, but new, policy considerations to achieve a more just society. So while Segundo's third step enlarges the second step's arena of suspicion, Riemer's third commitment concentrates more on prudential constitutional action, involving an attempt "to develop the superior constitutional principles that will guide the prophetic future."[50]

Still, the third commitment, to constitutional breakthroughs guided by certain normative principles, in Riemer's model accurately corresponds to the general ethical commitment of liberation theology's politics. For Segundo, however, this ethical commitment to political activism is present throughout liberation theology's model, since the praxis of liberation simultaneously involves both the hermeneutic circle and political activism; hence, the discussion of moral policy formation is not assigned to one specific step in the model.[51] Furthermore, the step of exegetical suspicion in the hermeneutic circle simply corresponds to one application of Riemer's commitment to fearless criticism—in this case, a realistic appraisal of the role of the Church in politics. Under Riemer's model, exegetical suspicion would be significant only as part of the broader commitment to criticize all aspects of society, and not as a separate commitment of its own, as under liberation theology. Segundo's third step, then, can be subsumed within Riemer's second commitment.

In the final step of the hermeneutic circle, Segundo calls for a new hermeneutic that takes into account the results of critical social scientific and exegetical analyses. The religious individual must take his or her newfound insights about church and society and develop a new hermeneutic for theological reflection.[52] The effects of the circle's first three steps have revealed how theological meanings are bound up in the daily activities of social life to such an extent that one aspect cannot be completely comprehended without an understanding of the other. The fourth step's new hermeneutic will now contribute to the development of a religious perspective influenced by a realistic appraisal of social conditions that follows the original commitment to human liberation. And with a realistic appraisal, the committed individual may act in a more prudent and effective manner. Riemer's final commitment, to prophetic scrutiny, reveals a similar intent as it encourages continuous reflection upon the achievements to date in any present or future attempt to establish a just social order.

With this application of the hermeneutic circle, then, liberation theology has proposed its own model of prophetic politics with which it may develop a prophetic movement, as it criticizes and denounces existing institutions and practices that perpetuate social injustice. Thus, it closely follows the pattern set by Riemer's model of prophetic politics when it uses its prophetic calling to adopt modern social sciences for radical critiques and to justify engagement in reformist or revolutionary activities.

Religion, Culture, and Radical Critique

The comparison of Segundo's and Riemer's models of prophetic politics—primarily with regard to Segundo's "ideological suspicion" and Riemer's "fearless criticism"—reveals a crucial dimension common to both: Each requires radical social science critiques, yet neither necessarily requires nor proscribes Marxist analysis. Furthermore, if Marxist analysis is adopted, neither model is limited to any particular version. The legitimacy of this dimension in turn reveals a crucial flaw in the assumptions of critics who fault liberation theology for its use of Marxist analysis: They have typically taken their understanding of Marxism from the arguments of orthodox Marxists and have assumed that liberation theologians have done the same. In fact, two important differences exist between liberation theology's use of Marxist analysis and the analysis of orthodox Marxists.

In the first difference, liberation theology's methodology relies on the hermeneutic circle, which requires a moral commitment as the initial point of departure for any reflection on, and critique of, society. In this alone, according to Maduro, liberation theology has reversed the typical orthodox Marxist approach to analyzing the dynamics of the state.[53] Unlike orthodox Marxism, liberation theology begins its social critique by evaluating society from within the broader context of religious culture, as opposed to evaluating religion from within the context of society and its economic base. In this way, religious concerns and categories will determine a priori, as indicated by the new hermeneutic, the appropriate degree to which Marxist analysis can, and will be, applied. Thus, in effect, religion is "in control" of the Marxist tradition, not the reverse.

In the second difference, liberation theology, now free from entanglement with materialist cosmologies, has engaged in what Maduro refers to as the "plundering" of Marxism (374–75). It has not approached the Marxist tradition as a body of moral philosophy that must be revered and held sacred, but as simply a set of tools that happens to contain useful approaches for analyzing Latin American social conditions. Furthermore, where needed, liberation theology has even modified certain aspects of various Marxist tools to meet better its own objectives. For example, similar to the revolutionary role of the proletariat, the use of the hermeneutic circle, with its second step of ideological suspicion, provides the religious individual with the opportunity to assume a role in the prophetic movement as both critic and agent of social change. As Maduro points out:

> Individuals appear in [Latin American liberation theology] as agents of reflection, decision and action, capable of grasping, criticizing and (at least partially) overcoming and transforming their social class structures. Therein, theological reflection is viewed as a privileged avenue through which such processes can take place, leading to the empowerment of the oppressed in their revolutionary struggles. (379)

Hence, in contradistinction to the position of orthodox Marxists, the revolutionary class need not necessarily be made up of the proletariat, but may come as well from peasants and others who are impoverished, oppressed, and guided by an act of will based on commitment to religious values. In effect, then, concludes Maduro, liberation theology is guilty for orthodox Marxists of "desacralizing" the true "faith." At the same time, to the chagrin of its critics, it would appear that liberation theology has "desatanized" Marxism.

Furthermore, reliance on "religious creativity," argues Maduro, goes far in affirming the ability of the oppressed to create a just culture of their own (379–80). Rather than relying on one preordained and inflexible ideological perspective from which to remake the world, the oppressed are free to create a new world as a result of their methodology of prophetic politics. That is, revolutionary social changes may occur as a result of the religious poor's reliance on the prophetic model's new hermeneutic, rather than with a narrow emphasis on developing appropriate class consciousness as tied to particular economic conditions. Consequently, religion will not necessarily disappear with the dissolution of capitalism and private property, as argued by orthodox Marxists, but may continue to be the revolutionary source of an authentic cultural and moral base for the reconstruction of society.

With regard to prophetic politics, James V. Spickard similarly maintains that liberation theology provides the most appropriate model of the kind of analysis most needed for understanding and changing the present social conditions in Latin America.[54] Spickard argues that liberation theology emphasizes the incorporation of social analysis—not the historical dialectic—in its critique of Latin American conditions. Indeed, it rejects orthodox Marxism's reliance on a historical analysis influenced by the principle of dialectical materialism. One consequence of this rejection by liberation theology's methodology is the retention and defense of the legitimacy of eschatological questions. Consequently, these theological questions survive and remain the proper domain of the institutional-ized Church with its unique spiritual interpretation, an interpretation out of reach of orthodox Marxism. With this refinement in its use of Marxism, accord-ing to Spickard, the prophetic politics of liberation theology continues to invig-orate "a democratic social movement that would usher in a truly human soci-ety."[55] This refinement is hardly a temporary "phase" of liberation theology's evolution during the 1970s and 1980s, as suggested by critics.

Quo Vadis?

As noted at the beginning of this chapter, the collapse of the former Soviet Union and other socialist regimes has brought to the fore the question of the validity and value of Marxism, and the future of Marxism may well call into question the future of those who employ it. In this vein, critics such as Paul Sigmund have called on liberation theology to abandon its appropriation of Marxism, as a result of the latter's tendency toward conflict, revolution, and misery.

Certainly, liberation theologians would agree with Sigmund's ethical con-cerns, but they would disagree with his theoretical assessment. They would emphasize the importance of finding remedies for chronic economic and polit-ical failures, regardless of the origins of those failures, as pointed up by the recent uprising led by the EZLN. These observations suggest that a proper methodology, such as Juan Luís Segundo's hermeneutic circle employed along the lines of Neal Riemer's model of prophetic politics, may continue to justify the careful appropriation of Marxist analysis. In this way, such a methodology will maintain the primacy of religious values and social commitments, while allying with Marxism or any other radical social critique for the compelling nature of its insights and contribution to social improvement.

The implications for an alliance between religion and radical social critique may be more optimistic than critics will admit. The social conditions in Latin America that gave rise to the clamor for liberation continue today as they did in the 1960s. And consequently, as Daniel H. Levine has argued, the appeal of liberation theology also continues, however muted may be its current public voice.[56] Indeed, liberation theology's appeal transcends intellectual issues such as the debate surrounding the incorporation of appropriate social science approaches, including Marxist analysis.

The debate surrounding the viability of Marxism, however, is not unim-portant to the construction of liberation theology's model of prophetic poli-tics. If the Marxist tradition were to be understood as referring to a large but disparate body of conflicting theories—as opposed to an all-encompassing, unified cosmology—then the collapse of the former Soviet Union would not necessarily be relevant to the debate over Marxism's apparent demise. In fact, the recent dissolution of the Soviet Union, along with its corruption of Marxist theory into a crude "religious" faith of its own, may, ironically, encourage the rejuvenation of radical social science approaches. Thus carefully examined, certain aspects of Marxist social analysis may still be relevant to liberation theology's model of prophetic politics. And relatedly, the future of religion itself, long nearly displaced by, and often at war with, orthodox Marxism and secular nationalism, may find—with assistance from the prophetic politics of liberation theology—a more effective role in the cultural and political life of society.

Notes

1. EZLN Directorate, Editorial, *Pasa-Montañas* [*sic*] 1 (February 1994): 1 (translation mine); cf. EZLN Directorate, "Democracia, EZLN y Sociedad Civil," *Paz-a-Montañas* 1 (March–April 1994): 5. Also, cf. José Antonio Cheibub, "Mobilizing and Sustaining Collective Action in the Mexican Revolution," *Politics and Society* 23 (June 1995): 243–58, on organizational problems faced by the armies during the Mexican Revolution of 1913–15; and Scott Cook and Jong-Taick Joo, "Ethnicity and Economy in Rural Mexico: A Critique of the Indigenista Approach," *Latin American Research Review* 30 (1995): 33–59, for a critical look at how to assess and discuss indigenous peoples in Mexico in light of the worldwide economic restructuring of capitalism, including the response of "neo-Zapatismo."

2. Editorial Collective, eds., *Zapatistas: The New Mexican Revolution* (Brooklyn: Autonomedia, 1994). The Mexican government has also continued to promise appropriations for social programs in impoverished areas; see, for example, Department of Economic Research of the Banco Nacional de México, "Mexico at the Crossroads," *Review of the Economic Situation of Mexico* 71 (April 1995): 135–36.

3. Tim Golden, "Mexican Church Accused of Role in Latest Revolt," *New York Times*, 9 January 1994, sec. A, p. 10.

4. Tim Golden, "Old Scores: Left Behind, Mexico's Indians Fight the Future," *New York Times*, 9 January 1994, sec. D, p. 6; cf. EZLN Directorate, "El EZLN ha sido apoyado por ideólogos y religiosos," *Pasa-Montañas* [*sic*] 1 (February 1994): 2–3. Indeed, in an apparent attack on Bishop Samuel Ruíz, who is attempting to mediate the dispute between the EZLN and the Mexican government, the government recently expelled three foreign priests working with the poor in Chiapas, according to Dennis Dunleavy and Karen Sauer, "Priests Expelled from Chiapas," communiqué from San Cristobal de las Casas, Chiapas, Mexico, 27 June 1995.

5. Gustavo Gutiérrez, *A Theology of Liberation: History, Politics and Salvation*, trans. Sister Caridad Inda and John Eagleson (Maryknoll, N.Y.: Orbis Books, 1973); originally published as *Teología de la liberación: perspectivas* (Lima: CEP, 1971).

6. John R. Pottenger, "Liberation Theology's Critique of Capitalism: The Argument from Gustavo Gutiérrez," *Southeastern Political Review* 17 (Fall 1989): 3–31.

7. Examples of the early writings of many of the most prominent theologians can be found in Sergio Torres and John Eagleson, eds., *Theology in the Americas* (Maryknoll, N.Y.: Orbis Books, 1976); and Rosino Gibellini, ed., *Frontiers of Theology in Latin America* (Maryknoll, N.Y.: Orbis Books, 1979). Also, see Alfred T. Hennelly, ed., *Liberation Theology: A Documentary History* (Maryknoll, N.Y.: Orbis Books, 1990). Perhaps the most recent and comprehensive collection of writings from liberation theologians can be found in Ignacio Ellacuría and Jon Sobrino, eds., *Mysterium Liberationis: Fundamental Concepts of Liberation Theology* (Maryknoll, N.Y: Orbis Books/Collins Dove, 1993).

8. For a clear but popularized overview of the relationship between the spiritual and social aspects of liberation theology, see Robert McAfee Brown, *Liberation Theology: An Introductory Guide* (Louisville, Ky.: Westminster/John Knox Press, 1993); cf. María Clara Lucchetti Bingemer, "La teología de la liberación: ¿Una opción por los pobres?" *Revista Latinoamericana de Teología* 9 (May–August 1992): 189–99. Liberation theologians often criticize behavioral social science for failing to identify the sin found in social structures themselves; cf. Jon Sobrino, "Liberation from Sin," *Theology Digest* 37 (Summer 1990): 141–45; and Jon Sobrino, "Iglesias ricas y pobres, y el principio-misericordia: Una Iglesia 'pobre' es una Iglesia 'rica en misericordia,'" *Revista Latinoamericana de Teología* 7 (September–December 1990): 307–23.

9. For an introduction to the relationship between Marxism and liberation theology, see John R. Pottenger, *The Political Theory of Liberation Theology: Toward a Reconvergence of Social Values and Social Science,* chap. 3 (Albany: State University of New York Press, 1989).

10. Ronald H. Nash, "The Christian Choice between Capitalism and Socialism," in *Liberation Theology,* ed. Ronald Nash (Grand Rapids, Mich.: Baker Book House, 1984), 49–67; cf. Hugh Lacey, "A Place for Liberation Theology in the New World Order?" *Cross Currents* 42 (Summer 1992): 252–55; and John O'Brien, *Theology and the Option for the Poor* (Collegeville, Minn.: Liturgical Press, 1992), 32–35.

11. For an intriguing argument in this regard, see Frank E. Manuel, "A Requiem for Karl Marx," *Daedalus* 121 (Spring 1992): 1–19; also, see Stephen White, Ian McAllister, and Olga Kryshtanovskaya, "Religion and Politics in Postcommunist Russia," *Religion, State and Society* 22 (1994): 73–88.

12. See, for example, Joseph Cardinal Ratzinger, Prefect for the Congregation for the Doctrine of the Faith, "Instruction on Certain Aspects of the 'Theology of Liberation,'" (Vatican: 6 August 1984); and Joseph Cardinal Ratzinger, "Instruction on Christian Freedom and Liberation" (Vatican: 22 March 1986).

13. Cf. Edward A. Lynch, *Religion and Politics in Latin America: Liberation Theology and Christian Democracy* (New York: Praeger, 1991); and Christian Smith, *The Emergence of Liberation Theology: Radical Religion and Social Movement Theory* (Chicago: University of Chicago Press, 1991), 230–33.

14. Clark H. Pinnock, review of *Liberation Theology at the Crossroads: Democracy*

or Revolution? by Paul E. Sigmund, *Calvin Theological Journal* 26 (November 1991): 475.

15. Alternatively, other critics insist that liberation theology was correct, in principle, to incorporate Marxist analytical techniques into its methodology, but they hold that it did so ineffectively. Thus, poor theoretical reasoning through the misapplication of Marxian insights has caused liberation theology to miss opportunities to effect meaningful social change; in this regard, see Alistair Kee, *Marx and the Failure of Liberation Theology* (London: SCM Press, 1990); cf. Alistair Kee, *Domination or Liberation: The Place of Religion in Social Conflict* (London: SCM Press, 1986), chap. 3.

16. Paul E. Sigmund, *Liberation Theology at the Crossroads: Democracy or Revolution?* (New York: Oxford University Press, 1990). An earlier statement of this thesis can be found in Paul E. Sigmund, "The Development of Liberation Theology: Continuity or Change?" in *The Politics of Latin American Liberation Theology*, eds. Richard L. Rubenstein and John K. Roth (Washington, D.C.: Washington Institute Press, 1988), 21–47.

17. Sigmund, *Liberation Theology at the Crossroads*, 29–32.

18. Ibid., 42–48.

19. See, for example, Stephen T. Worland, *The Preferential Option for the Poor: An Economist's Perspective* (Collegeville, Minn.: Saint John's University, 1987), 14.

20. See, for example, Michael Novak, *Will It Liberate? Questions about Liberation Theology* (New York: Paulist Press, 1986); cf. Mark Falcoff, "Political Systems and Economic Growth: The Case of Latin America," in *Liberation Theology and the Liberal Society*, ed. Michael Novak (Washington, D.C.: AEI, 1987), 194–200.

21. Sigmund, *Liberation Theology at the Crossroads*, 175.

22. Ibid., 177–81.

23. François Houtart, "Crisis in the FSLN: Class Conflict," *Envio* 13 (September 1994): 26–31; and José María Vigil, "What Remains of the Option for the Poor?" *LADOC* 25 (November/December 1994): 1–8.

24. For a statement of basic beliefs for liberation theology given the new worldwide conditions of capitalism in the form of neoliberalism, see Leonardo Boff, "Christian Liberation toward the 21st Century," *LADOC* 25 (March/April 1994): 1–14; cf. Miguel D'Escoto, "Neo-Liberal Wars in Central America," *Challenge* 3 (Fall 1992): 5–6; and Fernando Storni, "Capitalismo: ¿Cuál?" *Revista del Centro de Investigación y Acción Social* 41 (October 1992): 449–56.

25. David McLellan, *Unto Caesar: The Political Relevance of Christianity* (Notre Dame: University of Notre Dame Press, 1993), chap. 4; cf. Arthur F. McGovern, *Liberation Theology and Its Critics: Toward an Assessment* (Maryknoll, N.Y.: Orbis Books, 1989), xv–xviii.

26. Ibid., 59.

27. For example, when understood as cosmology, Marxism has had something to say on most subjects, both normative and technical, including religion. As a result, it has been denigrated by religious believers for its promulgation of atheism and materialism. If, indeed, Marxism entails a commitment to atheistic assumptions about creation and to materialistic or nonspiritual assumptions about human existence, then it would

appear that the theological adoption of Marxist analysis in whatever form would be incompatible with religion, as it must necessarily and ultimately result in the destruction of religion.

28. See, for example, Grigory Yavlinsky and Serguey Braguinsky, "The Inefficiency of *Laissez-Faire* in Russia: Hysteresis Effects and the Need for Policy-Led Transformation," *Journal of Comparative Economics* 19 (August 1995): 88–116; and Nathaniel C. Nash, "'A Wall in the Mind': Rising Resentment in the East Divides Germany," *New York Times*, 27 July 1995, sec. C, pp. 1, 18.

29. See, for example, Douglas Farah, "The Lost Decade: Central America Is Staggering under Its '80s Legacy," *Washington Post National Weekly Edition*, 14–20 June 1993, pp. 6–7.

30. Tomas A. Vasconi and Elena Peraza Martell, "Social Democracy and Latin America," *Latin American Perspectives* 20 (Winter 1993): 99–113.

31. See, for example, H. Mark Roelofs, "Liberation Theology: The Recovery of Biblical Radicalism," *American Political Science Review* 82 (June 1988): 549–66; Daniel H. Levine, "From Church and State to Religion and Politics and Back Again," *Social Compass* 37 (September 1990): 331–51; and William T. Cavanaugh, "The Ecclesiologies of Medellín and the Lessons of the Base Communities," *Cross Currents* 44 (Spring 1994): 67–84.

32. Michael Dodson, "Prophetic Politics and Political Theory in Latin America," *Polity* 12 (Spring 1980): 388–408.

33. Otto Maduro, *Religion and Social Conflicts* (Maryknoll, N.Y.: Orbis Books, 1982), chaps. 6, 25, 27, 30, 31, 33–35.

34. David McLellan, *Ideology* (Minneapolis: University of Minnesota Press, 1986), 1–9.

35. The most detailed exposition of these models can be found in Neal Riemer, *The Future of the Democratic Revolution: Toward a More Prophetic Politics* (New York: Praeger, 1984), chaps. 2–4; for a brief overview, see Neal Riemer, *Karl Marx and Prophetic Politics* (New York: Praeger, 1987), 3–6.

36. Riemer, *Future of the Democratic Revolution*, 223–24.

37. Ibid., 133; on Marxism, see p. 30.

38. José Severino Croatto, *Exodus: A Hermeneutics of Freedom* (Maryknoll, N.Y.: Orbis Books, 1981), 1, 10.

39. José Severino Croatto, *Biblical Hermeneutics: Toward a Theory of Reading as the Production of Meaning* (Maryknoll, N.Y.: Orbis Books, 1987), 13–35.

40. Juan Luís Segundo, *The Liberation of Theology* (Maryknoll, N.Y.: Orbis Books, 1976), chap. 1.

41. In fact, presumably only the poor can "do" theology; see Juan Luís Segundo, "Two Theologies of Liberation," *The Month* (October 1984): 322–27; cf. Elsa Tamez, "The Indigenous Peoples Are Evangelizing Us," *Ecumenical Review* 44 (October 1992): 458–66.

42. Segundo, *Liberation of Theology*, 81–90, 104–6.

43. With regard to the question of democracy, the *comunidades eclesiais de base* ([from Portuguese] Christian base communities, CEBs) provide a place for theological

and spiritual development as well as a social mechanism for developing a sense of democratic participation in neighborhood decision-making. On the theological and spiritual importance of CEBs, see Leonardo Boff, *Ecclesiogenesis: The Base Communities Reinvent the Church* (Maryknoll, N.Y.: Orbis Books, 1986); but cf. Richard Shaull, "The Christian Base Communities and the Ecclesia Reformata Semper Reformanda," *Princeton Seminary Bulletin* 12 (1991): 201–13. On the social mechanisms of CEBs, see Sonya Anne Ingwersen, "Not as Rulers among the Pagans: Authority and Base Church Communities," *St. Luke's Journal of Theology* 34 (December 1990): 41–59.

44. As mentioned above, liberation theologians use Marxist analysis as an analytical tool for describing and explaining Latin American social conditions. They do not use it as a philosophical framework, thus avoiding the problems of materialism and atheism associated with orthodox Marxism; cf. Segundo, *Liberation of Theology,* 47–62; and Ignacio Ellacuría, "Teología de la liberación y marxismo," *Revista Latinoamericana de Teología* 7 (May–August 1990): 109–35.

45. Riemer, *Future of the Democratic Revolution,* 240.

46. Juan Luís Segundo, "Revelation, Faith, Signs of the Times," in *Signs of the Times: Theological Reflections,* ed. Alfred T. Hennelly (Maryknoll, N.Y.: Orbis Books, 1993), 134–35.

47. Ibid., 137 (emphasis in original).

48. Segundo, *Liberation of Theology,* 7. There is irony in the academic approach, notes Segundo. Academic theology asserts its independence from the social sciences that explain the present state of religion, while retaining its dependence on the same sciences that explain the religious teachings of the past.

49. Ibid., 126–38.

50. Riemer, *Future of the Democratic Revolution,* 198.

51. For further discussion on liberation theology as an arena of mediation for sociology, theology, and ethics, see Leonardo Boff and Clodovis Boff, *Introducing Liberation Theology* (Maryknoll, N.Y.: Orbis Books, 1987), 24–42; cf. Rosino Gibellini, *The Liberation Theology Debate* (Maryknoll, N.Y.: Orbis Books, 1988), 8–12.

52. Segundo, *Liberation of Theology,* 75–81, 106–22, and 165–70.

53. Otto Maduro, "The Desacralization of Marxism within Latin American Liberation Theology," *Social Compass* 35 (September 1988): 375–76.

54. James V. Spickard, "Transcending Marxism: Liberation Theology and Critical Theology," *Cross Currents* 42 (Fall 1992): 326–41.

55. Ibid., 328.

56. See the review essay by Daniel H. Levine, "On Premature Reports of the Death of Liberation Theology," *Review of Politics* 57 (Winter 1995): 105–31.

10

Reinhold Niebuhr, Political Realism, and Prophetic Politics

Neal Riemer

Is the perspective provided by Reinhold Niebuhr—the most influential religious thinker on politics in the twentieth century—still the most cogent variety of political realism? Or must we—especially in light of developments attendant upon the end of the Cold War—move beyond Niebuhr's political realism toward a more prophetic politics?

I shall argue, in response to these questions, that the Niebuhrian perspective—despite its eminently sound contributions to political realism, despite the fact that it still has a great deal to commend it in the closing decade of the twentieth century—nonetheless inhibits our ability to respond creatively to opportunities opened up by the end of the Cold War and to serious problems confronting democratic America as it approaches the twenty-first century. Although profiting from Niebuhr's own prophetic insights, we need, I shall argue, to move beyond Niebuhr toward a more prophetic politics that can more readily facilitate our responses to these opportunities and problems.

In advancing this argument I seek not to repudiate key, enduring aspects of Niebuhr's political philosophy, but to emphasize why the time may be especially ripe to move beyond Niebuhr's telling critique of utopian Marxists, of naive liberals, idealists, pacifists, moralists, and of cynical realists. Marx's utopianism is no longer fashionable. The perverted variety of Marxism practiced in the Soviet Union has been pretty much discredited. The illusions of naive liberals, idealists, pacifists, and moralists—especially their naive faith in rationality, education, progress—no longer have appeal or staying power. Even cynical realism, rare in print if still operative in practical politics, has no appreciable intellectual or popular appeal. In a very significant sense, Niebuhr's battle on behalf of his variety of political realism has been won. This success, we must note, highlights the fact that Niebuhr's victory was largely, but not completely, a negative victory; that is, a victory *against* the illusions of utopians, liberals, idealists, pacifists, moralists, and *against* the unacceptable ethical posture of cynics.

The time is now very appropriate to reflect on the more positive agenda required to respond to new intellectual, religious, and political opportunities opened up both by Niebuhr's victory and by the circumstances attendant upon the end of the Cold War, a Cold War that played such a crucial role in the shaping and interpretation of Niebuhr's mature political realism. This agenda requires, for example, attention to the fuller achievement of peace, freedom, prosperity, ecological health, and excellence around the globe and to the roles in this endeavor to be played by the United States and an invigorated United Nations. The time is also ripe to reflect on the more positive agenda now demanded by a troubled American democracy confronting key problems—for example, an inadequate health-care system, malfunctioning welfare programs, criminal behavior, drug addictions, a disturbing budget deficit—still pressing for satisfactory resolution.

This reflection will, however, require us to take a critical look at Niebuhr's variety of political realism to see whether aspects of the mature Niebuhr's neo-orthodox approach may inhibit a sane prophetic response to current opportunities and problems: opportunities for creative breakthroughs on a number of fronts, breakthroughs with regard to problems involving global peace, human rights, economic well-being, ecological health, and social and cultural excellence.

Specifically, we may be unhappy about those aspects of Niebuhr's political philosophy that overemphasize human sin, that underscore too strongly our inability in this world to achieve complete justice, that overstress the crucial role of power and the need to balance power with power, and that too quickly reject the alleged illusions of utopians, idealists, pacifists, rationalists, and liberals. We may fear that such a realistic political philosophy—despite Niebuhr's own admirable intentions and his own, usually splendid, practical political courses of action—can lead, ironically, in both theory and practice, to a too complacent balance-of-power policy abroad and a too complacent pluralism at home, to an acceptance—however reluctant—of a tolerable status quo, of a timid conservatism. These conservative possibilities may emerge because we fear that if we reject Niebuhr's mature realism, we have no place to go. So we are tempted to hang on to Niebuhr's realism because, despite some shortcomings, his political philosophy is preferable to competing alternatives—for example, utopian Marxism, or naive liberalism, or illusory moralism, or callous cynicism. And so, liberal or conservative in our political orientation, we may come to celebrate as priests the great tough-minded tradition of American constitutional politics, and often to lose the prophetic impulse to criticize the existing order, the existing balance of power (whether domestic or international), and thus to call for—and act to achieve—the creation of a more prophetic order. We may lose the inspiration, the critical capacity, the creative statecraft to ask if we can move, as necessary—and only as necessary—beyond Niebuhr's political realism toward a more prophetic politics.[1]

Let me in the next two sections summarize a little more fully, and then criticize, the Niebuhrian perspective in order to lay a better foundation for my argument about the need to move beyond Niebuhr's political philosophy toward a more prophetic politics.

The Niebuhrian Perspective

Niebuhr wisely affirms that we must be on guard against, and reject, utopian assumptions about complete justice, harmony, peace, and perfection on this earth. We must continually be on guard against the abuse of power. We must recognize the tenacious grip of self-interest in politics, particularly on larger groups and especially on nation-states. We must guard against human sin and especially our human inclination to exceed our limits. The will to dominate is deeply rooted in humans and in human societies, and we must protect against it by balancing power with power. We must also appreciate that even the will to do good can lead to disastrous results. Such a will does not automatically lead to the good society. Nations seek to protect their vital interests, and these vital interests are not necessarily identical with the vital interests of all humankind in the good global commonwealth! Politics is a struggle for power among contending interests, and the larger interests—nation-states, corporations, trade unions, etc.—do not engage in this struggle according to the decent ethical considerations of the Sermon on the Mount, or the kinder ethical considerations that may more frequently motivate individuals in their intimate personal relationships. The principles of love, good will, altruism, idealism, pacifism, and rational ethics, which we may find in some moral individuals, do not operate for the larger organizations and the nation-states contending for power in our often immoral society and around the globe. Politics, then, must be seen as a self-interested struggle for power in which there are only "proximate solutions for insoluble problems."[2] In this struggle we may have to learn how to use wisely the insights and tools of the Children of Darkness: such insights as the inevitability of the struggle for power and the persistence of self-interest, and such tools as military, economic, and political power. We must also appreciate that the Children of Light, acting with the best of intentions, will not necessarily always do what is right, or achieve what they righteously seek. Balancing power with power may achieve some approximation of justice in this world, but never complete justice. Complete justice is only attained, for those with faith, in another domain. Of course, love, mercy, compassion, and faith remain to enlighten a realistic politics. They remain to prevent us from suc-cumbing to a callous or depraved cynicism or to the immorality of a ruthless Machiavellian politics. They remain to soften the harshness of political life.

So far so good! Given the hard and dreadful experience of the twentieth century, Niebuhr makes great sense. Domestically, entrenched, powerful capi-talistic forces—guarding their self-interest, their power, their profits—will not yield to sweet talk. Labor will have to organize and use its bargaining power against capital. Internationally, Hitler will not listen to sweet talk either. He, too, will seek to dominate if he can. Again power must be mobilized to combat power. If the conflict between labor and capital in America can be made to take place within a democratic and constitutional framework, with an approxima-tion of justice emerging from collective bargaining, the conflict with Hitler calls for armaments, support for nations resisting Hitler, and, eventually, war. In pluralist political communities with a democratic and constitutional tradi-tion, power may be used to balance power. Here a rough approximation of jus-tice may be hammered out within the democratic rules of the democratic game, a game in which a popular government may intervene to protect and advance legitimate interests lacking power. On the world scene, alas, such a democratic and constitutional community is lacking. Hence, a world govern-ment, although perhaps logically necessary, is practically impossible. Hence, an aggressive fascism, bent on military domination, must be resisted militarily and defeated. Moreover, communist expansion after World War II may have to be checked, when the risk of a third world war is not grave, and when Ameri-can national interests are truly engaged. Tough defensive measures may wisely involve political, economic, and military actions. But as we employ power to help the domestic weak or to oppose the expansionist global foe that poses a clear and present danger to our vital national interests, let us always keep in mind the dangers of our own good intentions. Let us not succumb to our own myths. Let us guard against the imprudence, the arrogance, the moral imperi-alism, the fanaticism of our own self-righteous power.

So the mature Niebuhr could emerge as a sagacious political philosopher, realistic and tough-minded and progressive on domestic issues, a founding father of Americans for Democratic Action in postwar America, as he had been a friend of labor, civil liberties, African Americans, and domestic reform ear-lier in his life. He could emerge, before World War II, as a father of political realism in foreign affairs, ever conscious of the need to protect the legitimate vital interests of the nation, clearly aware of the need for America to arm Hitler's foes and to fight and defeat the Nazi tyranny. He could remain an influ-ential voice of responsible realism after World War II, providing a perspective for the prudent use of American power in competition with the Soviet Union, with no illusions that the United Nations or a new world government could usher in utopia in the postwar world. And yet, in his last years, he could raise grave doubts about the wisdom of U.S. involvement in Vietnam because such involvement was not in our true national interest. And he could endorse the movement for fuller civil rights as an effort to do greater justice to those, especially African Americans, who lacked power in American society.

Niebuhr thus articulates a sane, sagacious, prudent, courageous, realistic political philosophy. He seems to understand so well the dangerous illusions of utopian, pacifist, naive liberal thought. Such thought ignores human sin, the frailty of human reason, and the reality of abuse of power. Although Niebuhr appreciates the need for a transcendent standard of judgment that can be brought to bear on politics, he perceives (as Marx could not) that the complete end of wage-slavery, alienation, egotism, and incomplete development could not be achieved in this world, and that there are real dangers in the attempt. Niebuhr suggests a balanced response: "Man's capacity for justice makes democracy possible; but man's inclination to injustice makes democracy necessary."[3] And Niebuhr insists that the constitutional principle be built into the very heart of democratic government: "It is the highest achievement of democratic societies that they embody the principle of resistance to government within the principle of government itself."[4] And so Niebuhr makes a case for the sense and legitimacy of democratic and constitutional government. All forms of government need to be on guard against injustice and need to provide a mechanism for redress of abuse of power. The "will to power" calls for sensible restraints on its legitimate exercise as well as safeguards against its abuse. The "will to live truly" is admirable insofar as one of its forms "is the desire to fulfill the potentialities of life . . . the realization of [a person's] own true nature . . . fulfillment in the lives of others . . . self-giving in relation to others."[5] But this will can also lead to evil if we are not careful; it can lead, ironically, to unintended evils, to "necessary" sacrifices in the name of a greater good. Niebuhr's counsel is thus a wise and salutary warning not only against authoritarians of the Left or Right, but also against a wide variety of do-gooders!

Critique of the Niebuhrian Perspective

Now what fuller critique of this very persuasive realistic Niebuhrian perspective is in order?

In my judgment, despite Niebuhr's healthy corrective to a wide variety of utopian, pacifist, liberal illusions, and despite his effort to incorporate a prophetic element in his own political philosophy, the balance that he too frequently strikes tends to diminish the liberating and transforming possibilities of the prophetic. Despite his own partially prophetic predilections, his variety of political realism too often leads to an emphasis on "proximate solutions," an emphasis that too frequently constitutes a too easy acceptance or a too generous toleration of existing politics and necessary evils. His variety of realism leads, I believe, to a failure (more noticeable, I concede, in some of Niebuhr's followers than in Niebuhr himself) to press even more vigorously on behalf of the least free, those who lack the power in a pluralist democracy to achieve Niebuhr's more tolerable balance of power. His variety of realism, despite his own recognition of the need to preserve a tension between *ought* and *is,* leads to a loss of power in that tension, to a loss of greater confidence in the legitimate transforming possibilities of politics, to a decline of prophetic imagination, and to a failure to achieve creative breakthroughs in politics.

Niebuhr's realistic position and its consequences stem—ironically—from Niebuhr's overemphasis on important truths about sin, pride, evil, power; about the stubborn persistence of diversity and conflict; about the naïveté and dogmatism of liberals, radicals, and pacifists convinced of the power of rational truth to prevail over stupid and oppressive self-interest; about the virtues of a philosophy of balance of power. Niebuhr and his followers (especially the less-sophisticated followers who forget Niebuhr's emphasis on the grandeur as well as the misery of our human radical freedom) are thus inhibited in exploring the possibilities of a genuinely radical politics that might be immune to Niebuhr's own legitimate criticism. Niebuhr had himself searched for such a genuine, but more substantial, radical politics in the late twenties and early thirties, and in important respects he championed it throughout his life, tragically limited by illness in his last years. So it is that Niebuhr to some extent, and some Niebuhrians more fully, fail to explore more creatively and courageously the possibilities of a more prophetic politics. Fundamentally, I suppose, they fail to explore the possibility of creative breakthroughs in politics because they are suspicious of bold, radical efforts to advance toward prophetic goals. They may deem these efforts foolishly utopian, not soundly prophetic. They are leery of procrustean efforts to shape a brave new world. They remain content to operate within the going democratic and constitutional system. The procrustean evils of Hitlerism and Stalinism make ordinary democratic and constitutional politics look very good by comparison—very safe and very sound. Some conservative followers of Niebuhr may be turned off by the possibility of creative breakthroughs in politics because they indiscriminately associate such bold efforts with radical modernity's betrayal of the wisdom of the prescriptive constitution. Crazy radical behavior by some in the 1960s and 1970s reinforced for these conservatives the sense and sobriety of the dominant forces of American democracy.

But is it possible to articulate a more prophetic politics that would avoid the real weaknesses and illusions of utopians, pacifists, radicals, and liberals to which Niebuhr has called our attention, and yet improve on the incomplete prophetic thrust in Niebuhr's political philosophy? Let me set forth next the commitments of a prophetic politics and continue my dialectical argument with Niebuhr and the Niebuhrians.

Toward a More Prophetic Politics

The commitments of prophetic politics are four in number: (1) a commitment to the universal applicability of such values as life, peace, freedom, justice, prosperity, excellence; (2) a commitment to fearless criticism of the existing order in light of these prophetic values; (3) a commitment to creative constitutional breakthroughs—to practical, sane action—to narrow the gap between prophetic values and existing reality; and (4) a commitment to continuous prophetic scrutiny and futuristic projection, via imaginative scenarios, in order to guard against future evils and to anticipate problems of even the best imaginable political order.[6]

Easier said than done! Let me, however, pursue my argument—my dialogue with Niebuhr—in order to suggest how a more prophetic politics (while respecting the sound ingredients in Niebuhr's political philosophy) can overcome what I believe are some disturbing shortcomings in Niebuhr's variety of political realism. Among the elements of Niebuhr's political philosophy that a prophetic politics must retain are the classic principles of constitutional government: a government that is limited in power (in the interest of freedom); responsible(in the interest of accountability); representative (in the interest of democracy); and sensitive (in the interest of staying in touch with legitimate human needs). Niebuhr is correct to emphasize that politics is wisely seen as seeking (I would add often if not always) "proximate solutions for insoluble problems." Given freedom, diversity, and conflict, democratic and constitutional accommodation—which attempts to strike a balance among contending interests—makes great sense. The need to guard against the abuse of power by tyrants must be matched by a recognition that, ironically, the road to hell is sometimes paved with angelic intentions.

And, of course, Niebuhr is correct to urge our recognition of human evil, of self-interest and power, of the weakness of human reason, and of the illusory natures of earthly harmony, perfectibility, and salvation.

Nonetheless, it seems to me that the Niebuhrian approach must be corrected in some respects so that we may avoid certain conservative consequences. These are the consequences, first, of a constitutional vision that is too limited; second, of a view of human nature that is too cribbed, of power too suspect, of a balance of power too trusting, of a science of politics too blind; and, third, of a statecraft too timid, inhibited, and sterile. Too great a concentration on human sin, weakness, and fallibility can lead, theoretically and psychologically, to a failure of vision, of creative imagination, and of social nerve. Too great a focus on the balance of power among contending interests can lead us to miss those whom Justice Hugo Black called the "poor, the ignorant, the numerically weak, the friendless, and the powerless,"[7] those who, because of their isolation and impotence, are invisible, who cannot compete easily in the struggle for power, and who therefore are often unable to affect public policies that are shaped so significantly by powerful organized group interests. Historically, our blindness to African Americans, Native Americans, women, and the poor has been notorious. A complacent, timid, frightened statecraft can easily be the outcome of both the lowering of our sights and our social-scientific blindness to the least free. A balance of power among organized and powerful interests will not do justice to the unorganized and the impotent. And in international politics, the balance of power—however much it may have (when rightly employed) historically preserved peace among the great powers—may not do justice to weak nation-states in conflicts between a great power and a weak one.

Let us take a somewhat fuller look at political realism in international affairs. Niebuhr, I believe, well illustrates political realism at its best. Moreover, he was quite aware of the reasons political realism did not always function at its best. In addition, he recognized—as a religious thinker in the Judaic-Christian tradition—that a standard other than the limited secular standard of the nation-state functions to judge the performance of political realists in this world.

Political realism at its best, as Niebuhr recognized, must seek to protect the genuine vital interests of the nation-state. It must also be attuned to the realities of power in its many dimensions and to the importance of the balance of power. And, above all, leaders of state must act prudently.

Niebuhr himself recognized, however, that leaders of state frequently depart from political realism at its best. They frequently lack the proper vision. They may succumb to idealistic illusions that can lead to political ineptness on one hand or foolish moral crusades on the other. They may also succumb to cynicism and a brutal and ruthless exercise of power. They normally focus (and understandably so) on protecting the vital interests of their own particular political community—their own nation-state—but frequently at the expense of other nation-states. Moreover, and ironically, leaders of state are handicapped by their own realistic social-scientific understanding of political realities. This is the understanding that stresses the crucial role of power and the balance of power. It is the understanding that highlights the historical complexities, genuine ambiguities, inevitable compromises, and admitted difficulties of living in the real world of politics, and of working out decent arrangements amidst the struggle for power. This understanding may inhibit more imaginative, more creative leadership. In addition, as a result of their narrow ethical vision and limited empirical understanding, leaders of state find it difficult to exercise prudent judgment in the present and in preparation for the contingent future.

Unfortunately, Niebuhr's own recognition of the reasons for the failure to achieve political realism at its best did not sufficiently encourage him to develop more fully a paradigm of prophetic politics that would serve to encourage leaders of state to achieve political realism at its best or to move, as necessary, beyond the limited perspective of political realism even at its best.

Consequently, Niebuhr, for the most part, stayed with the paradigms of political realism and the nation-state. To do so, unfortunately, is to accept too easily the narrow vision of protecting the vital interests of the nation-state. Leaders of state often seek such protection even to the detriment of the vital interests of other political actors in world politics: not only other nation-states, but other political actors such as functional organizations, international regimes, regional organizations, and such global organizations as the United Nations.

To stay with the paradigm of political realism creates a related problem. Political realists are limited by their inability to adjust more easily and generously to the important reality of the vulnerability, interconnectedness, and interdependence of nation-states in the contemporary world of international politics. These realities have had a shattering impact on the very ability of the nation-state to protect its own vital interests. It is not clear to me that the Niebuhrian variety of political realism—or, indeed, any variety of political realism—is yet adequately attuned to these important changes affecting the world of politics.

Finally, it is my judgment that the concept of prudence treasured by Niebuhrian political realists is neither imaginative enough, nor creative enough, nor bold enough, nor radical enough to respond to the changing world of politics.

For these reasons, I am arguing, we need to move beyond Niebuhrian political realism toward a more prophetic politics. This is most apparent in the domain of international politics, where the unparalleled opportunities for creative breakthroughs in politics are now most evident and vitally needed. But the move toward a more prophetic politics is also required in the domestic arena, not only in the United States, but also in other political communities around the globe. In the United States, for example, we urgently need breakthroughs on a number of crucial problems that we haven't so far been able to deal with satisfactorily—problems, for example, in the fields of employment, health, and welfare, not to mention persistent problems involving crime, drug addiction, racial and religious prejudice, a balanced budget, and a more responsible political system.

Such a prophetic politics, I believe, enables us to move beyond the political realism of ordinary democratic and constitutional politics at home. It also provides a standard in international politics for encouraging political realism at its best and, as necessary, for moving beyond even political realism at its best.

Such a prophetic politics is radical insofar as it takes seriously the prudent extension and universal applicability of prophetic values. What is involved here is a significant enlargement of the sphere of ethical concern, as well as a deepening of ethical concern within that larger sphere. It is radical, additionally, insofar as it searches more persistently for the fundamental ethical and scientific reasons for the gap between prophetic values and existing political realities; insofar as it focuses on sane and humane action—especially creative breakthroughs in politics—to diminish this disturbing gap; and insofar as it denies to even the best future human order an immunity to critical scrutiny as it simultaneously invites scenarios of imaginative futures.

Such a prophetic politics thus seeks to harness more fully the power of the prophetic idea in politics, as it explores the fuller meaning of that idea in politics. Religion, which suggested the root idea of the four commitments of prophetic politics, joins forces with a venerable philosophic, social-scientific, and scientific tradition to give fuller meaning and applicability to the prophetic idea in politics. Human beings are encouraged here on earth to build on the tested insights of the Judaic-Christian religious heritage, the enduring propositions of the noblest traditions of Western philosophy, and the prescriptive principles of democratic and constitutional government. Here I would emphasize that neither the rejection of naive utopianism nor the acceptance of wise Niebuhrian constitutional limitations means the repudiation of prophetic striving, especially the difficult search for creative breakthroughs in politics. Prophetic politicians can affirm with Niebuhr that we must strive toward heaven without ever being able to reach it in our earthly lives, but they will place greater emphasis on the striving than on the non-reaching. Similarly, adherents of prophetic politics can appreciate, as did Niebuhr, that we are required to stay out of hell on earth without the certainty that we can. This prophetic tension is the reality that we must learn to live with creatively: recognizing the tension, but committing ourselves to act vigorously to advance creative breakthroughs in politics.

Prophetic politics, I believe, represents an important shift in emphasis in comparison to the Niebuhrian perspective. It is not that the prophetic ingredient is absent in Niebuhr; it is that it is not properly emphasized and developed. The shift in emphasis is best seen in the prophetic insistence on effort, and particularly on effort to achieve creative breakthroughs in politics.

Great effort within legitimate limits—in articulating prophetic values, in criticizing the existing order, in seeking creative constitutional breakthroughs, in engaging in ongoing prophetic scrutiny, and in fashioning futuristic scenarios—is not simply permissible in prophetic politics. It is mandatory! The desirability of effort, trial, and experiment in seizing and shaping opportunities is rooted in the commandment in the prophetic tradition to fulfill prophetic values. Fulfillment demands both thought and action and opens up exciting vistas for the operation of human intelligence and will. Fulfillment makes mandatory a dynamic but sane view of politics, a strikingly democratic view, since we have no way of knowing for sure beforehand who will and who will not contribute to creative realization within the framework of the common good.

Limits to fulfillment (which, as Niebuhr has correctly warned us, are rooted in both our sinful natures and our failure to appreciate that good intentions alone are no safeguard against evil outcomes) are a reality that we ignore at our peril. Yet such limits provide no absolute discouragement to legitimate effort, for several good reasons.[8] First, we do not know, short of continued probing, the precise nature of the theoretical and practical limits to human realization. Second, we have by no means achieved the more favorable conditions for the expression of better-known potentiality that, currently, is obstructed by circumstances clearly capable of remedy. Third, if there is room and need for effort to advance human fulfillment, there is also need for effort to guard against retrogression and degeneration. Finally, humans must recognize, and compensate for, the deficiency involved in their tendency to fail to use their uniquely good and creative human talents and energies.

The Cold War tended to evoke a political realism that too often emphasized the negative—containing communism, using the power of nuclear weapons to deter the Soviet menace—and often led to questionable political and ethical policies, such as supporting authoritarian, anticommunist, right-wing regimes. Clearly, given the end of the Cold War, the time is ripe for a reassessment of political realism and its intellectual exponents, such as Reinhold Niebuhr. The time is ripe for a fresh look at the opportunities and problems we face, both internationally and domestically. The time is ripe for a reexamination of the oversimplified realist/idealist opposition. We need to see if the paradigm of prophetic politics, while including the sound elements in Niebuhr's political philosophy, can take us beyond the Niebuhrian model and help to respond more creatively to rare opportunities for building, not utopia, but a world freer of the scourge of war; political communities able to resolve their inevitable differences in peaceful and constitutional ways; a world of freer, more just, more prosperous, more ecologically healthy political communities.

Conclusion

We need, then, I am arguing, to move beyond Niebuhr toward a more prophetic politics.

In our critical assessment of Niebuhr we can wisely emphasize the radical and prophetic ingredients in his thinking. We cannot reject his understanding of the principles of love and justice, his appreciation of the powerful role of evil human nature in human affairs, his recognition of power and of social conflict, and his endorsement of the value of prudent constitutional accommodation.

We may, however, have to ask critical questions about the limitations of the perspective of political realism, especially, but not exclusively, in international politics. These are limitations that affect the vision of political realists, their fuller grasp—ironically—of the realities of international politics, and their frequently flawed prudential judgments. We may, moreover, have to reject those emphases in Niebuhr's realistic political philosophy that can lead his followers to accept too easily ethically questionable features of the rough, tough game of power politics, intolerable aspects of the status quo, the sometimes unjust operation of liberal democratic pluralistic politics, the frequent loss of that dynamic tension between *ought* and *is* that is so crucial for advancing creative breakthroughs in politics.

The time—in brief—is now especially ripe for a fresh look at the value and power of the prophetic idea in politics.

Notes

1. Beyond Niebuhr's own writings, a good place to begin a critical evaluation of his thought is Charles W. Kegley, ed., *Reinhold Niebuhr: His Religious, Social, and Political Thought* (New York: Pilgrim Press, 1984). This book first appeared in 1956 and includes a very valuable response by Niebuhr to his critics. It also includes a most helpful "Bibliography of the Writings of Reinhold Niebuhr." The 1984 edition contains updates by several of the contributors—e.g., John C. Bennett, Arthur Schlesinger Jr., and Kenneth W. Thompson. For more recent books, see Charles C. Brown, *Niebuhr and His Age: Reinhold Niebuhr's Prophetic Role in the Twentieth Century* (Philadelphia: Trinity Press International, 1992); Larry Rasmussen, ed., *Reinhold Niebuhr: Theologian of Public Life* (Minneapolis: Fortress Press, 1991); Kenneth Durkin, *Reinhold Niebuhr* (London: Chapman, 1990); Richard W. Fox, *Reinhold Niebuhr: A Biography* (New York: Pantheon, 1985); Richard John Neuhaus, ed., *Reinhold Niebuhr Today: Essays* (Grand Rapids, Mich.: Eerdmans, 1989); Richard Harries, ed., *Reinhold Niebuhr and the Issues of Our Time* (Grand Rapids, Mich.: Eerdmans, 1986). See also the perceptive assessments of Niebuhr in Ronald H. Stone, *Reinhold Niebuhr: Prophet*

to Politicians (Nashville: Abingdon Press, 1972); in Michael Joseph Smith, "The Prophetic Realism of Reinhold Niebuhr," chap. 5 in *Realist Thought from Weber to Kissinger* (Baton Rouge: Louisiana State University Press, 1986); in Joel H. Rosenthal *Righteous Realists: Political Realism, Responsible Power, and American Culture in the Nuclear Age* (Baton Rouge: Louisiana State University Press, 1991); and in John Patrick Diggins, "Power and Suspicion: The Perspectives of Reinhold Niebuhr," *Ethics and International Affairs*, 6 (1992): 141–61. For a perceptive Niebuhrian critique of mainline U.S. churches, see Allen D. Hertzke, "An Assessment of the Mainline Churches since 1945," chap. 2 in *The Role of Religion in the Making of Public Policy*, ed. James E. Wood Jr. and Derek Davis (Waco, Texas: Dawson Institute of Church-State Relations, 1991), 44–77.

2. The exact quotation, from which I have taken the quoted words, is as follows: "for democracy is a method of finding proximate solutions for insoluble problems." Reinhold Niebuhr, *The Children of Light and the Children of Darkness: A Vindication of Democracy and a Critique of Its Traditional Defenders* (New York: Scribners, 1960), 118.

3. Niebuhr, Foreword to *Children of Light,* xiii.

4. Quoted in Harry R. David and Robert C. Good, eds., *Reinhold Niebuhr on Politics* (New York: Scribners, 1960), 182.

5. Niebuhr, *Children of Light,* 19.

6. The paradigm of prophetic politics is developed more fully in Neal Riemer, *The Future of the Democratic Revolution: Toward a More Prophetic Politics* (New York: Praeger, 1984).

7. See *Chambers v. Florida,* 309 U.S. 227 (1940).

8. See Neal Riemer, *The Revival of Democratic Theory* (New York: Appleton-Century-Crofts, 1962), 84–85.

11

Intergenerational Justice and the Prophetic Tradition

Bruce E. Auerbach

The quest for intergenerational justice is among the best examples of the continued vitality of the prophetic tradition in the contemporary world. Intergenerational justice requires that our society become more universally just: that it consider not only the interests of existing persons, but also our obligations to past and future generations. The search for intergenerational justice requires a commitment to the higher value of justice and to a more universal application of that value. It requires that we critique both the comfortable politics of interest-group liberalism and the antigovernment politics of contemporary conservatives; and, ultimately, that we move beyond both dominant contemporary American political models.

The achievement of a more intergenerationally just world also requires creative breakthroughs. It has become apparent that despite, or even because of, our technological progress, the next generation may well face a planet that is more polluted and less safe for human existence than the one our recent ancestors inherited. Finally, a commitment to achieving intergenerational justice requires us to engage in futuristic projection. Without the ability to anticipate how our actions are likely to affect future generations, no meaningful pursuit of intergenerational justice is possible.

The contemporary interest in intergenerational justice represents a comparatively recent change in the thinking of Western nations in general and of the United States in particular. As recently as the 1960s, there was little discussion of intergenerational justice in the scholarly or popular literature.[1] In the ensuing decades, the concept of intergenerational justice has come to play an increasingly prominent role in our political thinking. As we have come to understand the toxic effects associated with our use of nuclear energy and chemicals such as DDT, academic interest in the question of intergenerational justice has grown. More recently, politicians, too, have begun talking about the question of justice to future generations.

Although the contemporary quest for a more intergenerationally just world unquestionably meets the definition of prophetic politics, there is some dispute as to how this quest fits into the prophetic tradition. Some thinkers argue either that the *problem* of intergenerational justice is new to the twentieth century or that the *concept* of intergenerational justice originated in the latter half of this century as a response to the unique problems of this century. Hans Jonas, for example, has argued that technology has so transformed and augmented humanity's powers as to open up a "whole new dimension of ethical relevance for which there is no precedent in the standards and canons of traditional ethics."[2] More recently, Peter Laslett and James S. Fishkin have argued that the concept of intergenerational justice, understood as "an obligation on all present persons to conduct themselves in recognition of the rights of all future persons, regardless of geographical and temporal position, . . . did not exist as a subject of analysis or discussion, or even as a concept, before the 1970s, or before the 1960s at the earliest."[3]

Although these thinkers do not attempt to place the quest for intergenerational justice within the prophetic tradition, it is clear that if they did, they would understand it as a search for new and superior values and public policies. They argue, and I agree, that the contemporary Western understanding of intergenerational justice as "an obligation on all present persons to conduct themselves in recognition of the rights of all future persons, regardless of geographical and temporal position"[4] is of recent origin and represents a morally desirable extension of contemporary understandings of justice. However, in contrast to these thinkers, I am convinced that the concept of intergenerational justice itself is not new. On the contrary, the concept of intergenerational justice has deep historical roots that date from the biblical prophets. The prophets understood intergenerational justice differently from us. For the prophets, intergenerational justice consisted primarily of the obligation, owed to God, to act justly in an intergenerational community. Despite the fact that our understanding of intergenerational justice is different from that of the prophets, the two understandings are sufficiently related that we can learn much about intergenerational justice from studying the prophetic writings.

If my argument is correct, it means that we have rediscovered, rather than invented, the concept of intergenerational justice. This fact does not diminish the importance of intergenerational justice for our era. Nor does it deny that intergenerational justice represents a superior ethical value for the late twentieth century. A value does not have to be invented in the twentieth century to be well tailored to the problems of this era.

My argument in this chapter focuses on establishing three major points. The first is that, contrary to the arguments of some contemporary thinkers, the concept of intergenerational justice is indeed a traditional concept with roots in the writings of the biblical prophets. Second, while contemporary understandings of intergenerational justice depart in significant ways from those of the prophets, our understandings also have much in common, most notably a concern with the effects of one generation's actions on future generations. Finally, while we cannot and should not seek to return to the conceptual framework of the biblical prophets, we can learn much from their understanding of intergenerational justice. Specifically, we would benefit greatly from adopting their understanding that we live in an intergenerational community.

The Historical Roots of Intergenerational Justice

We can trace the antecedents of our contemporary concern with the environment to biblical prohibitions against deforestation as a tactic of war (Deut. 20:19) and to the injunctions to allow the land to lie fallow every seven years (Exod. 23:10–11). Contemporary concerns with the effects of pollution on future generations have striking parallels to the concerns of the biblical prophet Jeremiah, who wrote that "the fathers have eaten sour grapes, and the children's teeth shall be set on edge" (Jer. 31:29).[5] More generally, we have inherited from the prophetic tradition an outlook toward nature and our fellow human beings that continues to influence our thinking on intergenerational justice and other ethical questions.[6]

An essential element in the biblical worldview was that membership in a community was the most important feature of the social and political world. The community was the conveyer of those values that made life worth living. The Hebraic community was based on membership in a tribe and on a shared history and covenant. Members of this community shared bonds that united them and that differentiated them from members of other communities. Members of a community shared habits and attitudes that developed when people were raised under similar conditions and shared common experiences.

Communities were understood to have an existence and a reality that extended beyond that of individual members of the community at any given moment. This was so in two senses. First, communities could perish even if the individuals who made up the community at any given time survived. Thus, if a people were conquered and dispersed or sold into slavery, the community would perish just as surely as if the city had been sacked and all the citizens killed. Second, communities were understood to be inherently intergenerational. Communities were made up not only of those alive at any given time, but also of those who had lived in the past and those who would live in the future. The intergenerational nature of community was not a mere abstraction; it was an essential part of what was meant by a community. Thus, the covenant that God made with Abraham extended not only to Abraham, but also to Abraham's descendants. The renewal of the covenant by successive generations was an essential part of fulfilling that covenant.

The prophets were concerned not only with the survival of Israel, but also with its health and justice. Indeed, the survival of the community and justice in the community were closely linked in the minds of the prophets, for justice was necessary for the long-term health and survival of the community. The prophets never ceased warning of the intergenerational consequences of injustice and of the benefits to the community of acting justly. For example, the prophet Jeremiah states, "[I]f you truly amend your ways and your doings, if you truly execute justice with one another, if you do not oppress the alien, the fatherless or the widow, or shed innocent blood in this place, and if you do not go after other gods to your own hurt, then I will let you dwell in this place, in the land that I gave of old to your fathers for ever" (Jer. 7:5–7).

Many of the specific injunctions of the Torah concern conduct that has an impact on future generations. As noted earlier, the Torah includes prohibitions against deforestation as a tactic of war and against cutting food trees for building siegeworks.[7] The Hebrew people also were prohibited from taking a bird and its chicks from a nest on the same day (Deut. 22:6–7). These prohibitions are complemented by affirmative obligations such as the requirement, previously noted, that the land be allowed to lie fallow every seven years (Exod. 23:10–11).[8] Together these prohibitions and injunctions indicate a concern with the impact of human actions on the natural environment that is comparable in many ways to contemporary concerns over the use of defoliants in war, with the impact of modern farming techniques on soil erosion, and with deforestation in the United States.[9] The biblical writers quite clearly were concerned with ensuring practices compatible with the long-term prosperity of their community.

The Torah also includes prohibitions and injunctions aimed at regulating policies that directly affect other human beings and other generations. For example, the Talmudic rabbis interpreted the biblical commandments regarding the conduct of war as prohibiting cutting off all paths of retreat when besieging a city.[10] War was not to be waged against future generations.[11] The Bible also enjoins fathers to teach their children to love and fear God (Deut. 6:1–9). These elements of biblical law are designed to ensure the perpetuation and survival of the intergenerational community that the covenant had established.

The most important function of the prophets was to admonish the Hebrew people to keep the covenant with God and to act justly. Their message was that if the Hebrew people did not mend their ways, they or their offspring would be punished by God. On the other hand, if the people did mend their ways, God would bless them and their descendants and restore them to prosperity.

An important characteristic of the biblical understanding is that reward or punishment for present actions was often understood to befall not only the present generation, but future generations as well. Thus in Exodus, God commands Moses:

> "I am the LORD your God, who brought you out of the land of Egypt, out of the house of bondage.
>
> "You shall have no other gods before me.
>
> "You shall not make for yourself a graven image, or any likeness of anything that is in heaven above, or that is in the earth beneath, or that is in the water under the earth; you shall not bow down to them or serve them; for I the LORD your God am a jealous God, visiting the iniquity of the fathers upon the children to the third and the fourth generation of those who hate me, but showing steadfast love to thousands of those who love me and keep my commandments." (Exod. 20:2–6)

The notion that future generations are punished or rewarded for the iniquities or righteousness of their ancestors is an essential element in the biblical understanding of the world. It was also profoundly troubling to some of the prophets. For example, in Ezekiel we read:

> Yet you say, "Why should not the son suffer for the iniquity of the father?" When the son has done what is lawful and right, and has been careful to observe all my statutes, he shall surely live. The soul that sins shall die. The son shall not suffer for the iniquity of the father, nor the father suffer for the iniquity of the son; the righteousness of the righteous shall be upon himself, and the wickedness of the wicked shall be upon himself. (Ezek. 18:19–20)

We see similar concerns expressed in the Book of Jeremiah in the form of a prophecy of a new covenant:

> "In those days they shall no longer say:
>   'The fathers have eaten sour grapes,
>   and the children's teeth are set on edge.'
> But every one shall die for his own sin; each man who eats sour grapes, his teeth shall be set on edge." (Jer. 31:29–30)

Although some of the prophetic writers were obviously troubled by the prospect of children being punished for the iniquities of their parents, the prophets recognized that the welfare of future generations, in fact, was tied to the justness of the present generation's actions. In this regard, the prophetic vision is not very different from our own concern that, unless we change our ways, future generations will inherit an environment rendered toxic by our pollutants.

However, an important difference between the biblical prophets' understanding of intergenerational justice and the contemporary understanding is that, for us, what makes a policy, such as the depletion of the ozone layer, intergenerationally unjust is precisely that future persons will be harmed by these actions. Indeed, only evidence that future generations might be harmed by the depletion of the ozone layer makes the elimination of chlorofluorocarbons (CFCs) a question of intergenerational justice. By contrast, for the prophets, a policy that caused ecological damage, thereby endangering future generations, would be unjust because it violated God's commandments by laying waste to the land and, in so doing, departed from the ways of righteousness. For us, the suffering of future generations is the evil, whereas for the prophets the failure to obey God's commandment was the evil, and the suffering of future generations was God's punishment for the iniquities of prior generations.

The biblical prophets' approach and most contemporary secular approaches to intergenerational justice also rest on different understandings of our relationship to posterity. The prophetic model assumes that the people care intensely about what happens to their community and their descendants. Indeed, the prophetic model assumes that people care at least as intensely about the fate of their descendants and their community as they do about their own fate. Otherwise, the prophetic warnings that God's punishment would fall on their descendants would not be an effective spur to action. For the ancient Hebrews, a prophecy that future generations would become "like strangers unto them" would have been a powerful condemnation of the actions of the present generation.

By contrast, few contemporary thinkers argue that we should, or do, care as much about future generations as we do about contemporary members of our community. Rather, most contemporary thinkers assume that our distant posterity will be strangers to us.[12] The understanding that future generations stand as strangers to us leads to the conclusion that we have more limited obligations to future generations than to our contemporaries. We generally recognize a greater obligation to promote the welfare of members of our family or our community than to promote the welfare of strangers. Indeed, even though the sense of community has been eroded greatly in the United States, we retain some vestigial understanding that the nation as a whole has an obligation to provide for the welfare of the poorest of our fellow citizens. By contrast, we recognize no comparable obligation to promote the welfare of those we consider to be strangers.

An extreme expression of the view that we have few obligations to future generations is found in the writings of Martin Golding, who argues that "one might go so far as to say that if we have an obligation to distant future generations it is an obligation not to plan for them."[13] More typical is the argument of Richard and Val Routley, who assert that

> to say that we are not responsible for the lives of future people does not amount to the same thing as saying that we are free to do as we like with respect to them, that there are no moral constraints on our action involving them. In just the same way, the fact that one does not have, or has not acquired, an obligation to some stranger with whom one has never been involved—that one has no responsibility for his life—does not imply that one is free to do what one likes with respect to him, for example to rob him or to pursue some course of action of advantage to oneself which could seriously harm him.[14]

According to most contemporary thinkers, our principal intergenerational obligation is to avoid acting in ways that harm future persons. Thus, the problem of intergenerational justice arises primarily when we become aware that our actions may cause such harm.

From the modern perspective, what is striking about the biblical prophets' understanding of intergenerational justice is that they did not conceive of the problem of intergenerational justice in terms of acting justly *toward* future persons. Certainly, this is not due to the failure of the ancient thinkers to be aware that the actions of one generation affect future generations. As we have seen, they understood quite well that the present generation's actions affect the welfare of posterity. Nor, clearly, were the prophets unconcerned with the welfare of future generations.

The prophets believed that if the survival and prosperity of the community were to be assured, the community must adhere strictly to the standards of justice. Communities that departed from those standards would inevitably suffer the consequences of their unjust actions. Those consequences might be felt by the present generation or by future generations. In either case, it was the community that would suffer God's punishment for its injustice. The biblical prophets did not conceive of the problem of intergenerational justice in terms of acting justly toward future persons or respecting the rights of future persons, primarily because they had a different understanding of the role of justice in the community. Their understanding linked the perpetuation of the community to the achievement of justice. For the prophets, intergenerational justice consisted primarily of achieving justice in an intergenerational community. They understood both justice and their community to be inherently intergenerational. In this sense, we might say that they had *an intergenerational conception of justice* rather than a separate and distinct conception of "intergenerational justice."

Many contemporary thinkers fail to recognize the ancient roots of the concept of intergenerational justice because they fail to recognize the prophets' understanding of "justice in an intergenerational community" as a legitimate and historically significant way of conceptualizing intergenerational justice. There is no doubt that the biblical prophets understood intergenerational justice differently from most contemporary thinkers; yet there is also little doubt that their understanding should be recognized as a concept of intergenerational justice.

Contemporary Understandings of Intergenerational Justice

We have seen that there are three important differences between the prophetic and contemporary approaches to intergenerational justice. First, the biblical prophets based the obligation to act justly on the religious duty to obey God's commandments. By contrast, most contemporary thinkers place the obligation to act justly on a more secular foundation. Second, the prophetic view of intergenerational justice was maximal in the sense that the prophets sought to ensure the future welfare of their community, Israel, in all its aspects. By contrast, most contemporary thinkers adopt a more limited understanding of our obligations to future generations, consistent with the belief that future generations will be strangers to us. More specifically, they focus on the obligation to avoid taking actions that might harm future persons. Finally, the biblical prophets sought justice in an intergenerational community. They conceived of both justice and their community as inherently intergenerational. By contrast, most thinkers who have written on intergenerational justice since the 1960s have abandoned the notion of an intergenerational community, focusing instead on the question of how our actions are likely to affect those *individuals* who will live in the future. This is to say that most contemporary understandings of intergenerational justice are based on person-affecting principles.[15]

A moral principle is a "person-affecting principle" if it considers to be morally relevant only the effects of actions on persons. Thus, an act would be considered wrong if, and only if, it harms some person. Conversely, an act would be considered good if, and only if, it makes some person better off. Actions that neither benefit nor harm persons, or actions that do not affect persons, are considered to be morally neutral. Most contemporary approaches to intergenerational justice are based on person-affecting principles insofar as they judge actions to be intergenerationally just if the effects of our actions meet our obligations to persons of remote generations, and intergenerationally unjust if the effects of those actions fail to meet our obligations to persons of remote generations. Unless present actions are likely to affect persons of other generations, contemporary theorists generally do not raise questions of intergenerational justice at all; nor do they raise questions of intergenerational justice unless they recognize us as having moral obligations to other generations in particular circumstances.

The central issue in the contemporary debate over intergenerational justice is the nature of our obligations to future persons. Thinkers from different schools of thought have dissimilar understandings of what we owe to future persons. Utilitarians argue that our obligations to future persons consist of acting in a manner that brings about the greatest amount of happiness (or good) for the greatest number of future persons. Thinkers in the individual-rights tradition argue that our obligation is to respect the rights of future individuals. Still others adhere to the view that we have an obligation to treat future persons as our equals.

The shift from a religiously based concern with community to a secular concern with obligations to individuals has a number of important consequences. One is that most contemporary thinkers are not concerned with the question of obligations to past generations. Our secular assumptions about the nature of life lead us to conclude that the actions of the living cannot affect those who have died.[16] While there is some debate among contemporary thinkers over the question of whether we can harm the dead,[17] the dominant view is that we cannot. Since person-affecting principles hold that actions that do not affect other persons are morally neutral, we are led to conclude that our actions can be neither just nor unjust to past generations.

Another important consequence of the shift from religious and community-based understandings of intergenerational justice to secular understandings is that by defining intergenerational justice as obligations to future persons, we enhance the probability of an opposition between the demands of justice and those of intergenerational justice. Future persons may have different interests from contemporaries. To give only one obvious illustration, it may be in the interest of the present generation to finance present consumption by long-term borrowing on the credit of the United States government, but it is most definitely not in the interests of future generations to inherit this debt.

While the traditional understanding of justice in an intergenerational community did not eliminate conflicts among generations, it tended to deny the imprimatur of justice to benefits that accrued to the present generation at the expense of posterity. By contrast, most contemporary understandings of intergenerational justice separate questions of justice and intergenerational justice and limit the latter to actions that affect future persons. This separation tends to diminish the salience of intergenerational justice to the present generation. This has potentially serious consequences. When presented with the conflicting demands of loggers (backed by lumber companies) for employment and of environmentalists for the preservation of the wilderness, it is easier for politicians to accede to the demands of present persons than to demands raised in the name of future generations.

A more subtle effect of the shift from traditional to contemporary understandings of intergenerational justice is to narrow what is meant by intergenerational justice. According to the contemporary view, in order to say that an action is intergenerationally unjust, we must be able to establish a link between that action and an undesirable consequence for some future person to whom we have an obligation. Unless we are concerned with how our actions will affect future persons or about whether our actions will meet our obligations to future persons, we do not raise questions of intergenerational justice. Thus, contemporary thinkers who are concerned about intergenerational justice focus typically on issues such as the effects of present energy policies on future generations or the effects of environmental pollution on future generations.

However, not all actions that shape the future of the human community take the form of actions that affect "actual but future" persons. Policies that seek to limit population size or alter the identity of future generations may do so by preventing the existence of certain categories of persons. Unfortunately, most contemporary understandings of intergenerational justice do not readily lend themselves to addressing the ethical issues that arise from our capacity to affect the size and the identity of the future population. One source of difficulty is that often it is not possible to describe the effects of our actions on population size and identity in terms of harms or benefits to future persons. The most dramatic example of this is that a nuclear war that exterminates the human species cannot be said to harm future persons, since no future persons would exist if such a war occurred. If we hold that the sole criterion by which we ought to judge intergenerational actions is the effect of those actions on actual future persons, then, by definition, a "species-exterminating" nuclear war could not be intergenerationally unjust.[18]

For similar reasons, it is not possible to understand the significance of actions that affect the identity of the future population exclusively in terms of benefits or harms to future persons. For example, we cannot explain why the Holocaust was intergenerationally unjust by focusing exclusively on the children and grandchildren of the survivors of the Nazi death camps or on the impoverishment of European culture that resulted from the destruction of the Jewish community in many parts of Europe. While the children and grandchildren of the survivors were affected by the experiences of their elders, and while European culture has been impoverished by the absence of a thriving Jewish community, neither is an adequate measure of the intergenerational impact of the Holocaust.

We also cannot explain why the Holocaust was *inter*generationally unjust by focusing on the harm done to the those who were exterminated in the Nazi death camps. While we can measure the *intra*generational injustice of the Holocaust in terms of what the Nazis did to its immediate victims, if we focus exclusively on the harm done to those who suffered and perished in the concentration camps, we ignore the intergenerational effects of the Holocaust. The purpose of the Nazis was not simply to kill individual Jews and other targeted peoples; it was to alter the identity of future generations by exterminating the Jewish people and other peoples. Unless we recognize this intergenerational dimension, we fail to comprehend the meaning of the Holocaust. To the extent that our moral understandings preclude us from assigning moral weight to such "missing victims,"[19] those understandings represent a poignantly inadequate foundation for a twentieth-century theory of intergenerational justice.

The fact that contemporary approaches to intergenerational justice have difficulty addressing the ethical dimensions of policies and actions that shape the size and the identity of the future population is especially ironic, for this century has seen a dramatic increase in our capacity to determine population size and identity. By no means should all methods of determining population size and identity be condemned. Birth control and genetic engineering may be used for both moral and immoral purposes. The role of ethical theory is to guide their use wisely. It is precisely here that most contemporary approaches to intergenerational justice let us down by limiting moral questions to those that affect "actual but future persons."

In many respects the prophetic understanding of intergenerational justice as justice in an intergenerational community was broader than the contemporary focus on future individuals. As a result, the biblical prophets' view actually may be better suited than contemporary understandings to address such twentieth-century evils as nuclear war and genocide and such twentieth-century technologies as birth control and genetic engineering.[20] The prophetic understanding of intergenerational justice included not only a concern with meeting one's obligations to past generations, but also with the present and future survival and development of the community. Since the community was seen as transcending the lives of the individual members and as giving meaning to those lives, actions that harmed the community were considered to be unjust.

A return to the understanding of intergenerational justice of the biblical prophets is not possible, and many people would not consider it desirable even if it were possible. A return is not possible because the traditional understandings of intergenerational justice grew out of a world and a worldview many contemporaries no longer share. An essential part of the biblical understanding of intergenerational justice was the belief that human beings occupied a special place in a divinely created and divinely ruled cosmos and the belief that

God punishes directly those who transgress his commandments. Relatively few contemporary thinkers understand the world in such theocratic terms.

The fact that we no longer accept the worldview of our ancestors does not mean we are incapable of reconciling and integrating a concern for justice to contemporaries with a concern for intergenerational justice. But it may mean that such a reconciliation is likely to be incomplete unless we move beyond the narrow view that intergenerational justice consists exclusively of not causing harm to future persons.

Toward a More Prophetic Understanding of Intergenerational Justice

A good place to begin the task of rethinking our understanding of intergenerational justice is by recognizing that there exists a close relationship between how we act toward future generations and whether future generations will have obligations to us. If the present generation acts justly and to the benefit of our descendants, our descendants are likely to value the traditions they have inherited from us and to recognize an obligation to build upon those traditions. By contrast, if we act selfishly and without consideration for how our actions will affect our distant descendants, those who inherit the planet from us are unlikely to recognize a moral obligation to preserve the institutions and practices they have inherited, or to honor our commitments.

It is true, of course, that it can make no difference *to us* whether distant future generations recognize an obligation to preserve our institutions and honor our commitments. But this does not mean it will make no difference *to future generations and their descendants* whether they find the institutions and commitments they will inherit worthy of preservation. By attempting to act justly toward future generations, we do more than seek to provide material benefits to future generations; we also establish the institutional and cultural foundations for a just intergenerational community. This should be our most important legacy to posterity.

An essential feature of a just intergenerational community is that remote generations recognize obligations to one another. We are responsible for how our actions will affect future generations and are obligated to consider their interests. What is much less widely accepted is that the present generation also has obligations to its ancestors. If past generations have sacrificed for our benefit—and if we have actually benefited from their actions—the most fundamental principles of comity require that we be grateful for those benefits.

The other side of the obligation to be grateful for the benefits we have received is that we should be prepared to criticize the failures of our ancestors or even to condemn their injustices. If the actions of our ancestors have proved to be harmful to us, or if past generations have acted without regard to their obligations to posterity, criticism, or even condemnation, is appropriate. Here, too, it cannot make any actual difference to distant past generations whether we condemn their actions as unjust. But the possibility that future generations *might* condemn the actions of their ancestors can serve to redirect the actions of a people concerned with the judgment of history.[21] Moreover, a willingness to criticize the failures of past generations is an essential part of living in an intergenerational community. Not only does such criticism serve as a cathartic, it also reminds us that our descendants will be affected by our actions, just as we have been affected by the actions of our ancestors.

While the questions of gratitude to, and criticism of, past generations present few conceptual problems, the question of repaying the debts we owe to our ancestors presents more difficulties. Because our actions cannot affect the dead, it is impossible for us to reciprocate directly either the benefits or harms we have received from past generations. On the other hand, *successive reciprocity* can exist among remote generations.[22] This is to say, the debts we owe our ancestors can be paid to our descendants, who in turn can repay to their descendants the debts they owe us.[23] In this manner, a truly intergenerational community can develop, in which the just actions of past generations bind future generations, not to the status quo, but to a tradition of intergenerationally just action.

However, we must go beyond merely recognizing the links between the existence of an intergenerational community and intergenerational justice. We must also recognize that the existence of an intergenerational community is a precondition for achieving intergenerational justice. Where an intergenerational community does not already exist, we should acknowledge an affirmative obligation to establish one. Where such a community does exist, we must seek to preserve and strengthen it.

The recognition that we have an obligation to establish or sustain an intergenerational community does not, by itself, determine the extent of our obligations to future generations, nor does it provide us much information about the nature of this intergenerational community. How we should define our intergenerational community is properly the subject of public debate, in the same way that how we define the social contract among contemporaries is an essential part of the political debate in every nation that aspires to popular sovereignty. The importance of recognizing an obligation to establish or sustain an intergenerational community is not that it provides us with a detailed blueprint for achieving intergenerational justice, but that it provides us with a moral framework by which we can understand, evaluate, and develop just intergenerational policies.

It is useful to contrast the minimal obligation to future generations that most contemporary theorists acknowledge with the more extensive understanding of our intergenerational obligations that I am advancing. Most contemporary theorists assert that our obligations to future generations are met if we avoid taking actions that are likely to cause harm to future persons. Clearly, this is an essential part of the meaning of intergenerational justice. However, to limit intergenerational obligations to avoiding harm to future persons is to treat future generations wrongfully as strangers to whom we have only minimal obligations. By contrast, I am arguing that we ought to understand future generations as standing in a very different relationship to us, namely, as members of our community, whose welfare we have an affirmative obligation to promote.

Our power to shape the future is too great to permit us to shirk or minimize our responsibilities by treating future generations as strangers to whom we have only the minimal obligation not to cause harm. If we are to act morally in the intergenerational sphere, we must accept that future generations are members of our moral community, and we of theirs. If our actions make it less likely that future generations will recognize us as members of their moral community, we should treat this, as the biblical prophets would have, as a powerful condemnation of our actions, and not as granting us license to ignore the needs and interests of future generations. The truest test of the morality of our intergenerational actions is future generations' recognition of those actions as just, and their recognition of us as their moral ancestors.

Any civilization that has an impact on its environment more enduring than its own life span must be concerned with the effects of its actions on future generations. Unless the present generation takes into consideration and gives due weight to the interests of future generations when framing its public policies, its actions will not be just to its descendants. While the obligations of future generations to their ancestors are more subtle, they are hardly less important. Unless future generations acknowledge, respect, and build upon the just intergenerational commitments of their ancestors, their actions may undermine their own ability to act justly toward their descendants. Little stock will be placed in the commitments of a generation that unjustly abrogates the commitments of its ancestors.

If our actions toward future generations are just, if we give due consideration to their interests and act toward them as toward members of our own community, future generations are likely (though not certain) to feel gratitude for our actions and an obligation to preserve the institutions and traditions that have served them well. On the other hand, if we ignore the interests of future generations and instead treat them as strangers to whom we owe little or nothing, future generations are likely to give us our due by reviling us and abandoning our institutions as unworthy of preservation.

If a community is a set of persons bound together by common understandings and mutual obligations, intergenerational justice requires that we seek to establish and preserve a truly intergenerational community. We do this by taking into consideration the interests of future generations when framing public policies, just as we take into consideration, or should take into consideration, the interests of contemporary members of our own community when framing present policies. While there is no guarantee that future generations will in fact see us as members of *their* intergenerational community, it is far more likely that they will do so if we treat them as members of *our* community to whom we have obligations and for whose welfare we bear some responsibility, than if we treat them as strangers for whom we have no obligations but the obligation not to plan.[24]

Indeed, under the present circumstances, to treat future generations as strangers for whom we bear no special moral responsibility and to whom we have no obligation but the obligation not to plan is to act in an intergenerationally unjust manner. For this view of posterity misrepresents the nature of our relationship to future generations, the extent to which our actions actually affect the future, and the extent of our responsibility for how our actions will affect the future. Future generations are neither our subordinates whom we are justified in treating as means to our own ends, nor strangers toward whom our only responsibility is not to cause harm. Rather, they are members of our extended community who will feel the effects of our actions. This does not mean that there is always an affirmative obligation to improve the conditions in which future persons will live. It is not intergenerationally unjust to tread lightly on the earth, limiting the effects of our actions to our remote generations as much as possible, and leaving the earth in essentially the same condition in which we found it.[25] Societies we call "primitive" have done so for hundreds of thousands of years.

However, we must appreciate that the time is long past when we have trod lightly on the earth. The effects of many of our actions will be felt by persons living centuries or even millennia from now. The burdens of environmental pollution, the rapid consumption of nonrenewable resources, and overpopulation will fall unjustly on future generations. Indeed, so profound are the effects of some of our actions (such as the decision to produce energy by nuclear fission) that they are certain to outlast our own community and be felt by generations who, in fact, will be strangers to us. To the extent that some present policies can be so characterized, we must conclude that these policies are intergenerationally unjust and ought to be reversed. Under modern conditions, there is no moral alternative to seeking to take into account the interests of future persons when framing our public policies, and seeking actively to shape the future in ways that promote the welfare of future generations.

Conclusion

My argument in this chapter has focused on establishing three major points. The first is that, contrary to the arguments of some contemporary thinkers, the concept of intergenerational justice is indeed a traditional concept with roots in the writings of the biblical prophets. Second, while most contemporary understandings of intergenerational justice depart in significant ways from those of the prophets, these understandings also have much in common. We have seen, for example, that the biblical prophets based the obligation to act justly on the religious duty to obey God's commandments, whereas most contemporary thinkers place the obligation to act justly on a more secular foundation. The prophets also had a broader concern with the welfare of future generations than do many contemporary thinkers, who accept the more limited view that our primary intergenerational obligation is to avoid harming future persons. A third difference is that the biblical prophets conceived of both justice and their community as inherently intergenerational, whereas most contemporary thinkers focus on the question of how present actions are likely to affect those individuals who will live in the future. Despite these differences, contemporary thinkers and the biblical prophets share a concern with how the actions of the present generation will affect the future, and a sense of moral outrage that the teeth of future generations will be "set on edge" by the iniquities of the present generation.

Finally, I have argued that while we cannot, and should not seek to, return to the conceptual framework of the biblical prophets, we can learn much from their understanding of intergenerational justice. Specifically, we would benefit greatly from adopting their view that we live in an intergenerational community whose welfare we have an affirmative duty to promote. If we do, there may yet be some hope that we will begin to act more justly toward past and future generations.

Notes

Parts of this chapter have been published previously in the author's *Unto the Thousandth Generation: Conceptualizing Intergenerational Justice* (New York: Peter Lang, 1995) and appear here with the permission of the publisher.

1. Ernest Partridge remarks on this fact in the introduction to *Responsibilities to Future Generations: Environmental Ethics,* ed. Ernest Partridge (Buffalo, N.Y.: Prometheus Books, 1980), 10.
2. Hans Jonas, "Technology and Responsibility: The Ethics of an Endangered

Future," in *Responsibilities to Future Generations*, ed. Ernest Partridge (Buffalo, N.Y.: Prometheus Books, 1980), 23.

3. Peter Laslett and James S. Fishkin, "Introduction: Processional Justice," in *Justice between Age Groups and Generations*, ed. Peter Laslett and James S. Fishkin. (New Haven: Yale University Press, 1992), 14–15.

4. Ibid.

5. All biblical citations are from the Revised Standard Version.

6. Among the more important perspectives we have inherited from the Hebraic traditions is the notion that human beings have dominion over nature.

7. "When you besiege a city for a long time, making war against it in order to take it, you shall not destroy its trees by wielding an axe against them; for you may eat of them, but you shall not cut them down. Are the trees in the field men that they should be besieged by you? Only the trees that you know are not trees for food you may destroy and cut down that you may build siegeworks against the city that makes war with you, until it falls" (Deut. 20: 19–20).

8. The principal stated purpose of the injunction to allow the land to lie fallow every seventh year is to feed the poor. The secondary stated purpose is to allow wild beasts to eat.

9. See Charles E. Little, *The Dying of the Trees: The Pandemic in America's Forests* (New York: Viking, 1995).

10. George Horowitz, *The Spirit of Jewish Law* (New York: Central Book Co., 1973), 150–51.

11. The exception to this rule is that the Hebrew people were commanded to exterminate the seven original tribes of Canaan so "that they may not teach you to do according to all their abominable practices which they have done in the service of their gods and so to sin against the Lord your God" (Deut. 20:18). As Horowitz points out, this was never carried out. Horowitz, *Spirit of Jewish Law*, 117.

12. See, for example, Martin P. Golding, "Obligations to Future Generations," in *Responsibilities to Future Generations*, ed. Partridge, 61–72; Terence Ball, *Transforming Political Discourse* (New York: Basil Blackwell, 1988), 143–60; and Richard Routley and Val Routley, "Nuclear Energy and Obligations to the Future," in *Responsibilities to Future Generations*, ed. Partridge, 277–301.

13. Golding, "Obligations to Future Generations," 69–70.

14. Routley and Routley, "Nuclear Energy," 284.

15. Derek Parfit, *Reasons and Persons* (Oxford: Clarendon Press, 1984), 393–95.

16. Some contemporary religions, among them Catholicism, hold that it is possible to intercede with God on behalf of the dead through prayer.

17. Among the contemporary thinkers who argue that the actions of the present generation can harm the dead are Barbara Baum Levenbook, "Harming Someone after His Death," *Ethics* 94 (1984), 407–19; Joel Feinberg, *Harm to Others*, vol. 1. (New York: Oxford University Press, 1984); Joel Feinberg, "The Rights of Animals and Unborn Generations," in *Responsibilities to Future Generations*, ed. Partridge, 139–50; George Pitcher, "The Misfortunes of the Dead," *American Philosophical Quarterly* 21 (1984),

183–88; and John O'Neill, "Future Generations: Present Harms," *Philosophy* 68, no. 263 (January 1993), 35–51.

18. Needless to say, the judgment that nuclear war is not *inter*generationally unjust does not imply that it is not *intra*generationally unjust. As Carl Sagan argues in "Nuclear War and Climatic Catastrophe: Some Policy Implications," (*Foreign Affairs* 62 [Winter 1983]: 291–92), even a relatively limited nuclear war could extinguish human life on this planet. The deaths of billions of noncombatants in a war that cannot be won is properly condemned as unjust.

19. While the term "missing victim" lacks analytic rigor, in the sense that those who are never born cannot be *actual* victims, the concept of a missing victim does have the heuristic value of calling our attention to the fact that some actions wrongfully prevent the existence of future persons, thereby creating a real "demographic deficit." It is true that the term "missing victims" cannot refer to identifiable hypothetical individuals, but it is also important to differentiate between (1) actions that affect the identity of the future population randomly or in a nondiscriminatory manner and (2) actions that effectively and wrongfully prevent the existence of future people in a specific demographic category.

20. Unlike nuclear war, genocide was not invented in the twentieth century. However, genocide does seem to have become an epidemic in the twentieth century.

21. On the other hand, an almost obsessive concern with how history would view him did not prevent the late President Richard Nixon from obstructing justice or from committing what amount to war crimes in Southeast Asia.

22. For a discussion of the applicability of successive reciprocity to questions of intergenerational justice, see John Rawls, *A Theory of Justice* (Cambridge: Harvard University Press, 1971), 284–93.

23. It is noteworthy that only the benefits we have received from past generations can be repaid justly to future generations. It would be unjust for us to harm future generations as "repayment" for the harm past generations might have caused us.

24. See Golding, "Obligations to Future Generations," 69–70.

25. In his *Theory of Justice,* John Rawls takes the opposite position, arguing that there is an obligation to save for future generations so that they may enjoy greater liberty than we (284–93).

12

The Prophetic Mode and Challenge, Creative Breakthroughs, and the Future of Constitutional Democracy

Neal Riemer

What light does the prophetic mode shed on the key problems of constitutional democracy? How can we respond wisely to the prophetic challenge? What model of politics may sensibly guide those concerned with the future of the constitutional democracy in the twenty-first century? What argument can be made on behalf of the guiding model of prophetic politics? These questions are particularly provocative as we approach a new millennium—the twenty-first century. A brief summary and critique of four competing political models— Machiavellian politics, utopian politics, liberal democratic politics, and prophetic politics—may help us as we seek to respond to these questions. I argue that the models of Machiavellian, utopian, and liberal democratic politics are, at best, inadequate, and, at worst, disastrous; that the model of prophetic politics—a superior democratic and constitutional politics—while true to its own commitments, can successfully incorporate the strengths and avoid the weaknesses of the other models.[1]

I reinforce my argument by highlighting the reality of creative breakthroughs in politics (past and present) in the tradition of prophetic politics and by exploring a prophetic scenario for a possible future creative breakthrough.[2] Historical and contemporary creative breakthroughs demonstrate that it is possible to do more than merely articulate prophetic values and criticize existing society and politics in light of those values. It is also possible to achieve significant constitutional breakthroughs, breakthroughs that succeed in sensibly resolving momentous problems that the "realistic" conventional wisdom declares incapable of resolution. Moreover, my examination of a proposed future breakthrough suggests that continuous prophetic scrutiny and futuristic projection, often criticized as utopian by Machiavellian realists and realistic liberal democratic politicos alike, not only are required by the model of prophetic politics but also are crucial to the continued health of constitutional democracy around the globe. Past and present creative breakthroughs, I argue, underscore the proposition that we must keep an open mind on the probability of the possibility of future break-throughs.

Machiavellian Politics: The "Lion and Fox" Politics of the Nation-State

Machiavellian politics is characterized by a supposedly "realistic" ethical commitment to the protection of the vital interests of the nation-state—its independence, security, power, and prosperity. It is based on a supposedly "scientific" recognition of politics as a struggle for power among contending interests. It is characterized by policy judgments that require statesmen to be beasts as well as men and to be both lions and foxes in the conduct of the affairs of state; that is, to be prepared, as circumstances warrant, to use both force and craft in protecting the vital interests of the state.

This model has much to offer those who seek a wise guiding model. It underscores the need to protect the genuinely vital interests of our own political community; to understand the character of the eternal struggle for power that is politics; and to avoid the confusion of *ought* and *is* in the formulation of policy. These strengths (which are normally evident in the foreign policy of any sensible nation-state and can be seen at work in domestic policy as well) are, however, offset by the weaknesses of Machiavellian politics. And these weaknesses raise doubts about the wisdom of its adoption as a model for the future. For example, Machiavellian politics is often characterized by idolatrous worship of the nation-state and of the narrow, parochial, short-sighted interests of the local political community. The practitioners of Machiavellian politics must often lower their ethical sights in order to make their objectives achievable. This amounts to a loss of civilizing vision in both theory and practice. The Machiavellians, moreover, do not hesitate to use brutal force and to employ the worst excesses of craft to achieve national security and to protect other alleged vital interests. In recent American history—to select one nation for purposes of illustration—Vietnam and Watergate point out dramatically the weaknesses of Machiavellian politics, and particularly a wrongheaded understanding of the meaning of a nation's vital interests.

We must conclude, then, that Machiavellian politics, despite some undoubted strengths, is, on balance, deficient. At best it may protect the vital interests of the nation, but at the expense of other peoples and nations. At worst, Machiavellian politics threatens to destroy both the nation and the globe.

Utopian Politics: The Harmonious Politics of Earthly Salvation

Many critics are tempted to flee from Machiavellian politics to some version of utopian politics. This model of politics is characterized by the dream of earthly salvation, of the harmonious state, of the conflict-less society. The Marxist conception of the communist society is the most influential illustration of this model in the modern world.[3] The harmonious community has a "scientific" foundation. Utopian thinkers hold that utopian politics can be brought about by an elite, in touch with the Truth, and able to "educate" a malleable people. This pattern is illustrated not only by Communist Party leaders but also by the philosopher-kings, Grand Inquisitors, and Fraziers of the world of literature and politics.[4] After utopia has been achieved, the need for significant judgment in politics declines.

The strengths of utopian politics are considerable: an inspiring conviction of a better world; a plan for the present; confidence in the truthfulness, fruitfulness, and power of the utopian dream. However, serious weaknesses undermine its strengths. These include (1) a defective vision, which manifests itself in a maddening pride, a tendency to hubris; (2) a serious divorce from reality, illustrated by the loss of a sense of the existent, of power, of the possible; and (3) a loss of prudent judgment, seen in the utopian's failure to calculate costs and to perceive the need for a democratic and constitutional order in utopia. In attempting to fulfill utopian ideals, utopians are tempted to violate the very traditions of civility they profess to honor and, ironically, to succumb to Machiavellian tactics of "lion and fox." Troublemaking poets will be banned from the harmonious republic. Dictatorship will be necessary for the transition to the classless communist society. Miracle, mystery, and authority will be required to overcome unhappiness brought on by the burden of freedom. The gospel of operant conditioning, as practiced by a scientific savior, will usher in the new Garden of Eden. Other utopians, confronted by the difficulty of achieving the reign of harmony, become disillusioned with the real world of conflict, and desert politics entirely.

And it is even the case that some aspects of the perfectly harmonious society—for example, the decline of judgment in a world without sin—might prove to be undesirable, and deadly dull. My allusions have already identified several varieties of utopian politics: platonic, old (Marxist) Left, old (authoritarian) Right, Skinnerian (*Walden Two*). Other varieties abound. They all share a conviction of the need for the triumph of the true faith against its benighted foes.

A critical assessment of utopian politics leads to a gloomy set of conclusions: (1) Certain utopian ends may not be desirable. (2) Even if utopian politics is desirable, it is not achievable. (3) Even if utopian politics is desirable and achievable, the cost of its achievement may be too high. (4) The serious utopian is confronted with bleak alternatives: disillusionment, impotence, costly sacrifice!

Liberal Democratic Politics: The Conservative Politics of Pluralistic Balance

Can we, however, avoid jumping from the frying pan of Machiavellian politics into the fire of utopian politics by adopting liberal democratic politics—what we might also call ordinary constitutional politics? Will such a politics enable us to protect the genuinely vital interests of the political community while still holding open the possibility of sane fulfillment of at least some defensible utopian ideals?

Superficially, the answer seems to be affirmative. Those who believe in liberal democratic politics—as illustrated, for example, by the United States—are dedicated to the "more perfect union." They are committed to balancing liberty and authority. They are convinced that we must see politics as a civilizing process. They believe that they have succeeded in establishing, in an imperfect world, a government that is limited, representative, responsible, and popular—no mean achievement! Such a government does guard, with reasonable success, against arbitrary power. It does seek to balance responsibility to God, nation, people, interests, local communities. It does realistically perceive the legitimate appeals of conscience, people, party, and the need to balance these in the pursuit of justice. Those who practice liberal democratic politics see the well-established need to umpire the struggle for power according to sound rules that have emerged from our historical constitutional experience and have been ratified over time by a fundamentally sound electorate. They acknowledge the inevitable need to balance competing equities in politics. They appreciate the well-grounded need to cultivate and exercise wise judgment on public policy issues in the absence of The Truth that all agree is the only standard in politics. Moreover, some twentieth-century theorists, in the pluralist and scientific tradition, argue that they have been able to overcome what they hold to be the unrealistic and utopian views of Enlightenment democrats. Wise democratic leadership can compensate for a foolish reliance on popular participation by inevitably uninformed and passionate voters. Public policy in the public interest is wisely hammered out amidst the pushes and pulls of contending interests. And a reformed welfare state, a regulated capitalism in a "mixed economy," can respond wisely to human needs and keep an exploitative economic system and defective welfare policies under control. In these ways, we can sensibly cease to worry about popular participation, the common good, and economic and social justice.

Thus, the strengths of liberal democratic politics seem to be considerable. This pattern strikes a needed balance between individual freedom and the community's interests. This model operates to overcome the worst features of both Machiavellian and utopian politics and to incorporate their strengths. It recognizes both the strengths and weaknesses of self-interest. It incorporates a capacity for realistic reform. It provides an arena—an open society—for human fulfillment. It makes constitutional government a living reality. These are great and historic achievements.

However, a more candid, and more incisive, assessment of liberal democratic politics calls our attention to a number of crucial weaknesses: its limited ethical vision, its deficient empirical understanding, and its timid, conservative appraisal of problems and "proximate solutions."

(1) Liberal democratic politics—and here I have in mind both "conservatives" and "liberals" in the liberal democratic tradition—is too often complacent about its own ethos and processes. It is too tolerant of existing evils. It lacks a powerful vision of a more desirable future. It is too often the politics of rich, powerful, white men. (2) Despite rhetoric about change and reform by "conservative" or "liberal" politicos, liberal democratic politics, almost obsessed with the idea of pluralistic balance, is inclined to favor the status quo, the existing powerful forces, and to ignore weaker, recessive forces—especially the "least free," particularly poor people, nonwhite people, women. Consequently, the practitioners of liberal democratic politics have a deficient scientific understanding of past, present, and future. Their understanding of change, and what it may take to emancipate those who are genuinely among the least free, is especially deficient. (3) From the perspective of wise practical action, and despite rhetoric about change, those engaged in liberal democratic politics are too conservative, too hesitant, too slow in a world where, at crucial times, more radical, decisive, and speedy judgments are required. Liberal democratic politicians, by and large, no longer illustrate a desirable tension between what "ought to be" and "what is" in their outlook and judgment. In the United States, for example, such liberal democratic politicians are to be found in both major parties and among 99 percent of our politicos.

On balance, then, although liberal democratic politics is a great historical achievement—and one that should not lightly be undercut—it is not good enough for the fulfillment of the democratic revolution in the twenty-first century. Its weaknesses suggest that we can do better. The dangers of the proliferation and misuse of nuclear weapons, the still onerous burden of armaments, the continuing ugly reality of genocide, the plight of the least free (in America and throughout the world), the persistence of poverty around the globe, ecological malaise, and the failure to improve the quality of our lives in all areas—

these factors suggest that we can do better in the arenas of peace, human rights, economic justice, ecology, and excellence.

Prophetic Politics: The Radical Politics of Life, Growth, and Fulfillment

Prophetic politics is characterized by four major commitments: (1) to values of a superior domestic and universal order; (2) to fearless criticism of existing political orders (in light of the prophetic paradigm); (3) to creative constitutional breakthroughs (to narrow the gap between prophetic paradigm and contemporary reality); and (4) to continuous prophetic scrutiny and futuristic projection via imaginative scenarios (in order to anticipate and cope with present and future problems and to ensure our future political health).

These commitments owe a great deal to biblical prophets and to the Judaic-Christian religious tradition. They also owe a debt to Greek philosophy and the tradition of natural law, each of which developed independently of the Judaic-Christian tradition, and yet linked up with that religious tradition in Western thought. They also owe a great debt to those movements of philosophical, social, and political thought we call the Enlightenment as it encapsulates, and brings to fulfillment, aspects of a superior constitution in theory and practice. Finally, they owe a great deal to modern science and our long tradition of social science as tools for human understanding, social criticism, and human prognosis.

Superior Ethical Vision

First, prophetic politics is characterized by a superior ethical vision. Although this vision is currently perceived only by some, it is nonetheless a vision capable of influencing all people. In this sense, the vision is universal and applicable to all people. Unlike Machiavellian politics, prophetic politics does not stop with the protection of the vital interests of the nation-state. Unlike utopian politics, the outlook of prophetic politics, although it seeks shalom, does not assume the achievement on earth of complete harmony, of universal salvation, and of human and social perfection. Unlike liberal democratic politics, prophetic politics is not so enamored of the existing order that it is inhibited in battling on behalf of peace, freedom, justice, prosperity, and excellence. Its vital interests are the vital interests of all peoples—not simply of the rich, of the powerful, of whites, of men. But it believes these vital interests are best secured within the framework of a superior democratic and constitutional order. This order requires the maximization of self-government in all spheres of human activity. It requires attention both to human needs and human fulfillment *and* to a common good that involves the future as well as the present; and it demands superior patterns of accommodation between individual and group interest and such a common good. This order also looks to sound experimentation to determine the worth of current and proposed social, economic, and political principles, institutions, and practices. The standard for judgment in this superior democratic and constitutional order is civilized life, healthy growth, and creative fulfillment.

Fearless Criticism of the Existing Political Order

Second, prophetic sensitivity opens up exciting ethical and scientific vistas. A sensitivity to the least free requires criticism of all political orders—whether liberal democratic, socialist, capitalist, communist, Western or Eastern, Third World or Fourth World, white or black or brown—in which the least free are struggling for emancipation and fulfillment. Prophetic criticism involves several most difficult and exacting tasks: clarifying and justifying the standards, values, norms, and rules that orient ethical and empirical investigation and permit meaningful appraisal; exploring the necessary and sufficient conditions of human life, peace, freedom, justice, prosperity, ecological health, and excellence; formulating the social-science theory that enhances understanding and explanation. It is particularly important to understand the gap between prophetic standard and contemporary reality, and the reasons for this gap. And it is crucially important to understand the process of sensible constitutional change and to examine and then choose from well-articulated alternatives for human action. Such a theory of criticism is characterized by a more realistic, and yet a more generous, understanding of political reality: of what has been, of what is, and of what can be. Political life is to be understood in terms of our purposes and rules as well as our actual behavior. Political life is to be understood, too, in terms of political becoming as well as political being. Such criticism thus points toward possibility (and probability) as well as toward impossibility (and improbability). Perfect earthly harmony and secular salvation are impossible, but a more prophetic world order is not. An earthly hell is quite possible, but so is human effort to avoid the degradation or destruction of the human race. Conflict may be ineradicable, but success in overcoming the most disastrous conflicts is possible. The probability of movement toward a superior democratic and constitutional order always remains to be tested.

As prophetic values set the stage for prophetic criticism, so prophetic criticism sets the stage for constitutional action and for creative constitutional breakthroughs in politics.

Creative Constitutional Breakthroughs

Third, those committed to prophetic politics are committed to creative constitutional action to narrow the gap between prophetic paradigm and contemporary reality. Long before Marx, the biblical prophets demanded action to change the world, action based on prophetic values and rooted in covenantal commandments. In Western thought, the covenant at Sinai has served as a prototype of all sound constitutions. We have inherited the tradition of action that must be creative, sane, superior, constitutional. Such actions, at their most significant, we might properly call creative breakthroughs in politics.

By a creative breakthrough in politics I mean a significantly fruitful resolution of a major problem. The breakthrough produces a momentous change in outlook and behavior. It results in our fuller understanding of political values; in our deeper understanding of patterns of cooperation, accommodation, and conflict; and in our more thorough understanding of the possibilities of public policy. The major problems are the familiar ones of war and peace, of liberty and authority, of majority rule and minority rights, of national sovereignty and a global common interest, of self-interest and the public interest, of poverty and prosperity. The success of the breakthrough is always measured in the light of its ends, its means, and its fruits. Wisely employed, creative breakthroughs can be attempted with minimum defections to the weaknesses of Machiavellian, utopian, and ordinary liberal democratic constitutional politics.

Prophetic breakthroughs are invariably a response to troublesome problems that seem to defy resolution. They are problems that the political priests of the existing order are not able to cope with. Today we do not have trouble identifying the problems. Can we safeguard the very life of mankind on earth? Can we obtain a more secure peace between sovereign nation-states, within a framework of freedom, and at a sensible cost? Can we move toward a superior global constitutional order? Can we achieve a global human rights regime capable of protecting against genocide? Can we advance political freedom and economic justice in all political and economic orders? Can we achieve a healthy ecological balance around the globe? Can we more generously sustain the pursuit of excellence—in moral virtue as well as in scientific and literary achievement—in mass societies? These questions suggest that there is much to be done in moving beyond the weaknesses of the sovereign nation-state system, of liberalism and socialism, of capitalism and communism. And there is much to be done in moving beyond societies too frequently characterized by violence, crime, drug addiction, irresponsible family life, and too often satisfied with mindless mediocrity.

These questions anticipate the creative breakthroughs required: (1) the breakthrough to a global community that is constitutional, democratic, and equipped with minimal but effective powers (in the interest of civilized survival); (2) the breakthrough to national and local political communities that can significantly enhance the well-being of the least free (in the interest of healthy growth); and (3) the breakthrough to a higher standard of excellence in all spheres of human endeavor (in the interest of moral and creative fulfillment).

Although too rare, creative breakthroughs in politics have occurred, and are still occurring. These breakthroughs are never perfect in the sense that they usher in a perfect world. But they do lead to momentous consequences. Thus, at least in certain areas of the world, the breakthrough to religious liberty puts an end to religious persecution, religious warfare, and an unhealthy connection of church and state. The breakthrough to the extensive republic enables the United States to reconcile liberty and large size. The breakthrough to European Union helps to ensure fifty years of peace, prosperity, and constitutional government in Western Europe. Let us examine a few of these creative breakthroughs to illustrate concretely that a more prophetic politics is not a utopian illusion; that we need not be resigned to a cynical Machiavellian realpolitik; and that we need not be inevitably stuck in the often limited conventional wisdom of ordinary constitutional politics.

Roger Williams and Religious Liberty. Roger Williams illustrates splendidly a seventeenth-century breakthrough.[5] The very real problem that Roger Williams faced was this: Is it possible to reconcile the ideal of religious orthodoxy (the belief that there is only one true faith) and political order (premised on acknowledgment of the one true faith) with the facts of religious diversity, religious persecution, and political conflict? The conventional wisdom affirmed that there was only one true religious faith and that it was the duty of the secular state to enforce that true faith, even if it meant intolerance, persecution, and sometimes war! The reality of life in Williams's seventeenth century was, however, characterized by a splintering of Christian faith and by religious and political battles about what religious group—Catholic or Protestant, and what Protestant denomination—possessed the true faith and had the power to enforce it. The reality, moreover, was religious persecution, political disorder, and warfare.

Hugo Grotius, writing in 1625 in the midst of the devastating Thirty Years' War (a war not unconnected to religious divisiveness), had protested the "license in making war of which even barbarous nations would have been ashamed." James Madison in 1784 would deplore the "[t]orrents of blood . . . spilt . . . in vain attempts of the secular arm to extinguish religious discord." Jefferson, in his *Notes on Virginia,* would note: "Millions of innocent men, women and children, since the introduction of Christianity, have been burnt, tortured, fined, imprisoned; yet we have not advanced one inch toward uniformity." In 1947 the U.S. Supreme Court, in the *Everson* case, would comment eloquently: "The centuries before and contemporaneous with the colonization of America had been filled with turmoil, civil strife, and persecution, generated in large part by established sects determined to maintain their absolute political and religious supremacy. With the power of government supporting them, at various times and places, Catholics had persecuted Protestants, Protestants had persecuted Catholics, Protestant sects had persecuted other Protestant sects, Catholics of one shade of belief had persecuted Catholics of another shade of belief, and all of these had from time to time persecuted Jews. In efforts to force loyalty to whatever religious group happened to be on top and in league with the government of a particular time and place, men had been fined, cast in jail, cruelly tortured, and killed."[6]

Williams's breakthrough occurs when he denies a key premise of the conventional wisdom—namely, that it is the duty of the secular rulers in the political community to enforce the true faith in this world. Williams argued on behalf of religious liberty (and democratic governance) on religious and political grounds. Christ, the Prince of Peace, did not come into the world to coerce consciences. Judgments on religious truth and behavior should not be made by earthly rulers in this mortal life, but by God in another life. Moreover, enforcement of the supposedly true religious faith by secular rulers produced disorder, conflict, war in the political community—a way of life incompatible with Christ, the Prince of Peace. The sensible alternative, Williams argued, was religious liberty, separation of church and state, and democratic governance—not religious persecution, linkage of church and state, and authoritarian rule. Williams, moreover, put his alternative into practice in what was to become Rhode Island; and in time this alternative became a crucial part of the First Amendment and the American constitutional order.

Reflection on this creative breakthrough strongly suggests the need in politics—and in political science—to be open to, and willing to test, new possibilities for living together better in the political community. James Madison was another person willing to test such new possibilities.

James Madison and the "Extensive Republic." James Madison, in the American generation of 1776–87, illustrates a brilliant creative breakthrough at the very beginning of our history as a nation.[7] He, too, illustrated unmistakably that creative breakthroughs in politics are possible. The problem that faced James Madison in 1787 was this: Is just republican government in a large state possible? Could one maintain free, strong, and popular government in the huge expanse of the American domain? This problem illustrated the two horns of a terrible dilemma: *either* a despotic empire as a necessity of government in a large state, *or* faction, injustice, and weakness as the inevitable outcome of a confederate republic with major power residing in the thirteen states. What Americans wanted—just and strong republican government in a large state—seemed to the conventional wisdom to contradict the evidence of history and the testimony of political philosophers. According to the conventional wisdom, the political science of the day, republican government (based on popular self-government and liberty) was possible *only* in a small political community (e.g., Athens or Venice or Geneva). But, alas, the new United States was a large state! Moreover, according to the conventional wisdom, a large state could be governed *only* under the authority of a monarch or a despot and within the framework of a nonrepublican empire, one clearly incompatible with the self-government and liberty that Americans had fought their revolution to secure. Anything less than such republican self-government and such republican liberty was a state of affairs that good American republicans could never accept!

What to do? Others had refused to face up to the problem, and to move beyond the conventional wisdom, because they believed the problem insoluble. Thus, Patrick Henry and other antifederalists argued that republican government is possible only in a small political community. They therefore opposed the new constitution of 1787 and the stronger government it created. They did not lift their sights beyond the loose political confederation of the Articles of Confederation. They rejected the possibility of a greatly strengthened, but republican, central government.

Alexander Hamilton and John Adams and other advocates of "high-toned" government maintained—before the adoption of the new constitution—that only an empire, or a strong central government on the British model, could hold together a political community as large as the new American nation. Confederations, they insisted, were notoriously weak, unstable, and detrimental to the interests of justice. If Henry and his friends argued that great strength in a central government jeopardized republican self-government and liberty, Hamilton and Adams and their friends held, initially, that faction prevailed in the small political community and jeopardized both the public good and the Union.

Madison's theory of the extensive republic—the federal republic—constituted a creative breakthrough because it demonstrated that Americans need not be impaled on either horn of the dilemma—either a despotic empire or faction, injustice, and weakness in a loose confederation. The new federal republic could cope with the dangers of disunion, large size, faction, and antirepublican forces. A greatly strengthened central government could cope with the danger of disunion. A new kind of federal government could cope with the problem of large size. An extensive, representative, constitutional, federal republic, in which a multiplicity of interests contended for power, could cope with the problem of faction. And, as Madison amended his political theory in the 1790s, a theory of democratic politics (relying upon basic freedoms and a two-party system) could cope with the danger of antirepublican forces' controlling the central government. Thus, a strengthened central government organized on the right republican and constitutional principles could keep the government together and avoid centralized despotism. Citizens in the thirteen states would have ample freedom to govern themselves and be free of factional injustice.

Toward Western European Union: A Creative Breakthrough in Process. But what of Western European nations? Could they move beyond war and destructive political and economic rivalry toward permanent peace, enduring prosperity, and solid constitutional democracy? This problem facing Europeans took on a momentous urgency after two catastrophic world wars.[8]

World War II had followed a devastating World War I that severely weakened Europe and opened the door to Communism in Russia and Fascism in Italy and Germany. World War II also followed the worldwide Great Depression that began in 1928. That great economic catastrophe, fed by protectionist policies, further weakened European nations and facilitated the advent of Nazism in Germany. Hitler's war of aggression in Europe also led to the German domination that facilitated the worst systematic butchery of all time—the Holocaust. The consequences of war, economic malaise, and political authoritarianism in twentieth-century Europe have been frightful.

Yet, disturbingly, after World War II, the "realistic" conventional wisdom continued to affirm that war will always be with us, that economic and political rivalry and war among the great powers are inevitable. The "realistic" conventional wisdom affirmed that the best that sovereign nation-states can achieve in international relations is a tolerable balance of power. The "realistic" conventional wisdom affirmed that political, ideological, geographical, and economic rivalry leads invariably to military clashes.

According to the "realistic" conventional wisdom, traditional nationalism—with its worship of the sovereign nation-state—is too powerful to allow any significant movement toward European Union to occur. A transnational or supranational authority is impossible. Economic rivalry and economic autarchy (self-sufficiency) cannot be avoided. The "realistic" conventional wisdom thus affirmed, fundamentally, that the present and the future will reproduce the past, that it is simply impossible in Western Europe to avoid nationalistic rivalry, economic conflict, and war. More pessimistic purveyors of the conventional wisdom also declared that devastating economic depressions, ineffective democratic governments, and authoritarian regimes are also inevitable.

Yet, despite the skepticism of the "realistic" purveyors of the conventional wisdom, a momentous breakthrough did occur in Western Europe after World War II: first, with the Coal and Steel Community (Schuman Plan, 1950; Treaty of Paris, 1951); then with the European Common Market (Treaty of Rome, 1957, 1958); then with the Single European Act (1985, 1987); and most recently with the Maastricht Treaty on European Unity (1991, 1992). The central objective in these efforts was to so integrate the economies of key participants—particularly France and Germany—as to make war impossible, to enhance trade and economic prosperity, and to advance their political (that is, their democratic and constitutional) health. The Paris treaty started with the integration of coal and steel. The Rome treaty aimed at a customs union. The Single European Act sought to advance the achievement of a single market. The Maastricht treaty aimed at a monetary and economic union and at a common foreign and security policy.

This breakthrough is still in process. Complete economic integration in Western Europe has not yet been achieved. More nearly complete political union in Western Europe remains an elusive goal. And the fuller economic and political integration of *all* of Europe is an even more distant prospect.

Nonetheless, the breakthrough has already facilitated fifty years of peace in Western Europe, enhanced economic prosperity, and strengthened democratic and constitutional institutions in the European Union. Four major propositions are now undeniable: (1) War between Germany and France, or between other nations in Western Europe in the European Union, is now clearly impossible. (2) Despite difficult economic times through which the European Union has passed or will pass, the economic strength of community members has been significantly enhanced, and members of the community are now better positioned economically to compete and prosper in Europe and in the larger world. (3) Constitutional democracy has been tremendously strengthened in all members of the community. (4) The European Union is better positioned to aid the cause of peace, economic advance, and constitutional democracy in other parts of Europe and in other parts of the world.

Futuristic Projection: Toward a Global Human Rights Regime and Protection against Genocide

Fourth, given the commitment to continuous prophetic scrutiny and futuristic projection, we are encouraged to do more than simply picture a more messianic age, where swords will be beaten into plowshares and spears into pruning hooks. We can begin to do what in the past we have only rarely done: project the scenarios (positive and negative) of the world we would like to create (or avoid) and—by anticipating problems—work through difficulties we now foresee, and perhaps even uncover some not currently in sight.

For example, as we attempt now to break through to more cooperative global patterns, we must look ahead to the evolution, and eventual achievement, of a modest but effective world political community. As we explore new steps to achieve greater democratic self-management in our political, economic, and social affairs, we also need to look ahead to the real problems involved in such self-management: problems involving conflicts between one democratic decision-making unit and another, between central planning and decentralized autonomy, and so on. For example, as we begin to satisfy basic human needs and enhance democratic governance, we need to be on the alert for ways to deal with clashes between ecological health and rapacious depletion of resources, between excellence and popular rule, between quality of life and hedonistic appetites. It is not too early to begin to explore imaginatively the politics and political philosophy of the twenty-first century. That exploration might benefit from the search for a breakthrough to protection against genocide.

A major concern that calls for a future breakthrough is the horrendous problem of genocide.[9] Can an effective global human rights regime be put into place both to prevent and to stop genocide? This is the terribly neglected, and excruciatingly difficult, problem that calls for a creative breakthrough in the future of international politics. Persistent, systemic, egregious violations of human rights—for example, genocide—must not only be outlawed (as in the rhetoric of United Nations pronouncements) but be made subject to effective international actions to end genocide. "Thou shalt not commit genocide" must join the prophetic commandment "Thou shalt not make nuclear war." In my affirmative answer, outlined in the futuristic scenario that follows, I shall argue that the creative breakthrough supporting such an affirmative answer calls for strengthened institutions in a global human rights regime, guided by a cogent theory of prudent prevention, an operative theory of effective staged implementation, and a wise theory of just humanitarian intercession.

The problem to be explored here is underscored by the tragic failure of the international community to develop an effective response to the evil of genocide in a post–World War II world traumatized by the Holocaust, a world that saw the passage of the United Nations' convention against genocide, but a world still characterized by genocide. Here I focus primarily on the imperative of developing a global human rights regime capable of dealing with genocide. My assumption is that if we can break through and deal effectively with genocide, we can then consolidate that breakthrough and deal with other flagrant violations of human rights.

The UN Convention on the Prevention and Punishment of the Crime of Genocide (adopted 1948, in force 1951) defines genocide as "any of the following acts committed with the intent to destroy, in whole or in part, a national, ethnic, racial, or religious group" by, for example, "Killing members of the group"; "Causing either bodily or mental harm to members of the group"; or "Deliberately inflicting on the group conditions of life calculated to bring about its physical extermination in whole or in part."[10] Moreover, by interpretation or amendment, the antigenocide convention should also clearly protect political groups or economic classes from genocide.[11]

I take for granted that the problem of genocide is real. First, genocide persists. Despite the global revulsion against the Nazi extermination of six million Jews and other target groups in the Holocaust—a revulsion that contributed to the UN Convention on the Prevention and Punishment of Genocide—genocide has continued in the post–World War II world. It continued in Cambodia, in East Pakistan (now Bangladesh), in Bosnia, in Iraq, Rwanda, and in other areas.[12]

Second, the problem of genocide remains because of the continuing dominance of a shortsighted conventional wisdom. This conventional wisdom too often "realistically" notes the seeming inevitability of egregious violations of human rights, the principle of noninterference in the internal affairs of nation-states, the absence of a national self-interest in humanitarian intercession, the weaknesses of the United Nations, and the costs and dangers of intervention.

The persistence of the problem of genocide prompts us to address four neglected needs and thus to outline the key features of a creative breakthrough required to attend to these needs.

Strengthened Institutions. The first need is the need to strengthen the institutions of the global human rights regime. By a global human rights regime I mean all those actors—for example, the United Nations, key nations, certain regional organizations, committed nongovernmental organizations—dedicated to the protection of human rights. These actors are committed to those norms, principles, institutions, policies, and practices concerned with the protection of human rights.[13] The norms, for example, are articulated in the UN Declaration of Human Rights, in the UN convention against genocide, and in other key UN documents. Here I will concentrate on institutions and the will to make them work. Key principles, policies, and practices will become clearer as I subsequently address theories of prudent prevention, staged implementation, and just humanitarian intercession.

Currently, we have a number of diverse political actors who respect and try to abide by these norms: certain nation-states committed to the protection of human rights; certain regional actors (e.g., the European Union) equally respectful of human rights; most organs of the United Nations; a number of nongovernmental organizations (e.g., Amnesty International) highly dedicated to human rights. Focusing only on the most promising of global human rights organizations, the United Nations, we find, however, that its key institutions are weak and often untested. Thus, the UN Security Council is potentially strong, but actually weak, in its ability either to prevent or to intercede against genocide. The UN Commission on Human Rights lacks strong enough powers to be effective.[14] The recently created UN High Commissioner on Human Rights is untested. UN policies and practices are theoretically promising, but weak in actuality. Clearly, there is a need—especially in the most promising global organization, the United Nations—to develop stronger institutions, policies, and practices that could make prudent prevention, effective staged implementation, and just humanitarian intercession genuinely meaningful.

The breakthrough I envisage requires a UN Security Council with the will to act; and this, in turn, means a will to act on the part of the permanent members of the Security Council. If the Security Council has power but often lacks will, other key UN institutions lack both power and will. The creative breakthrough proposed here envisages a strengthening of the UN High Commissioner for Human Rights and the UN Commission on Human Rights. The UN High Commissioner, in particular, working closely with an empowered UN Commission on Human Rights, has an especially important role to play in monitoring the status of human rights and in using the power of publicity. The strategy here would be to increase the powers of these organs to investigate and publicize genocidal threats or acts. The UN High Commissioner for Human Rights, working with the UN Commission on Human Rights, would then be required to recommend to the UN Security Council more stringent actions to prevent or stop genocide.

Several new UN institutions also need to be created. For example, to make monitoring more effective, a UN human rights monitor needs to be established for every region of the world in order to cover every country. A UN human rights protection force needs to be established to be ready to move in the event that protection against genocide requires its use. Similarly, a UN protectorate agency needs to be established to ensure temporary guardianship of a country after a genocidal regime is removed and until a regime that respects human rights is put into place.[15]

As key institutions of the global human rights regime are strengthened or developed, it will be helpful to address more clearly the broader operative political theory—the key principles, policies, and practices—that will guide those institutions. Again, neglected needs highlight the imperative of appropriate responses.

Prudent Prevention. The second neglected need is the need to articulate a cogent theory of prudent prevention of genocide.[16] My argument here is simple and compelling: It is far better to prevent genocide than to have to cope with it after it has occurred!

A theory of prudent prevention rests on three cardinal principles. First, there is a need to encourage the development of mature constitutional democracies. This is the best preventive principle because mature constitutional democracies do not practice genocide against their own citizens. Thus, with the growth of mature constitutional democracies, the danger of genocide would decline. Moreover, a world of mature constitutional democracies would contribute to a peaceful world because such democracies do not wage war on each other; and war is unquestionably the condition that makes possible the worst violations of human rights, including genocide.[17]

The world's existent mature constitutional democracies, regional organizations sensitive to the protection of human rights, the United Nations, and committed human rights NGOs—key members of a global human rights regime—have an ethical and prudential reason to foster constitutional democracies in a host of ways. The protection of human life is an ethical imperative. Prudentially, such actors recognize that such protection makes the global climate safer for each nation's vital interests, and safer, too, for the vital interests of regional organizations and the United Nations. These vital interests are clearly served when humanitarian intercession is not needed and when the costs and dangers of legitimate intercession are either eliminated or minimized.

The global human rights regime would have the important, yet delicate, task of monitoring the evolution of constitutional democracies around the globe, and of supporting national, regional, and UN policies to assist in the maturation of constitutional democracies. The monitoring would look to the existential status of nations around the globe, with particular emphasis on genocide. Monitoring would also look to the empirical investigation of the necessary and sufficient conditions—social, cultural, political, economic—for the development and maturation of constitutional democracies. National, regional, and global policies to achieve these conditions would then logically flow from such monitoring. At a minimum such policies would stress the development of democratic civil societies, healthy economic and social systems, and functioning democratic constitutions and political institutions.

Second, there is a need to develop the philosophy and practice of deterrence of genocide. Deterrence is the next best preventive medicine. Deterrence is based on the premise that mature constitutional democracies will not come into existence immediately, or all over the globe. Authoritarian and despotic regimes will continue to operate for many years. Consequently, a strategy of prevention must also contemplate additional ways of stopping egregious human rights violations—specifically acts of genocide—before they occur. A policy of deterrence is one such way. A policy of deterrence would warn potential genocidal violators of human rights that they will pay a high price for such violations. Deterrence would be premised on reliable monitoring to identify potentially genocidal violations. Publicity, in turn, would signal violators, as well as the global community, that the global human rights regime is aware of dangerous conditions and that egregious violations are unacceptable. The high price of egregious violations would include an escalating series of actions—political, economic, judicial, military. The credible threat of such actions would be designed to forestall genocidal violations.

Third, there is a need to develop the philosophy and practice of preemptive action in the event that deterrence doesn't work. Preemptive action is a fallback preventive strategy. All three principles of a theory of prudent prevention rest on the irrefutable proposition that it is better to prevent genocide than to stop it once it has occurred.

Preemptive action could include political, economic, and judicial sanctions, with military intercession being the ultimate sanction. Military intercession would be based on overwhelmingly credible evidence of a clear and present danger of genocide. The fuller conditions under which deterrence and preemptive action can occur, and policies and practices of implementation, will be spelled out as I speak to the following needs and thus speak to the issues of effective staged implementation and just humanitarian intercession.

Effectively Staged Implementation. The third need is the need to work out an operative theory of wisely staged implementation. Such a theory would guide the global human rights regime, and particularly the relevant UN organs of that regime. Several key points in such a theory can be identified.

First, there is a crucial need to develop effective and respected machinery for monitoring/investigating/reporting. Ideally, the UN High Commissoner on Human Rights, working with an empowered UN Commission on Human Rights, would coordinate the diverse national, nongovernmental, and United Nations monitoring that is currently going on in the arena of human rights. Reliable information about potential or actual genocide is the primary basis for a sensible response.

Second, the power of publicity must be employed to deter potential genocidal violations—where there is a clear and present danger of the eruption of genocide—and to solidify global support for just humanitarian intercession to stop genocide in progress. Such publicity would also be employed in cases of actual acts of genocide. Key UN organs (the UN High Commissioner on Human Rights, the UN Commission on Human Rights, the UN Security Council), effective regional organizations, key nations, and NGOs would function to publicize egregious violations.

Third, effective remedies—political, judicial, economic, military—must be on hand, to be prudently chosen and employed to prevent or stop genocide. To have any chance of success, such remedies must have the support of UN members willing and able to implement decisions of the UN Security Council. These decisions may involve such political actions as withdrawal of diplomatic recognition, such judicial remedies as trial and punishment of those guilty of genocide, such economic sanctions as a trade embargo or freezing of a country's assets, and such military sanctions as the use of force to stop genocidal actions.

Fourth, there is a crucial need to work out the problem of what might be called "human rights consolidation," namely, what it takes to ensure that human rights will continue to be respected after initial efforts at prevention or intercession have been successful. Consolidation might involve temporary maintenance of a UN human rights protection force in the country involved, placing the country involved temporarily in the status of a UN protectorate, or other prudent measures.

Just Humanitarian Intercession. The fourth tragically neglected need is the need to articulate a cogent theory of just humanitarian intercession.[18] Such a theory would include the following eight principles: First, an appropriate authority is required to bring the doctrine of just humanitarian intercession into action. The UN Security Council, for example, would be such an appropriate authority. Second, just humanitarian intercession could only be invoked in support of a just cause—for example, intercession to prevent or stop genocide. Third, military intercession would normally function as a last resort, after other pacific means—political, economic, judicial—have been tried and found wanting. Fourth, the consent of parties at risk—for example, targeted victims and their supporters—would normally be required for just humanitarian intercession. Fifth, the appropriate authority interceding would be required to make a prudent appraisal of the benefits and costs of intercession. Sixth, just humanitarian intercession must be based upon the expectation of a reasonable chance of success—immediate success in preventing or stopping egregious violations. Seventh, the interceding authority must employ humane and proportionate means to prevent or stop egregious violations, in the interest of minimizing harm, especially to the innocents involved in the conflict. Eighth, just humanitarian intercession must also calculate the long-run reasonable chance of success—success, for example, in putting into place a human rights–respecting regime to ensure the ongoing protection of human rights.

These eight principles of just humanitarian intercession are, of course, easier to state than to implement. Yet it is important to set forth the larger philosophy that guides both the deterrent and preemptive aspects of prudent prevention, and the conditions for actual intercession when preventive measures fail.

These four interrelated needs urgently call for the development of a responsible and effective human rights regime. The difficulties attendant upon the very endeavor to fulfill these four needs are daunting. Devotees of the "realistic" conventional wisdom are very skeptical about the possibility of the breakthrough outlined here. They argue that very little can be done; that the world lacks adequate policy, machinery, and will; that the costs of protection are too high; that nations (realistically concerned with protecting their own vital national interests) are not going to stick their humanitarian necks out for foreigners; that the United Nations is ill equipped to handle such problems; that it is unwise, dangerous, unlawful to meddle in the internal, domestic affairs of sovereign nation-states; etc.

Yet, despite this skepticism and despite the cogency of some of the arguments above, it is important to begin to confront the problem in order to see whether a creative breakthrough is possible. If we cannot break through on protection against genocide, then effective global protection of other human rights is placed in jeopardy. On the other hand, if we can break through to protection against genocide, we may have worked out the policy and machinery that can be employed to protect a wider range of human rights.

In undertaking the tasks of continuous prophetic scrutiny and futuristic projection, it is important to underscore the need to avoid the idolatries of nationalism, materialism, and narcissism without succumbing to falsely utopian notions about creating an angelic new person in a miraculous new earthly society where all conflict, tyranny, want, imbalance, and egoism have been entirely eliminated. Difficult as present and future tasks are, those pursuing a more prophetic politics must operate on the reasoned faith that we can—and, indeed, must—succeed in reducing the dangers of nuclear proliferation and nuclear war, in abolishing such gross tyrannical acts as genocide, in more equitably distributing power and wealth, in cleaning up our ecological home, and in achieving greater moral and cultural responsibility.

It is also important to face up to the very real difficulties of developing the pattern of prophetic politics. These difficulties remain to puncture an easy optimism. They can best be put in the form of nagging, troublesome questions that plague students of prophetic politics and challenge their creative response. They are especially the questions that political scientists concerned with continuous prophetic scrutiny and futuristic projection must continuously grapple with. (1) What conception of the prophetic paradigm can command the support of the diverse forces of the modern world—religious, philosophical, social, economic, political, scientific? (2) How shall fearless criticism go forward in the best ethical and scientific fashion? (3) Can prophetic values, principles, institutions, if theoretically sound, be successfully translated into superior constitutional practice—without prophetic politics itself becoming idolatrous, perfectionist, and complacent? (4) Are continuous prophetic scrutiny and futuristic projection really possible and genuinely fruitful? (5) Is it the paradoxical case that prophetic politics is necessary but impossible, or, if possible, highly improbable? These questions outline a future agenda for political philosophy in the tradition of prophetic politics.

Conclusion

Tough questions about the model of prophetic politics must be faced, but they must not paralyze our creativity. We must have a prudent confidence in the view that—wisely employed—the pattern of prophetic politics can protect genuine vital interests and elevate, refine, and harness the struggle for power, while avoiding idolatrous worship of the nation-state and the worst uses of force and craft. In this fashion, too, prophetic politics can again provide us with an inspiring image of a future world, a fruitful and powerful image that can enlighten the past, orient the present, and highlight future possibilities, while avoiding the sin of hubris. Prophetic politics may also assist us to move toward the more nearly perfect union, pursuant to time-tested notions of limited, representative, responsible, popular government, in accord with the sensible mandate to balance human equities, while avoiding the limited vision, deficient understanding, and timid assessment of liberal democratic politics.

The future of constitutional democracy in the twenty-first century will not be secure unless we are willing to explore, in theory and practice, the probability of the possibility of a more prophetic politics. As I have argued, a powerful case can be made for moving beyond Machiavellian politics, the "lion and fox" politics of the nation-state. We need to protect the truly vital interests of human beings, and local political communities have an important role to play in such protection. But we can no longer convincingly argue that nations—uniformly and adequately—always protect those vital interests. Nation-state idolatry remains an obstacle to human life, human rights, and fulfillment of human needs around the globe. We must also remember that utopian politics, the harmonious politics of earthly salvation, is wrongly rooted in the premise of an eventual conflict-less society. We cannot abolish conflict. We can articulate superior patterns of accommodation among contending interests. The history of constitutionalism leads us to appreciate that it is an evolving concept. It is a mistake, however, to assume that the constitutional pattern of liberal democratic politics (as it is currently practiced) is the end of the constitutional line. Despite its weaknesses, it is very good; but it is not good enough. Attempts by some pluralist political scientists or by "conservative" or "liberal" politicos (arguing perhaps from different perspectives) to make it more "realistic" and more responsive should not blind us to the weaknesses of the conservative politics of pluralist balance. Although this balance clearly has its virtues, it too often is a balance that suits the rich, the powerful, the white, the male; but poor people, weak people, most black people, and many women cannot conclude that liberal democratic politics is operating adequately on their behalf.

As we consider the probability of the possibility of a more prophetic politics, it is important to keep in mind the distinction I have tried to establish between prophetic and utopian politics. It is lamentable that the fear of messianic madness—whether in Left or Right totalitarianism—has led us to equate "utopian" and "prophetic" and to reject them both. We have failed to see that the prophetic impulse does not lead to Marx, Lenin, Stalin, and the Gulag Archipelago, or to the Grand Inquisitor, Hitler, and Auschwitz, or to *Walden Two*! It is also sad that—rejecting utopian politics and disgusted with Machiavellian politics—we have been tempted to conclude that liberal democratic politics is our safest harbor in a world in which false prophets preach "miracle, mystery, and authority" or in which cheap prophets preach easy, painless victories over persistent evils. It is sad because that harbor is not the safest harbor. Indeed, if we are to safeguard the future of constitutional democracy, if we are to respond to the challenges of twenty-first-century politics, we are called to voyage, not to rest. Only if we see that we can distinguish between prophetic and utopian politics can we move away from Machiavellian politics without embracing utopian politics, and without concluding that liberal democratic politics (as currently practiced) is the way to achieve the right balance in the politics of the twenty-first century. The recovery of the prophetic may be the precondition for a sound and creative, a superior democratic and constitutional, politics in the twenty-first century. The possibility is a live one. Our challenging task in the prophetic tradition is to demonstrate the probability of that possibility.

Notes

1. See Neal Riemer, *The Future of the Democratic Revolution: Toward a More Prophetic Politics* (New York: Praeger, 1984) for a fuller exposition of the model of prophetic politics. In this chapter I have expanded upon my earlier argument. Earlier versions of my model of prophetic politics have appeared in "Prophetic Politics: On the Political Philosophy of Stavrianos, Ferkiss and Falk," *Alternative Futures* 2, no. 4 (Fall 1979): 66–82; in "Prophetic Politics and Foreign Policy," *International Interactions* 8, no. 1–2 (1981): 25–39; in a special issue, "Religion and Politics," edited by Robert Booth Fowler, of *Humanities in Society* 6, no. 1 (Winter 1983): 5–18; and in "The

Prophetic Mode and Challenge in Religion, Politics, and Society," *Drew Gateway* 55, nos. 2 & 3 (Winter 1984/Spring 1985): 1–12.

2. See Neal Riemer, "Creative Breakthroughs in Politics" (paper presented at the annual meeting of the American Political Science Association, New York, September 1994); and Neal Riemer, *Creative Breakthroughs in Politics* (Westport, Conn.: Praeger, forthcoming).

3. See Neal Riemer, *Karl Marx and Prophetic Politics* (New York: Praeger, 1987).

4. See Neal Riemer, "Some Reflections on the Grand Inquisitor and Modern Democratic Theory," *Ethics* 67, no. 4 (July 1957): 249–56.

5. See Neal Riemer, *The Democratic Experiment* (Princeton, N.J.: Van Nostrand, 1967), 78–89; Perry Miller, *Roger Williams: His Contribution to the American Tradition* (Indianapolis: Bobbs-Merrill, 1953); Irwin H. Polishook, *Roger Williams, John Cotton and Religious Freedom: A Controversy in New and Old England* (Englewood Cliffs, N.J.: Prentice-Hall, 1967). See also my article, "Religious Liberty and Creative Breakthroughs: The Contributions of Roger Williams and James Madison," in *Religion in American Politics,* ed. Charles W. Dunn (Washington, D.C.: Congressional Quarterly Press, 1989), 15–23. For perspective on continuing problems involving religious liberty, see also Luís E. Lugo, ed., *Religion, Public Life, and the American Polity* (Knoxville: University of Tennessee Press, 1994); my chapter, "Madison: A Founder's Vision of Religious Liberty and Public Life" (37–50) throws light on Madison's debt (direct and indirect) to Williams's argument.

6. See Hugo Grotius, *The Law of War and Peace*, quoted in Francis W. Coker, *Readings in Political Philosophy* (New York: Macmillan, 1938), 409. The quotations from Madison and Jefferson can be found in Leo Pfeffer, *Church, State and Freedom* (Boston: Beacon Press, 1953), 27, 95. *Everson v. Board of Education,* 330 U.S. 1 (1947).

7. See Neal Riemer, *James Madison: Creating the American Constitution* (Washington, D.C.: Congressional Quarterly Press, 1986). For other perspectives on Madison, see Richard K. Matthews, *If Men Were Angels: James Madison and the Heartless Empire of Reason* (Lawrence: University Press of Kansas, 1995); Drew R. McCoy, *The Last of the Fathers: James Madison and the Republican Legacy* (Cambridge: Cambridge University Press, 1989); Robert A. Rutland, *James Madison: The Founding Father* (New York: Macmillan, 1987); Ralph L. Ketcham, *James Madison: A Biography* (New York: Macmillan, 1971); Irving Brant, *James Madison,* 6 vols. (Indianapolis: Bobbs-Merrill, 1941–61).

8. On the European Community and Union, see Jean Monnet, *Memoirs* (London: Collins, 1978); François Duchene, *Jean Monnet: The First Statesman of Interdependence* (New York: Norton, 1994); Desmond Dinan, *Ever Closer Union? An Introduction to the European Community* (Boulder, Colo.: Lynne Rienner, 1994); John Pinder, *European Community: The Building of a Union* (Oxford: Oxford University Press, 1992).

9. See Leo Kuper, *Genocide: Its Political Use in the Twentieth Century* (New Haven: Yale University Press, 1981); Leo Kuper, *The Prevention of Genocide* (New Haven: Yale University Press, 1985); Herbert Hirsch, *Genocide and the Politics of*

Memory (Chapel Hill: University of North Carolina Press, 1995); Lucy S. Davidowicz, *The War against the Jews* (New York: Bantam, 1975); Helen Fein, *Accounting for Genocide* (New York: Free Press, 1979); and Helen Fein, *Genocide Watch* (New Haven: Yale University Press, 1992).

10. The full text of the Convention on the Prevention of the Crime of Genocide may be found in Kuper, *Prevention of Genocide*, Appendix 1, 241–46.

11. On this point I follow Kuper, *Genocide: Its Political Use,* especially pp. 9–10, and chap. 8, "Related Atrocities," 138–60.

12. See U.S. Department of State, *Country Reports on Human Rights Practices* (Washington, D.C.: U.S. Government Printing Office, yearly).

13. On the concept of an international regime, see Stephen Krasner, ed., *International Regimes* (Ithaca, N.Y.: Cornell University Press, 1983).

14. For the weaknesses of the UN Commission on Human Rights, see Jack Donnelly, *International Human Rights* (Boulder, Colo.: Westview Press, 1993).

15. Although in my scenario I concentrate on the UN, I do not exclude attention to protection against genocide at the level of effective regional organizations. The strengthening of comparable institutions at the regional level is quite in harmony with my argument.

16. Although my focus is on genocide (as the most egregious violation of a basic human right, the right to life), the ethical vision that animates a global human rights regime is also captured in such other UN documents as the International Covenant on the Elimination of All Forms of Racial Discrimination (adopted 1965, in force 1969); the International Covenant on Civil and Political Rights (1976); the International Covenant on Economic, Social, and Cultural Rights (in force 1976); the UN Convention against Torture and Other Cruel, Inhuman or Degrading Treatment or Punishment (signed 1984, in force 1987).

17. See David P. Forsythe, *Human Rights and Peace: International and National Dimensions* (Lincoln: University of Nebraska Press, 1993); see also David P. Forsythe, *Human Rights and World Politics*, 2d ed. (Lincoln: University of Nebraska Press, 1989). To anticipate one criticism, let me note that mature constitutional democracies do engage in war, not with other mature constitutional democracies, but with other countries. Moreover, historically, the track record of *maturing* constitutional democracies (such as the United States) in dealing with Native Americans, blacks, or women has by no means been exemplary! And, of course, a similar point could be made—historically—of other maturing constitutional democracies—the United Kingdom, France, Belgium, Holland.

18. See Fernando R. Teson, *Humanitarian Intervention: An Inquiry into Law and Morality* (Dobbs Ferry, N.Y.: Transnational Publishers, 1988); Richard B. Lillich, ed., *Humanitarian Intervention and the United Nations* (Charlottesville, Va.: University Press of America, 1973); R. J. Vincent, *Human Rights and International Relations* (Cambridge: Cambridge University Press, 1984); Hirsh, *Genocide and the Politics of Memory.* Clearly, this view of just humanitarian intercession owes a great deal to just-war theory; and all the difficulties that confront just-war theory also confront just humanitarian intercession.

Select Bibliography

Auerbach, Bruce E. *Unto the Thousandth Generation: Conceptualizing Intergenerational Justice.* New York: Peter Lang, 1995.

Augustine, Saint. *The City of God.* New York: Modern Library, 1950.

Arendt, Hannah. *The Human Condition.* Chicago: University of Chicago Press, 1958.

Bercovitch, Sacvan. *The American Jeremiad.* Madison: University of Wisconsin Press, 1978.

Berdyaev, Nicolas. *The Meaning of History.* New York: Scribners, 1936.

Blenkinsopp, Joseph. *A History of Prophecy in Israel from Settlement in the Land to the Hellenistic Period.* Philadelphia: Westminster Press, 1983.

Bonhoeffer, Dietrich. *Ethics.* London: SCM Press, 1955.

Brown, Charles C. *Niebuhr and His Age: Reinhold Niebuhr's Prophetic Role in the Twentieth Century.* Philadelphia: Trinity Press International, 1992.

Brown, Robert McAfee. *Liberation Theology: An Introductory Guide.* Louisville: Westminster/John Knox Press, 1993.

Brueggemann, Walter. *The Prophetic Imagination.* Philadelphia: Fortress Press, 1978.

Buber, Martin. *The Prophetic Faith,* trans. from the Hebrew by Carlyle Witton-Davies, New York: Macmillan, 1949. Reprint. New York: Harper Torchbook, 1960.

Byrnes, Timothy. *The Catholic Church and Human Rights.* New York: Garland, 1988.

Castelli, Jim. *The Bishops and the Bomb.* New York: Image Books, 1983.

Clements, R. E. *Prophecy and Tradition.* Atlanta: John Knox Press, 1975.

Coggins, Richard, Anthony Phillips, and Michael Knibb, eds. *Israel's Prophetic Tradition.* Cambridge: Cambridge University Press, 1982.

Croatto, José Severino. *Biblical Hermeneutics: Toward a Theory of Reading as the Production of Meaning.* Maryknoll, N.Y.: Orbis Books, 1987.

Davis, Harry R., and Robert C. Good, eds. *Reinhold Niebuhr on Politics.* New York: Scribners, 1960.

Dinan, Desmond. *Ever Closer Union? An Introduction to the European Community.* Boulder, Colo.: Lynne Rienner, 1994.

Donnelly, Jack. *International Human Rights.* Boulder, Colo.: Westview Press, 1993.

Douglass, Frederick. *Narrative of the Life of Frederick Douglass, an American Slave.* London: Joseph Barker, 1846.

Duchene, François. *Jean Monnet: The First Statesman of Interdependence.* New York: Norton, 1994.

Ellacuría, Ignacio, and Jon Sobrino, eds. *Mysterium Liberationis: Fundamental Concepts of Liberation Theology.* Maryknoll, N.Y.: Orbis Books/Collins Dove, 1993.

Falk, Richard A. *This Endangered Planet.* New York: Random House, 1971.

Formicola, Jo Renée. *The Catholic Church and Human Rights: Its Role in the Formulation of U.S. Policy, 1945–1980.* New York: Garland, 1988.

Forsythe, David P. *Human Rights and World Politics.* 2d ed. Lincoln: University of Nebraska Press, 1989.

———. *Human Rights and Peace: International and National Dimensions.* Lincoln: University of Nebraska Press, 1993.

Fowler, Robert Booth, ed. "Religion and Politics." *Humanities in Society.* 6, no. 1 (Winter 1983).

Fredrickson, George M. *The Inner Civil War.* New York: Harper & Row, 1965.

Friedrich, Carl J. *Transcendent Justice: The Religious Dimension of Constitutionalism.* Durham, N.C.: Duke University Press, 1964.

Friedrichs, Robert W. *The Sociology of Sociology.* New York: Free Press, 1972.

Garrison, William Lloyd. *Thoughts on Colonization.* Boston: Garrison & Knapp, 1932.

Greene, Anne. *The Catholic Church in Haiti.* East Lansing: Michigan State University Press, 1993.

Gutiérrez, Gustavo. *A Theology of Liberation: History, Politics, and Salvation.* Maryknoll, N.Y.: Orbis Books, 1973.

Hadden, Jeffrey K., and Anson D. Shupe, eds. *Prophetic Religions and Politics.* New York: Paragon House, 1986.

Hanson, Paul D. *The Dawn of Apocalyptic.* Philadelphia: Fortress Press, 1975.

———. *The Diversity of Scripture: A Theological Interpretation.* Philadelphia: Fortress Press, 1982.

———. *The People Called: The Growth of Community in the Bible.* New York: Harper & Row, 1986.

———. *Old Testament Apocalyptic.* Nashville: Abingdon Press, 1987.

———. *Isaiah 40–66.* Louisville, Ky.: John Knox Press, 1995.

Hertzke, Allen D. "An Assessment of the Mainline Churches since 1945." Chap. 2 in *The Role of Religion in the Making of Public Policy*, edited by James E. Wood Jr. and Derek Davis. Waco, Texas: Dawson Institute of Church-State Relations, 1991.

Heschel, Abraham J. *The Prophets.* New York: Harper & Row,1962; reprint (in 2 vols.) New York: Harper & Row Torchbook 1969 and 1971.

———. *Prophetic Inspiration after the Prophets.* Hoboken, N.J.: Ktav, 1990.

Hofrenning, Daniel J. B. *In Washington But Not of It: The Prophetic Politics of Religious Lobbyists.* Philadelphia: Temple University Press, 1995.

Hyfler, Robert. *Prophets of the Left: American Socialist Thought in the Twentieth Century.* Westport, Conn.: Greenwood Press, 1984.

Johansen, Robert C. *The National Interest and the Human Interest.* Princeton, N.J.: Princeton University Press, 1980.

Pope.John XXIII. *Pacem in Terris.* New York: Paulist Press, 1963.

Kee, Alistair. *Marx and the Failure of Liberation Theology.* London: SCM Press, 1990.

Kegley, Charles W., ed. *Reinhold Niebuhr: His Religious, Social, and Political Thought.* New York: Pilgrim Press, 1984.

King, Martin Luther, Jr. *Stride toward Freedom.* New York: Harper, 1958.

———. *Why We Can't Wait.* New York: Harper & Row, 1964.

———. *Where Do We Go from Here: Chaos or Community?* New York: Harper & Row, 1967.

Koch, Klaus. *The Prophets.* New York: Harper & Row, 1962.

Kuper, Leo. *Genocide: Its Political Use in the Twentieth Century.* New Haven: Yale University Press, 1981.

———. *The Prevention of Genocide.* New Haven: Yale University Press, 1985.

Laslett, Peter, and James S. Fishkin, eds. *Justice between Age Groups and Generations.* New Haven: Yale University Press, 1992.

Lindblom, Johannes. *Prophecy in Ancient Israel.* Oxford: Basil Blackwell, 1962.

Lugo, Luís E., ed. *Religion, Public Life, and the American Polity.* Knoxville: University of Tennessee Press, 1994.

Manuel, Frank E. *The Prophets of Paris.* Cambridge: Harvard University Press, 1962.

Manuel, Frank E., and Fritzie P. Manuel. *Utopian Thought in the Western World.* Cambridge: Harvard University Press, 1979.

McFeely, William S. *Frederick Douglass.* New York: Norton, 1991.

McLellan, David. *Unto Caesar: The Political Relevance of Christianity.* Notre Dame: University of Notre Dame Press, 1993.

Merrill, Walter M. *Against Wind and Tide.* Cambridge: Harvard University Press, 1963.

Merrill, Walter M. and Louis Ruchames, eds. *The Letters of William Lloyd Garrison.* Cambridge: Harvard University Press, 1971–81.

Mische, Gerald, and Patricia Mische. *Toward a Human World Order: Beyond the National Security Straightjacket.* New York: Paulist Press, 1977.

Morken, Hubert. "Prophetic Politics: Three Models." *Drew Gateway.* 55, no. 1 (Fall 1984).

Morse, J. Mitchell. *The Sympathetic Alien: James Joyce and Catholicism.* New York: New York University Press, 1959.

———. *Prejudice and Literature.* Philadelphia: Temple University Press, 1976.

National Council of Catholic Bishops. Hugh Nolan, editor. *The Pastoral Letters of the United States Catholic Bishops.* Vols. 1-5. Washington, D.C.: United States Catholic Conference, 1984, 1984, 1983, 1984, 1989.

Niebuhr, Reinhold. *Moral Man and Immoral Society.* New York: Scribners, 1932.

———. *The Children of Light and the Children of Darkness: A Vindication of Democracy and a Critique of Its Traditional Defenders.* New York: Scribners, 1944.

———. *The Nature and Destiny of Man.* New York: Scribners, 1941; reprint (2 vols. in 1), New York: Scribners, 1949.

Olan, Levi A. *Prophetic Faith and the Secular Age.* New York: Ktav, 1982.

Parfit, Derek. *Reasons and Persons.* Oxford: Clarendon Press, 1984.

Parsons, Howard L. "The Prophetic Mission of Karl Marx." In *Marxism and Christianity*, edited by Herbert Aptheker. New York: Humanities Press, 1968.

Partridge, Ernest, ed. *Responsibilities to Future Generations: Environmental Ethics.* Buffalo, N.Y.: Prometheus Books, 1980.

Patterson, John. *The Goodly Fellowship of the Prophets.* New York: Scribners, 1948.

Polak, Fred L. *The Image of the Future.* 2 vols. New York: Oceana, 1961.

Rasmussen, Larry, ed. *Reinhold Niebuhr: Theologian of Public Life.* Minneapolis: Fortress Press, 1991.

Regan, Tom, ed. *Earthbound: New Introductory Essays in Environmental Ethics.* New York: Random House, 1984.

Riemer, Neal. *The Revival of Democratic Theory.* New York: Appleton-Century-Crofts, 1962.

———. *The Democratic Experiment.* Princeton, N.J.: Van Nostrand, 1967.

———. *The Future of the Democratic Revolution: Toward a More Prophetic Politics.* New York: Praeger, 1984.

———. *James Madison: Creating the American Constitution.* Washington, D.C.: Congressional Quarterly Press, 1986.

———. *Karl Marx and Prophetic Politics.* New York: Praeger, 1987.

———. *Creative Breakthroughs in Politics.* Westport, Conn.: Praeger. Forthcoming.

Rogers, William B. *"We Are All Together Now": Frederick Douglass, William Lloyd Garrison, and the Prophetic Tradition.* New York: Garland, 1995.

Rosenthal, Joel H. *Righteous Realists: Political Realism, Responsible Power, and American Culture in the Nuclear Age.* Baton Rouge: Louisiana State University Press, 1991.

Ruether, Rosemary Radford. *The Radical Kingdom: The Western Experience of Messianic Hope.* New York: Harper & Row, 1970.

―――. *Liberation Theology: Human Hope Confronts Christian History and American Power.* New York: Paulist/Newman, 1972.

―――. *New Woman, New Earth: Sexist Ideologies and Human Liberation.* New York: Paulist Press, 1975.

―――. *To Change the World: Christology and Cultural Criticism.* New York: Crossroad, 1981.

―――. *Contemporary Roman Catholicism: Crises and Challenges.* Kansas City, Mo.: Sheed & Ward, 1987.

―――. *Gaia and God: An Ecofeminist Theology of Earth Healing.* San Francisco: Harper, 1992.

Scott, Robert B. Y. *The Relevance of the Prophets.* Rev. ed. New York: Macmillan, 1968.

Segers, Mary, ed. *Church Polity and American Politics.* New York: Garland, 1990.

Segundo, Juan Luís. *The Liberation of Theology.* Maryknoll, N.Y.: Orbis Books, 1976.

Sigmund, Paul E. *Liberation Theology at the Crossroads: Democracy or Revolution?* New York: Oxford University Press, 1990.

Sikora, R.I., and Brian Barry, eds. *Obligations to Future Generations.* Philadelphia: Temple University Press, 1978.

Smith, Christian. *The Emergence of Liberation Theology: Radical Religion and Social Movement Theory.* Chicago: University of Chicago Press, 1991.

Smith, Michael Joseph. *Realist Thought from Weber to Kissinger.* Baton Rouge: Louisiana State University Press, 1986.

Stone, Ronald H. *Reinhold Niebuhr: Prophet to Politicians.* Nashville: Abingdon Press, 1972.

Teson, Fernando R. *Humanitarian Intervention: An Inquiry into Law and Morality.* Dobbs Ferry, N.Y.: Transnational Publishers, 1988.

Tillich, Paul. *Political Expectation.* New York: Harper & Row, 1971.

Tinder, Glenn. *Community: Reflections on a Tragic Ideal.* Baton Rouge: Louisiana State University Press, 1980.

———. *Against Fate: An Essay on Personal Dignity*. Notre Dame: University of Notre Dame Press, 1981.

———. *The Political Meaning of Christianity: An Interpretation*. Baton Rouge: Louisiana State University Press, 1989.

———. *Political Thinking: The Perennial Questions*. 6th ed. New York: Harper Collins, 1995.

———. *Tolerance and Community*. Columbia: University of Missouri Press, 1995.

U.S. Catholic Bishops. *Pastoral Letter on Nuclear Weapons*. Washington, D.C.: Office of Publishing and Promotion Services, 1983.

———. *Pastoral Letter on Catholic Social Teaching and the U.S. Economy, 1984*. Washington, D.C.: Office of Publishing and Promotion Services, 1985.

Von Rad, Gerhard. *The Message of the Prophets*. New York: Harper & Row, 1967.

Waldo, Martin. *The Mind of Frederick Douglass*. Chapel Hill: University of North Carolina Press, 1984.

Walters, Ronald G. *American Reformers, 1815–1860*. New York: Hill & Wang, 1978.

Walzer, Michael. *The Revolution of the Saints: A Study in the Origins of Radical Politics*. Cambridge: Harvard University Press, 1965.

———. *Obligations: Essays on Disobedience, War, and Citizenship*. Cambridge: Harvard University Press, 1970.

———. *Radical Principles: Reflections of an Unreconstructed Democrat*. New York: Basic Books, 1980.

———. *Exodus and Revolution*. New York: Basic Books, 1985.

———. *Interpretation and Social Criticism*. Cambridge: Harvard University Press, 1987.

———. *The Company of Critics: Social Criticism and Political Commitment in the Twentieth Century*. New York: Basic Books, 1988.

———. *Just and Unjust Wars: A Moral Argument with Historical Illustrations*. 2d. ed. New York: Basic Books, 1992.

———, ed. *Toward a Global Society*. Providence, R.I.: Berghahn Books, 1995.

Waskow, Arthur. *Rainbow Sign: The Shape of Hope*. New York: Schocken Books, 1985.

Weber, Max. *Ancient Judaism*. Translated by H. H. Gerth and Don Martindale. Glencoe, Ill.: Free Press, 1952.

Weinfeld, Moshe. *Social Justice in Ancient Israel*. Jerusalem: Magnes Press and Minneapolis: Fortress Press, 1995.

West, Cornel. *Prophesy Deliverance! An Afro-American Revolutionary Christianity*. Philadelphia: Westminster Press, 1982.

———. *Prophetic Fragments*. Grand Rapids, Mich.: Eerdmans, 1988.

———. *The American Evasion of Philosophy: A Genealogy of Pragmatism.* Madison: University of Wisconsin Press, 1989.

———. *Keeping Faith: Philosophy and Race in America.* New York: Routlege, 1993.

———. *Race Matters.* Boston: Beacon Press, 1993.

Wilson, Robert R. *Prophecy and Society in Ancient Israel.* Philadelphia: Fortress Press, 1980.

Wojcik, Jan, and Raymond-Jean Frontain, eds. *Poetic Prophecy in Western Literature.* Madison, N.J.: Fairleigh Dickinson Press, 1981.

Index

About the Contributors

BRUCE EDWARD AUERBACH is an associate professor of political science at Albright College in Reading, Pennsylvania. He received his B.A. and M.A. degrees in political science from Drew University and his Ph.D. in political science from the University of Minnesota. Dr. Auerbach is the author of numerous articles and papers in political philosophy and constitutional law, and—most recently—of the book *Unto the Thousandth Generation: Conceptualizing Intergenerational Justice.*

JO RENÉE FORMICOLA is associate professor of political science and chair of the Department of Political Science, Seton Hall University. She is the author of *The Catholic Church and Human Rights: Its Role in the Formulation of U.S. Policy, 1945–1980* and of many significant articles on American Catholic political theology and other religious and political themes.

PAUL D. HANSON is Florence Corliss Lamont Professor of Divinity and professor of Old Testament in the Divinity School and in the Department of Near Eastern Languages and Civilizations of the Faculty of Arts and Sciences, Harvard University, and master of John Winthrop House, Harvard College. He is the author of *The Dawn of Apocalyptic; Dynamic Transcendence; The Diversity of Scripture; The People Called: The Growth of Community in the Bible; Ancient Israelite Religion; Old Testament Apocalyptic;* and *Isaiah 40–66;* and editor of books on the prophets Micah and Jeremiah.

J. MITCHELL MORSE is professor of English, emeritus, Temple University. He is the author of *The Sympathetic Alien: James Joyce and Catholicism; Matters of Style; The Irrelevant English Teacher;* and *Prejudice in Literature.*

JOHN R. POTTENGER is associate professor of political science, University of Alabama in Huntsville, where he teaches courses in political philosophy. Dr. Pottenger is the author of *The Political Theory of Liberation Theology* and numerous articles on political theology, moral philosophy, and social theory.

NEAL RIEMER is Andrew V. Stout Professor of Political Philosophy, emeritus, Department of Political Science, Drew University. His books include *The*

229

Revival of Democratic Theory; The Democratic Experiment; The Future of the Democratic Revolution: Toward a More Prophetic Politics; Karl Marx and Prophetic Politics; James Madison: Creating the American Constitution; and *Creative Breakthroughs in Politics.* He is also coauthor of *The New World of Politics;* and editor/coauthor of *New Thinking and Developments in International Politics: Opportunities and Dangers.*

WILLIAM B. ROGERS is assistant dean, Graduate School, Drew University. He is the author of *"We Are All Together Now": Frederick Douglass, William Lloyd Garrison and the Prophetic Tradition.* He previously served with the Association of Independent Colleges and Universities in New Jersey. His academic background includes a B.A. in political science and English from Hartwick College, an M.P.A. from the Maxwell School at Syracuse University, and an M.A. in political science and a Ph.D. in intellectual history from Drew University.

ROSEMARY RADFORD RUETHER is Georgia Harkness Professor, Garrett-Evangelical Theological Seminary, and graduate faculty, Northwestern University. Among her books are *The Church against Itself; The Radical Kingdom: The Western Experience of Messianic Hope; Liberation Theology; Religion and Sexism; Faith and Fratricide: The Theological Roots of Anti-Semitism; New Woman, New Earth: Sexist Ideologies and Human Liberation; Women and Religion in America; To Change the World; Texts for Woman Church; Contemporary Roman Catholicism: Crises and Challenges;* and *Gaia and God: An Ecofeminist Theology of Earth Healing.* She is also coauthor of *God and the Nations.*

GLENN TINDER is professor of political science, emeritus, University of Massachusetts—Boston. He is the author of *Against Fate: An Essay on Personal Dignity; Community: Reflections on a Tragic Ideal; The Political Meaning of Christianity: An Interpretation; Political Thinking: The Perennial Questions;* and *Tolerance and Community.*

MICHAEL WALZER is a professor at the School of Social Science, Institute for Advanced Study, Princeton, New Jersey. He is the author of *The Revolution of the Saints: A Study in the Origins of Radical Politics; Obligations: Essays on Disobedience, War, and Citizenship; Radical Principles; Exodus and Revolution; The Company of Critics: Social Criticism and Political Commitment in the Twentieth Century; Interpretation and Social Criticism; Just and Unjust Wars;* and *Thick and Thin: Moral Argument at Home and Abroad;* and editor of *Toward a Global Society.*

CORNEL WEST is professor of religion, Divinity School, and professor of Afro-American studies, Harvard University. He is the author of *Prophesy Deliverance! An Afro-American Revolutionary Christianity; Prophetic Fragments; The American Evasion of Philosophy: A Genealogy of Pragmatism; Keeping Faith: Philosophy and Race in America;* and *Race Matters.*